The Mystery of Edwin Drood

The Mystery of Edwin Drood

Charles Dickens' unfinished novel and our
endless attempts to end it

Pete Orford

PEN & SWORD HISTORY

First published in Great Britain in 2018 by
PEN AND SWORD HISTORY
an imprint of
Pen and Sword Books Ltd
47 Church Street
Barnsley
South Yorkshire S70 2AS

Copyright © Pete Orford, 2018

ISBN 978 1 52672 436 6

Printed and bound in the UK
by T J International, Padstow, Cornwall, PL28 8RW

Typeset in Times New Roman by
Aura Technology and Software Services, India

Pen & Sword Books Ltd incorporates the imprints of Pen & Sword
Archaeology, Atlas, Aviation, Battleground, Discovery,
Family History, History, Maritime, Military, Naval, Politics, Railways,
Select, Social History, Transport, True Crime, Claymore Press,
Frontline Books, Leo Cooper, Praetorian Press, Remember When,
Seaforth Publishing and Wharncliffe.

For a complete list of Pen and Sword titles please contact
Pen and Sword Books Limited
47 Church Street, Barnsley, South Yorkshire, S70 2AS, England
E-mail: enquiries@pen-and-sword.co.uk
Website: www.pen-and-sword.co.uk

Contents

Acknowledgments

It is inevitable that writing about an unfinished book should raise anxieties that your own work should find a similar fate, and many has been the time that I have worried this might be the case. The fact this is not so is down to the generous support of those around me.

My interest in Dickens began as an undergraduate when I enrolled for a module taught by Professor Malcolm Andrews. At the end of the first lecture he laid down his notes and proclaimed that first and foremost Dickens should be *enjoyed*, and accordingly ending the session by giving a spirited reading from *The Pickwick Papers* of Sam Weller and his father writing a valentine's letter. That singular moment has remained the keystone to my career in Dickens ever since. Accordingly, after completing a PhD in Shakespeare and wanting a break from the bard, I returned to Dickens for what was supposed to be one article before settling down to a long career as an Early Modern scholar. What actually happened is that one article turned into books, conference papers and an introduction into a whole new world of nineteenth-century academics, and what could have easily been a tragic tale of one scholar stepping out of his field and meeting a frosty reception instead became a fish-out-of-water comedy in which I found myself welcomed and encouraged. I like to think Dickens would have been proud of the collegial spirit present among his scholars.

My work on *Drood* began at the tail end of the bicentenary when Professor John Drew welcomed me aboard at Buckingham to conduct research into this unfinished work and its solutions. He has been a supportive mentor ever since, along with the rest of the English department, who have always been on hand to offer advice, encouragement and coffee in equal measures. In turn, my students have patiently listened to my occasional *Drood* deviations in the middle of a lecture on Victorian melodrama or Greek tragedy, and the feedback I have received from postgraduate seminars has been fruitful and enthusiastic.

The main outlet to date for my work on *Drood* has been online at www.droodinquiry.com, which would not have been possible without the generous support of both the Dickens Fellowship and the University of Buckingham's Dennison Fund, not to mention the contributions of fellow scholars and enthusiasts to the reading blog and to the associated conference held in September 2014. Particular thanks go to the web developer Thomas Palmer, and the incredible work of Alys Jones, who vividly brought the whole project to life with her wonderful illustrations. To then have the work from that site developed into an exhibition was a dream come true, and thanks is therefore gladly offered to the staff of the Charles Dickens Museum for their support and expertise. Equally, no scholar could do any of the work they do without librarians, and in addition to the fantastic resources in the Suzannet Research Library at the Charles Dickens Museum I must also offer gratitude to the British Film Institute, Senate House Library, the University of Buckingham library, and the always friendly and helpful staff at the Bodleian. Due acknowledgments are also made specifically to the Charles Dickens Museum and Proquest for their help sourcing the illustrations and generous permission to use them. In the final stages of the book, the publishing team at Pen and Sword proved to be insightful and enthusiastic in their support.

Such is the generosity of my fellow Dickensians in offering their time and conversation that to note everyone down would stretch the acknowledgments out to over half the book, but particular thanks must go to Beatrice Bazell, Anne-Marie Beller, Emily Bowles, Jonathan Buckmaster, Verity Burke, Beth Carney, Don Richard Cox, Louise Creechan, Emma Curry, Hadas Elber-Aviram, Holly Furneaux, Helen Goodman, Paul Graham, Jenny Hartley, Camilla Ulleland Hoel,

ACKNOWLEDGMENTS

Gwyneth Hughes, Frankie Kubicki, Leon Litvack, Hazel Mackenzie, David Madden, David Paroissien, Jo Parsons, Bob Patten, Chris Pittard, Louisa Price, Jo Robinson, Paul Schlicke, Beth Seltzer, Joanne Shattock, Michael Slater, Tom Ue, Cathy Waters, Tony Williams, Carl Wilson, Ben Winyard and Claire Wood.

Last but not least are my family and friends, for providing a sounding board for, or distraction from, my work as required. My children Cade, Ned and Lirael have ensured that my telescopic knowledge of *Drood* was balanced at all times by a broader awareness of dinosaurs, Pokémon and CBeebies. But it is my wife Jodie who has been, and remains, the most constant support and motivation throughout my career. It is to her, therefore, that I dedicate this book and hereby promise, now it is done, that I will finally mow the lawn.

Introducing the Mystery

This is a book about fanfiction, and the extraordinary response of readers to Charles Dickens' final – and unfinished – book, *The Mystery of Edwin Drood*. Since its publication in 1870, there have been hundreds of theories about the existing fragment of the book, trying to argue for how they think the story might end. Depending on your level of cynicism, the volume of responses is either a damning indictment of reader infatuation and conspiracy theories, or a standing testament to the continued admiration and relevance of Dickens and his works. In truth, it is a little of both, and one of the more remarkable aspects of researching the many theories of *Drood*'s end is the recurring pattern in their structure – be it an article or monograph, the first ten percent of the argument is always a well-argued, objective overview of the theories that have come before, coupled with a sound recognition of how those earlier authors all lost objectivity and succumbed to their own ideas at the expense of any real evidence. The final ninety percent is then a slow descent into subjectivity as the author ultimately becomes everything they have just criticised, pushing their own ideas with the same manic level of certainty in their veracity. Indeed, for many years now *Drood* studies have been seen in relation to Dickens scholarship much as alchemy is seen to science – an important forebear to the field, of which many prominent figures have previously indulged, but one that most modern-day counterparts try to distance themselves from. Like Frankenstein, or any other scientist of the Hammer Horror genre, he who decides to investigate *Drood* is looked upon with an element of pity by those who know the ultimate end of all who try to unlock its mysteries, as methodical research in quiet libraries slowly but surely leads to standing in the laboratory of a lightning-struck castle screaming 'He's alive! EDWIN'S ALIIIIIIIIVVVVVEEE!'

It is my intention not to follow this same path, for understandable reasons. This book is therefore *not* my theory of how *Drood* ends. It is rather an account of all that has gone before, partly to bring the casual reader of Dickens up to speed with the full story of his final novel, but also to see exactly what these many theories tell us about Dickens, his reputation, and his readers over the last century-and-a-half. In charting the history of *Drood* solutions, it will by necessity offer a glimpse at the wider frame of Dickens criticism since his death. Sometimes the two work in harmony, but often the mania for ending *Drood* acts in direct opposition to attempts to move scholarly discussion of his works forward. As will be shown, there is a tension that emerges in this narrative between enthusiasts and academics. I should like to note here that it has been my great pleasure to find that this tension is entirely historic, and that in the pursuit of this research I have personally found great support and enthusiasm from both camps. Dickens is that rare thing, a writer who can be enjoyed and celebrated by the general public while probed and critiqued by the academy, without detriment to either side.

This union of enthusiast and academic is a key element of my own approach to Dickens and one of the driving forces behind this book. Though I do not intend to discuss my own ideas of *Drood*'s end, in the interest of objectivity I should proclaim my own stance towards the novel and the many suggested conclusions. My approach varies between celebration and bemusement. Some of the ideas that will be discussed are utterly bizarre, but it needs to be recognised that most, if not all, have been created out of an earnest desire to honour Dickens or share the author's enthusiasm with a wider community, and this is no bad thing. In the time since Dickens' death we have seen countless conflicts and historical atrocities, and against this backdrop the heated exchanges of literary fans debating the fate of a fictional character are comfortingly harmless. You might ask how people can get so worked up about a book. I would say that arguing about literature is a far more positive experience than physical conflicts over geography and politics. I come here, therefore, not to sneer at the Droodists from the sidelines, but to champion the movement, with any gentle mocking coming from one among them. Ultimately, it is my contention that every response is valid simply for being a response. It shows us how Dickens is received by his readers, and every reader has the right to his or her personal response. As much as we can recognise the benefits of objective analysis in literary studies, there is no arbitrator who can dictate how a reader should personally react and relate to a novel.

The book in your hands is therefore not so much a book about Dickens, but of those who have read him. The existing half of *Drood* spans just over 200 pages, but the non-existent half has been expanded to thousands of pages presented in letters to the national press, journal articles, monographs, novels, erotic fiction, not to mention movies, plays and musicals. Dickens' book is open-ended, albeit unintentionally, and that has meant a colossal library of works exploring the wide unknown of *Drood*'s conclusion. The history of *Drood* is of one book by Dickens surrounded by, sometimes lost in, the works of hundreds of followers who have, for the past 150 years, generated this remarkable response. But nor is Dickens to be completely absent from the discussion. The incredible response to his last work is also a testament to the Droodists' passion for Dickens and the hold he maintains over his readers. For nearly 150 years, the characters of Dickens' final story have stood suspended in their plot, with no end before them they gather potential energy, ready for the reader to take them where they will. And for the Droodists, this potential for multiple ending has been utilised greatly.

So while this book focuses on life after Dickens, at its heart is a tale of deep admiration for Dickens' work that has fuelled and prompted fierce debate. Quite often the Droodists have gone too far and lost sight of both the original text and any semblance of objectivity. A lot of the ideas you are going to read about in this book get very silly, very fast. Fun as that may be (and it is), it comes at a cost, and has for a long time had a detrimental effect on *Drood*. Too many people have come to see the book purely in terms of the half that has not been written, either as a call to arms to join the fray and put forward their own ideas, or as a solemn warning to steer clear from the whole thing. Even among fans of Dickens, many will simply not bother reading what is ultimately going to be a book that they know they will never finish. But for those who do, the frequent reaction I have found in discussion is surprise at how good the book actually is. Dickens' last work has some fantastic characters, and moments of writing that is as strong as anything else in his career. To some extent it is a great shame that of all his books, this had to be the one he didn't finish. Therefore, in taking the Droodists head-on and recounting their theories, there is a secondary motive in this book of attempting to exorcise the ghost of the second half in order to allow both fans and critics to enjoy the first half. In chapter four I discuss how this sort of approach is now becoming more common, and it is my hope to see further work written on *Drood* that explores the themes and characters within the fragment that we have, rather than trying to extrapolate a plot that we do not have. Dickens was a wonderful writer, but predominately it is not his narrative we applaud, but his narration. Even without an end, *Drood* offers a great read.

A brief note on terminology

Throughout this book I will refer to solutions and completions as two distinct ideas. My definition of a solution is where someone has expressed their ideas about how *Drood* might end, whereas a completion is where they have attempted to realise those ideas as a fully fictionalised second half. The difference between them is not in length, but breadth. Some completions can be relatively brief, while many solutions will span an entire book as the author exhaustively lays out all of their reasoning and the various clues they have found both within and without Dickens' text. Irrespective of length, solutions will focus on just the aspects of the plot that are of interest to them, which is usually the fate of Edwin, the identity of Dick Datchery, and any romantic pairings and marriages they believe will feature in the book's closing chapters. A completion, however, has to consider not just the areas of interest to the author, but what is going to happen to *all* of Dickens' characters. In a completion, we can read more about the Billickin's feud with Miss Twinkleton, or the rise and fall of Mayor Sapsea. Completions must also attempt to cater for the reader's desire to not only see what might happen next, but to have it presented in an enjoyable and engaging manner, rather than a simple breakdown of plot points. Completions, therefore, open themselves up to far more criticism, but for that very reason of bravery in the face of certain criticism, they have my far greater respect, whatever their conclusion.

In attempting to make sense of a century-and-a-half of both solutions and completions, I have identified four overarching movements of thought: the Opportunists, the Detectives, the Academics, and the Irreverent. Each will form the focus of the succeeding chapters. As will be seen, early responses leapt on the opportunity for sales while showing less concern for Dickens' intentions, something that was then addressed with a vengeance by the crusade of the Detectives. This second wave scoured the text to 'solve' the mystery and find the 'true' end. This in turn would be challenged by the next wave, and the Academics' growing insistence that the end of *Drood* is no mystery after all, but a psychological portrait of a killer. The Academics' work would then be upturned again by the most recent wave of deliberate irreverence, in which a number of new completions have gleefully and knowingly ignored Dickens to see what else can be done with the remainder of his story. Like all labelling, this titling of these four movements is arbitrary, as is division into four rather than five or three, and to be taken with a pinch of salt. The work of the Detectives has extended far beyond the 1930s, where chapter two ends. Equally there are works that can be seen to qualify both as Academic and Detective, depending on which part of it you are reading. As a group, we are all individuals. But as a loose framework it is nonetheless useful for starting to make sense of the many solutions under consideration. I would defend it as a useful scaffold for building a sense of the deluge of theories on *Drood*, but not a scaffold to march individual ideas to if they deviate.

Before *Drood*

The majority of this book will be devoted to what came after *Drood*. The remainder of this introduction will now pause to consider what came before. Written and published in 1870, *Drood* came five years after the publication of Dickens' previous novel, *Our Mutual Friend*. This was the longest pause between Dickens' novels in his career (in the early days, publication of novels even overlapped, with the early parts of *Oliver Twist* arriving while the later parts of *The Pickwick Papers* were still being published). The reason for this long hiatus can be explained by the reading tours Dickens embarked on across the UK and the US. The opportunity to hear the author performing his own works was one eagerly lapped up by readers, and the tours were a great success. Dickens equally enjoyed the sensation, gaining at once that instant feedback on his works that had previously been missing. He finally got to see the reaction of readers for himself. Malcolm Andrews notes: 'The Readings indeed confirmed that sense of a community of interests and mutual friendship between Dickens and his public.'[1] These tours confirmed Dickens' celebrity status as the most prominent (and certainly recognisable) author of his age. In that sense, the tours were the perfect prelude to the release of a new work in 1870.

Conversely, the tours are often seen as a driving factor in Dickens' death. The sheer amount of travelling in itself was cause for exhaustion, while Dickens' near-fatal experience as a passenger in the Staplehurst train crash left the author deeply unsettled about train travel for understandable reasons. Moreover, the readings themselves were involved and energetic, and while the majority of them were comic or pleasant in tone (*A Christmas Carol* was the most frequent reading), towards the end of the tour Dickens introduced *Sikes and Nancy* into his repertoire. This reading, in which he portrayed the vicious death of Nancy at Sikes' hands, electrified and terrified audiences in equal measure, and placed Dickens under further strain: 'I shall tear myself apart,' he said before his final performance of the piece.[2] It was noted that his pulse would race and he would need to rest thoroughly after such readings. The tours had taken a darker tone, and the combination of the punishing schedule and the intensity of the readings themselves resulted in Dickens being told by doctors that he had to stop the tours for his own health. Accordingly, the author reluctantly bade farewell to his public on 15 March, 'with feelings of very considerable pain', but announced his return in book form in the new upcoming novel *The Mystery of Edwin Drood*:

> *Nevertheless, I have thought it well in the full flood tide of your favour to retire upon those older associations between us which date much farther back than these, and thenceforth to devote myself exclusively to the art that first brought us together.*
>
> *Ladies and Gentlemen, – In two short weeks from this time I hope that you may enter in your own homes on a new series of readings at which my assistance will be indispensable; but from these garish lights I vanish now for evermore, with a heartfelt, grateful, respectful, and affectionate farewell.*[3]

Sadness at leaving his audience was compensated by the thought of re-entering their homes in a more intimate manner. As will be seen in chapter one, Dickens' excitement of a return to 'the art that first brought us together' was shared by his contemporary reviewers and, we can presume, his readers too. But in retrospect, we have come to wonder to what extent Dickens suspected his own mortality at this time. A proviso in his contract with Chapman and Hall for *Drood*, which discusses what should happen 'If the said Charles Dickens shall die during the composition of the said work of The Mystery of Edwin Drood' has raised such suspicions, although further research has shown that a similar proviso was also in place for *Our Mutual Friend*.[4] Then again, just a week before his death in June 1870, Dickens changed his will, in which he left his journal *All the Year Round* to his eldest son Charley. So whether or not he actually felt death was imminent, he was certainly thinking of his legacy at this time. It is certain that a combination of Staplehurst, the reading tours and his ill health may have made Dickens more morbid, but we will never know whether there was anything more concrete to his concerns. At any rate, it is popular to consider *Drood* as being written by the author in his dying throes, which I willingly attempt to debunk in chapter one by contrasting with the early responses to the book.

The other significant personal influence that critics have increasingly turned to whenever discussing anything related to Dickens' later life is his relationship with Ellen Ternan. Her name will crop up especially in chapter three as critics hail the darker side of Dickens in contrast to the previous conception of a jolly good-hearted fellow. There has been great temptation to read autobiography in John Jasper's desperate attempts to maintain his public persona as a respectable community figure while harbouring deeply-held romantic feelings for a young girl. There is certainly an argument for this, as will be discussed in chapter three, but the warning is nonetheless needed for reading too much of the author in his work. There is almost certainly some influence, but we can never certain how much (or little).

So much for the personal influences. Since the book's publication, critics have also noted earlier works that seem to contain similar themes. I will discuss the debate over both Wilkie Collins' *The Moonstone* and Fyodor Dostoevsky's *Crime and Punishment* as potential models or parallels for *Drood* in the course of chapter three, but of particular interest is the lesser known works with which Dickens had a direct involvement. The first of these, Emily Jolly's 'An Experience', was published in *All the Year Round* on 14 and 21 August 1869, a time at which Dickens was planning his novel. In a letter to his friend and biographer John Forster, Dickens called it 'a very remarkable story'.[5] Though the tale is different from *Drood* in many respects, telling as it does the story of a grieving mother seeking revenge on the surgeon she holds accountable for her child's death, there are clear parallels to be seen too. After the death of the child, the surgeon falls ill and – to his horror – the mother acts as his nurse, holding a powerful and mesmeric charm over him too:

> *It was fear. I now experienced – there is no denying it – a*
> *most horrible fear. A shrinking of the spirit and of the flesh.*
> *Why was I given over to her?*

Was this another world, in which she had power given her to torment me? Was this my hell?

I, weak as a child, was alone with her. That awful woman with the terrible eyes, and the arms uplifted to curse me! The woman of my dread and dreadful dreams and fever-fancies.[6]

All of which can be seen, potentially, as an early germ of the idea of John Jasper's nurturing/controlling relationship with both his nephew and Rosa Bud, with equally dire consequences. Also of interest is Robert Bulwer-Lytton's story 'The Disappearance of John Ackland', which again was published in *All The Year Round*, between 18 September and 16 October 1869.[7] It should have gone on for longer, but Dickens himself called it short when he apparently realised the story had been done before. Several scholars have searched with no avail, for such a story that tells, as Bulwer-Lytton's story does, the tale of a man supposedly on friendly terms with another man, who he then kills and hides, only to be discovered thanks to the presence of the victim's watch. As I say, searches have been made but none can find what the precursor to this story might be that Dickens worried was being copied. Accordingly, the more popular theory is that Dickens actually dropped Bulwer-Lytton's story not because it copied another, but because it *anticipated* his own.

Other aspects to be considered regarding *Drood*'s conception relate to the author's statements to friends and family about the plot, which will be covered in detail in chapters one and two, and the author's own manuscript notes. Though Dickens had pretty much winged it with his early plots, from *Dombey and Son* onwards there is a much clearer sense of an overarching plot, supported by the surviving manuscript notes for these works where we can see Dickens' attempts to plan out the monthly numbers. When it comes to *Drood*, we have the manuscript plans for numbers one to six…but nothing for the final six instalments. Given that Dickens was writing approximately three months ahead of each instalment's publication, this is certainly unusual and several conspiracy theories abound, usually blaming Forster for deliberately suppressing the end. Many people have therefore turned to the surviving notes, and in particular the alternative titles considered by Dickens for potential ideas on the projected plan for the book: *The flight of Edwyn* [sic] *Drood*; *The loss of Edwin Drood*; *The Disappearance of Edwin Drood; The Mystery in the Drood Family*; *Dead? or alive?* All feed the ambiguity over Edwin's fate, and provide plenty of material for the Droodists to debate whether the hero is due to return or doomed forever. But discussions of interpretation bring us into the realm of *after* the book, for now we are looking *before*. Suffice it be said, then, that of *Drood*'s origins we have indications of potential literary inspirations, and an author exhausted and hiding his own secret, but also savouring the public affection seen first-hand on tours and enjoying the return to the novel. Ultimately, as much as we know about the origins of *Drood*, the amount we don't know is significantly more, and that gap has left an open invitation for theories and conspiracies as much as the absence of an ending has.

Finally, before we proceed with looking at those theories of what Dickens might have written, it makes sense to recap what he actually did write. *Drood* was originally published in six monthly instalments, beginning in April 1870 and finishing in September 1870, three months after the death of Dickens. The following summary is presented not to suggest one particular theory, but to attempt to give a fair synopsis of the plot as a useful *aide de memoire*.

No. 1, April 1870 (see fig. 1)

The first number opens in a London opium den, where a bedraggled figure wakes from a drug-induced vision of Cloistcrham, swiftly leaving only to reappear in the next scene as the respectable choirmaster of Cloisterham Cathedral, John Jasper. His exit from the morning service is watched by the dean, the verger Mr Topes, and the reverend Septimus Crisparkle, who all notice Jasper's ill state. Jasper himself is visited by his nephew and ward Edwin Drood. Edwin has long been spoilt by Jasper, as is noted by Jasper's landlady Mrs Topes (the verger's wife), but the devotion of the uncle is destined to face a great test, for Jasper is in love with Edwin's fiancée Rosa Bud. The engagement is a loveless match, done at the request of Edwin and Rosa's dead parents. While Edwin dreams of travelling to Egypt to work as an engineer, Jasper feels trapped in his life in Cloisterham. The next day we see Edwin visit Rosa at a boarding school (run by Miss Twinkleton, aided by Miss Tisher), where the young pair quarrel, both frustrated by their forced engagement. As they walk, they approach the cathedral where Edwin marks Jasper's voice among those singing, an observation which disturbs Rosa who wishes to leave the area at once.

Finally, we meet Mr Sapsea, pompous auctioneer, who is planning a grand epitaph to his deceased wife. For this purpose, he has asked Jasper to read the epitaph for his opinion of it, and while discussing this they are joined by the stonemason Durdles, who will be making the epitaph. As stonemason, Durdles has keys and access to the tombs of Cloisterham Cathedral, and as he and Jasper walk home, Jasper learns of Durdles' remarkable knack of tapping the walls of the crypt to determine the location of bodies in the tombs. Their discussion is disturbed by the ragged rogue Deputy, who throws stones at the pair. Jasper rages at the boy, but the child's actions are at Durdles' own request as it keeps him in check. Jasper leaves Durdles with a request to meet him again one night for a tour of the cathedral vaults. The final scene of the number is Jasper, home once more and watching his sleeping nephew 'with a fixed and deep attention'.

No. 2, May 1870 (see fig. 2)

The second number opens with the Reverend Crisparkle conducting his regular exercise routine, before having breakfast with his mother, with whom he has a close relationship. She has a letter from Mr Honeythunder, a rabid philanthropist who is sending them two young orphans from Ceylon, the appropriately named Landless twins. The twins are being entrusted to the Crisparkles' care. The girl, Helena, will be enrolled at Miss Twinkleton's school, and the boy, Neville, will live with the Crisparkles. Reverend Crisparkle and his mother arrange a welcome party for Neville and Helena, to also include Jasper, Rosa, Edwin and Miss Twinkleton, and are somewhat disconcerted when Honeythunder himself arrives with the twins and invites himself to the party, where he dominates the conversation with his bullish manner. On Honeythunder's leaving, Neville confides to Crisparkle how much he hates Honeythunder, and how he and his sister's life has been one of woe and mistreatment, and how in turn they had planned to run away from Crisparkle, but have been impressed with his manner and have chosen to stay. Meanwhile, Jasper is playing the piano and Rosa is asked to sing, as Jasper has been tutoring her, but she becomes nervous under the gaze of her music teacher and falters, whereupon Helena comes to her aid.

At the end of the night Rosa and Helena are escorted home to Miss Twinkleton's, where Helena confronts Rosa about Jasper's obvious attraction to her, and vows to keep her safe. Meanwhile, having escorted the ladies home, Edwin and Neville quarrel in the street. Neville admires Rosa and thinks Edwin does not deserve her, while Edwin resents Neville's prying into his affairs. Jasper stops them and invites them to his lodgings to calm the situation. However, after he prepares them a drink, they become even more wild (by nineteenth-century standards) with a glass smashed by Neville as he grows angrier with Edwin. Neville leaves with no more violence but Jasper rushes to Crisparkles the next morning scandalised by the brutish behaviour of young Neville to his beloved nephew. The final chapter of the number returns to Rosa and the boarding school where gossip about the beastly young Neville and his savage attack are interrupted by the arrival of Rosa's guardian, Mr Grewgious, who awkwardly asks after her wellbeing and hints, for the first time, that the marriage need not go ahead if the couple don't wish it. Before leaving Cloisterham, Grewgious visits Jasper, as Edwin's guardian, and the conversation is...uncomfortable. Jasper is all too aware of Rosa's awkwardness around him, and his surly response 'God save them both' leaves Grewgious confused and anxious.

No. 3, June 1870 (see fig. 3)

The third number opens with Mrs Crisparkle expressing her concerns over Neville Landless to her son, who defends his young ward. Reverend Crisparkle then sees Neville and Helena while out on a walk and advises him to make peace with Edwin. Neville confesses his love for Rosa to Crisparkle, which he sees as ill-advised and best kept secret. Helena expresses her gratitude for Crisparkle's concern by kissing his hand and he gets very bashful in response. Crisparkle asks Jasper to help with the reconciliation by hosting a dinner for the two young men, which he begrudgingly agrees to organise, but not before showing Crisparkle extracts from his diary in which his fears of Neville are made explicit. In the next chapter, we see Edwin in London visiting the offices of Mr Grewgious in Staples Inn (the door to which is identified by the headstone outside with the mysterious initials PJT). Grewgious again advises that the engagement is not binding, and while giving Edwin Rosa's mother's ring, to be used as the engagement ring for Rosa, he stresses to Edwin that the marriage should not be entered into lightly. Then we are back to Cloisterham for the next chapter, and Jasper's promised tour with Durdles around the cathedral tombs. On the way, they spy Neville and Crisparkle at a distance and, following Jasper's lead, they pause and watch the pair from the shadows, Durdles being somewhat disconcerted by the intensity of Jasper's stare as he looks upon them. Once in the cathedral crypt, Jasper plies Durdles with drink, upon which Durdles feels mysteriously tired and has a lie-down, where, half-awake, half-dreaming, he perceives Jasper take his keys from him and disappear for a length of time before returning to wake him so they can leave. Jasper is a little angered to find that Deputy is outside, and is worried as to how long he has been watching.

No. 4, July 1870 (see fig. 4)

The fourth number opens at Miss Twinkleton's where the girls are all leaving for the holidays, save Rosa. Edwin comes to see her and they agree to break off the engagement, after which they are immediately more relaxed with each other than they have been before. At their parting, Rosa gives Edwin a kiss, immediately after which Edwin notices Jasper watching them from afar. The next chapter opens on Christmas Eve, and the night of the promised reconciliation between Edwin and Neville. Neville is preparing for a long walk the next day, and has bought a large walking stick, which Crisparkle ominously suggests is far too heavy. Edwin wanders Cloisterham, first going to a jeweller to have his watch fixed, only to be told that his uncle was in not so long ago and knew exactly what jewellery Edwin carried (namely the watch, chain and shirt-pin). Later that day Edwin bumps into Princess Puffer – owner of the London opium den – who asks him for money, and after learning his name warns him that Ned is a bad name, and that there is a Ned who is in great trouble. Edwin is a little disconcerted at the suggestion that his name is trouble, especially as the only person to call him Ned is his beloved uncle. Jasper, meanwhile, seems in much happier spirits, as Crisparkle notes upon seeing him. Jasper, Edwin and Neville all enter Jasper's lodgings, and while we don't see what happens inside, we are told that a great storm hits Cloisterham that night.

The next morning, as the town's residents gather outside the cathedral to look at the broken clock on the cathedral, damaged by the storm, Jasper appears, raving, and banging on Crisparkle's door asking after his nephew – for Edwin has disappeared. Neville, meanwhile, is already gone on his walk, where he finds himself followed by a group of men who promptly try to arrest him. He fights them off with his suspiciously heavy stick, and blood is spilt. He is immediately brought to Crisparkle and Jasper, who are nearby, and Jasper points at the now-bloodied stick (suspiciously, of course). Neville is brought in front of Mr Sapsea, who has not become mayor of Cloisterham but is still great friends with Jasper, and while no evidence exists against young Landless, he is clearly seen as guilty of murder. Later that evening, Grewgious arrives at Jasper's lodgings and tells him that the engagement had been called off by Rosa and Edwin, in response to which revelation Jasper collapses, unconscious, while Grewgious maintains his position by the fireplace, looking on.

No. 5, August 1870 (see fig. 5)

The fifth number continues with this same scene. Jasper comes to and expresses his shock at the news, but also a new hope that, in light of this, perhaps Edwin himself has run away, afraid to tell his uncle the disappointing news of the broken engagement. While this discussion is taking place, Crisparkle is exercising (again). This time it is swimming in Cloisterham Weir, where he spots Edwin's watch and shirt-pin discarded in the water. He takes them to Jasper, who once more fears his nephew is dead, and appoints himself avenger of his dear boy, not resting until the murderer is destroyed.

In the next chapter, we move once more to London. Crisparkle first visits Honeythunder, as the guardian of the Landless twins, only to see the philanthropist wash his hands of the troublesome pair, to which Crisparkle has a choice few words to say. He leaves the blustering hypocrite and goes straight to Staple Inn, where Grewgious has been lodging Neville, who has long-since fled Cloisterham under the general suspicion of the whole town. Grewgious tells Crisparkle that Jasper has been to London several times, spying on Neville, and is outside the office at that very moment. At this point Dickens introduces a new character, Tartar, a former sailor, who makes friends with his new neighbour Neville. In the next chapter, we meet another new character, Datchery, a stranger in Cloisterham with a conspicuous shock of white hair, who poses various questions about the recent mystery in an entirely innocent way and, seeking lodging, asks to stay in the apartment below Jasper's, for which he then goes to visit Sapsea and Jasper to get their recommendation for the Topes as landlords. His initial travel around the town also brings him into contact with Durdles and Deputy. In the final chapter of the number, Rosa's peace is further disturbed by the arrival at the nun's house of Jasper, who accosts her by the sundial in the garden and confesses his passionate obsession with her, vowing that he will give up his crusade of hounding Neville is she will have him, or destroy young Landless if she does not. Horrified, Rosa flees Cloisterham to the safety of Grewgious in London.

No. 6, September 1870 (see fig. 6)

The next morning, Grewgious and Rosa are deciding what to do. His assistant, Bazzard, we are told, is away on leave. They are joined by Crisparkle, who has received a note from Rosa. They are limited in their movement by their knowledge that Jasper spies upon the building. But at that moment Tartar arrives, having recognised in Crisparkle a former school friend who saved him from drowning as a boy, and on the sailor's entrance Grewgious comes up with a plan. Rosa will go into Tartar's home, from which she can go to the balcony and talk to Helena, who is with Neville in his lodgings next door, thus allowing Rosa to see her friend without Jasper knowing it. Rosa is thrilled to be in Tartar's apartment, and Helena notes the breathless excitement in her friend. Grewgious then takes Rosa to find more suitable accommodation at a boarding house run by the tyrannical Billickin, a widow who refuses any prefix. Rosa is joined by Miss Twinkleton, who is to be a companion and guardian for her in London, and they in turn are invited by Tartar for a lovely boat trip out, accompanied by his man Lobley and Grewgious. Time spent in the company of the handsome sailor see Rosa developing new sensations of feelings.

In the final chapter, 'The Dawn Again', we go back to Jasper, who has returned to the opium den, much to the joy of Princess Puffer, who seems to have another agenda. She questions Jasper in his drug-induced state, and he talks about a task he has long thought of doing, only now that it is done, it is not as he imagined. The next day Jasper leaves to return to Cloisterham, and Princess Puffer follows him, realising in doing so that he is a respectable choirmaster. Her endeavours attract the attention of Datchery, who follows her in turn and sees her absolute glee as she stands at the back of the cathedral watching the unknowing Jasper and recognising him. Equally pleased by this revelation, Datchery returns to his lodgings and makes some sort of tally mark, suggesting progress in his investigation, before beginning a lovely breakfast prepared by Mrs Tope. And that's where it all ends – and a much bigger story begins…

Dick Datchery:
The dawn again (and again...and again...)

> Mrs Tope's care has spread a very neat, clean breakfast ready for her lodger. Before sitting down to it, he opens his corner-cupboard door; takes his bit of chalk from its shelf; adds one thick line to the score, extending from the top of the cupboard door to the bottom, and then falls to with an appetite.

Mr Datchery chews the food in his mouth carefully. He had read that one should chew food thirty-two times before swallowing; to date he has been chewing it for 148 years, but you can never be too careful. He sits back in his chair while his jaws continue to work on the food, always present, never swallowed. His appetite remains unquenched, but he takes great satisfaction in the latest development in his investigation. He has him now for sure, that was certain. His observation of Princess Puffer had been most interesting, and he is now on the brink of solving it. But first, he has to eat. He falls to with an appetite.

Of course, there is still a great deal to do. The whereabouts of Drood, dead or alive, still needs to be uncovered. But there is time for that. Now that he knows to keep an eye on Jasper, it will only be a short while before the rest of the mystery is resolved. Yes, this will soon be a closed case. But nothing was ever resolved on an empty stomach. He falls to with an appetite.

Then there's that unfortunate Landless fellow, exiled to London while the town holds him under suspicion. There is a wrong that needed righting – or an end that needed writing? He shakes his head, his mass of white hair fanning out as he does so, and empties his mind of such silly thoughts. Writing indeed! This is a serious mystery, and time is of the essence to unmask the culprit and save any further anguish on the part of the many victims. Yes, he will bring it all to an end, just as soon as he has finished breakfast. He falls to with an appetite.

The watch and shirt-pin had certainly caused confusion, to begin with – a very clever twist that. But you have to get up pretty early in the morning to fool Dick Datchery, and he will soon show everyone the true story explaining their presence in the weir. It is remarkable to think of the impact this could have on the sleepy town of Cloisterham, as justice is finally served, and such a long time coming too. And as for poor, persecuted Rosa – well! This too will be resolved. He falls to with an appetite.

As Datchery chews – forever chewing – a nagging doubt buzzes in the back of his mind. He has been eating for such a long time now, perhaps it is time to act, not think? To leave the table and put his plan into effect? His discovery earlier this morning ...no, yesterday morning ... no, last week? ...year? ...century? ...calls for immediate action. He must act. He will act. All this will end. There is so much to do, always so much still to do. It shall be done. It will be done. He will go and solve the whole thing – now. He must prepare. But the food is laid out so cleanly. And though he has been chewing all this time, he still has yet to actually eat. He will have no strength unless he eats. Yes, breakfast first, then immediately afterwards all this will be solved. The Mystery of Edwin Drood will be no more...

...

He falls to with an appetite.

CHAPTER ONE

Nostalgia and Opportunism: The Early Solutions 1870–1885

Famous last words

'The Late Charles Dickens'

I
Dickens is dead. Who has not lost a friend?
Far, far too early seems this sudden end
Of one whom all men loved. The fatal hour
Arrives too soon for him,
Whose glance had not grown dim,
Whose heart and brain preserved their fresh and
*   liberal power.*

II
'Whom the gods love, die young' – so wise men
*   hold:*
This man dies young, who never could grow old.
Genius like his to the last hour receives
The golden gift divine;
And to the last there shine
The love within his heart, the life upon his leaves.

III
Such life. Old Chaucer was his prototype:
But Geoffrey's verse in Charles' prose grew ripe.
He gave us Pickwick, Quixote of the day –
Weller, the Sancho Panza
Of a new extravaganza –
Quilp, the half-human goblin, devilishly gay.

IV
Micawber, too, the strangely sanguine scamp –
The ebrious Swiveller, the garrulous Gamp –
Pecksniff's low tricks, and Skimple's dainty
thirst:
Latest, to move our Wonder,
Crisparkle, Honeythunder –
Men whom we all have met, though DICKENS
drew them first.

V
His canvas glows with many charming girls,
But surely, choicest of these pretty pearls
Is little Rosa of the cloistered City –
A wayward gay coquettish
Provoking loving pettish
Darling of life's young spring, creature to scold
and pity.

VI
Ay, the final hand! – it had not lost its cunning:
Ah! But the strong swift life-blood ceased
running –
Pass quick away the pathos and the mirth:
When shall we see again
One whose creative brain
Adds such a chapter to the Bible of the Earth?[8]

CHAPTER ONE

Dickens was dead: to begin with. After working on the latest instalment of *Drood* on the morning of 8 June 1870, in the chalet across the road from his home in Gads Hill, he then suffered a seizure that afternoon, dying later in the early hours of the following day. The private passing of the man swiftly became the public sensation of the press, with obituaries of great sentiment and hyperbole: 'The prince and the great man had fallen, and the shock experienced by hundreds of thousands on Thursday morning was an event never to be forgotten.'[9] Several even extended to poetry, such as the entry above from *The Period*. Awful as the verse may be, the sentiments expressed are very much in line with several articles of the time in its depiction of Dickens as a friend of the people, his death as a personal loss for all of his readers, and his last work as promise of more of the same beloved characters: 'ay, the final hand! – it had not lost its cunning'. This golden-hued interpretation of *Drood*, which would not persevere, is very much coloured by the event of his passing. The book gained great import by being his last words, which ultimately is not a reflection on the text itself but its timing.

Other contenders to Dickens' last piece of writing were also appearing in the press. *The Times* reported that: 'His last letter to the manager of *All the Year Round*, Mr Holdsworth, a gentleman who has been connected with Mr Dickens for a quarter of a century, was dated the day before his death, and asked him to purchase at 'one of those Great Queen-street shops' – who knew so well as Dickens about London brokers and their wares? – a writing-slope for Gadshill such as he had in use at the office.'[10] It's hardly the most insightful prose. Clearly, the interest of the letter lies in its context, not its content (Victorian furniture enthusiasts excepted). Similarly, John Makeham wrote excitedly to the *Daily News* to share a letter in his possession written by Dickens on 8 June, the publishing of which allowed Makeham a brief moment in the spotlight, which he savoured with a simpering praise that might make Uriah Heep blush: 'I cannot but be glad to have in my possession Charles Dickens' last words – and such words – and to be able to lay them before his thousands of admiring and mourning friends.'[11] The words themselves were but a reply to Makeham's own letter concerning a religious passage quoted in *Drood* (and actually Dickens' letter is disagreeing with Makeham's interpretation of the passage). Makeham was not a friend or confidante of Dickens but a reader being written to for the first time; that he should have, or make claim to have, 'Dickens' last words' is sheer dumb luck. However, as with the unremarkable request for a writing-slope, these words gain far greater significance for Dickens' readers simply by being amongst the last, as would prove to be the case for *Drood* in its unintended position as Dickens' final novel. Where the letters of Holdsworth and Makeham are disappointingly functional and uninspiring in content, *Drood* has the advantage of a developed narrative that allowed early readers to probe and extract last words of wisdom or a melancholy foreshadowing of the author's own death.

But it was not always so, and contemporary reactions to the story when it first began to appear – and Dickens was still alive and well – were quite different indeed. The first monthly part of *Drood* was published on Thursday 31 March 1870, and the reviews that came out of this initial instalment in April were not only positive, but exuberant. 'Really, Messrs. Chapman and Hall!' cried the *John Bull*'s review:

> *Please revise the announcement of Dickens's last work! The Mystery of Edwin Drood! Of course it did, a work from the pen of Boz is always sure to draw. Please alter: – 'the mystery of Edwin' drew – you may add, if you like, immensely.*[12]

Drood marked the return of Dickens to writing novels after that unprecedented five-year gap while he had been engaged on his reading tours, so, as the *Illustrated London News* noted in its one-paragraph review, 'all the world is eager to welcome Mr Dickens back to the domains of serial fiction, and so far as we can judge from the first number of his work, public expectation is not likely to be disappointed'.[13] *The Times*, in a longer review, concurred both with the sense of anticipation and the pleasant realisation that this book would live up to the hype:

> *The novel reading world have been on the tiptoe of expectation since the announcement of a new work by their favourite author. We have perused the first instalment, and venture to express the public pleasure, and to thank Mr Dickens for having added a zest to the season.*[14]

The early readers did not read the book looking *ahead* to Dickens' death, as we do, but looking *back* on Dickens' life so far, bringing the heritage of the Dickens canon with them. Consequently, the review, not only in *The Times* but also in the *Athenaeum*, are both very nostalgic, writing respectively that:

> *As he delighted the fathers, so he delights the children, and this his latest effort promises to be received with interest and pleasure as widespread as those which greeted those glorious Papers which built at once the whole edifice of his fame.*[15]

> _____

> *It is a positive pleasure to see once more the green cover in which the world first beheld Mr Pickwick, and to find within it the opening chapters of a tale which gives promise of being worthy of the pen which sketched, with masterly hand, the course of Mr Pickwick's fortunes.*[16]

Not only do these reviews look back with fondness, but they link *Drood* back right to the beginning, with Dickens' first full novel *The Pickwick Papers* – not a comparison one would expect as its light-hearted comic episodes seem a world away from the dark, murderous streets of Cloisterham. In recent years, as will be seen, it is more frequently *Our Mutual Friend* that is drawn upon as a comparison for *Drood*, as a result of the love triangles and the murder plots contained within both, and its status as the novel that immediately precedes *Drood*. But in 1870, the reviewers cared less for the social commentary of *Our Mutual Friend* and more for the popular comedy of *Pickwick* and the early novels, and there is a sense in which the reviewers' identification of *Drood* with *Pickwick* speaks as much of their own preoccupations as it does of the book's content.

At any rate, these reviewers certainly noted a much higher content of comedy in *Drood* than subsequent critics of the book would heed. The *Illustrated London News* concludes that the 'most successful of the character portraits is Durdles', who *The Times* likewise applauds as 'a thoroughly original conception'.[17] Even in the *Athenaeum*'s lengthier review, those scenes that we have come to think of as key in the first instalment – Jasper in the opium den, his conversation/confession with Edwin, the references to the Sapsea memorial, Jasper's plan to visit the tombs, and the closing image of Jasper watching his nephew in the dark – prove of little interest. Just one line of the review is given to Jasper, and that is by means of discussing the comical scene with Mr Sapsea. Instead, according to the *Athenaeum* in April 1870, the key moments in are the high humour of Durdles, Sapsea, and the delightful scene of young Rosa and Edwin: 'There is, moreover, a touch of the old Boz humour in that exquisitely promising Rosa Bud.' Humour and nostalgia – this was the way in which *Drood* was first read.

By the time of the third instalment in June 1870, the *Illustrated London News* was still singling out praise for 'the dissipated mason, Durdles' for being 'the only character, so far, that can be regarded as a creation, in Mr Dickens' characteristic style'.[18] Likewise, consider again that opening poem from *The Period* and the three characters out of the novel who it singles out for praise: Rosa, Crisparkle…and Honeythunder. The identifying of these three characters in particular shows the impact of serialised reading. Even with the fragment we now have, we still have a better idea of the whole than readers in June 1870, who only had three of the six instalments to draw on. Thus, to them, Grewgious was yet to emerge as a prime mover in the defence of

Rosa; Datchery had not yet appeared; Edwin was just a spoilt young man; and Neville had yet to endure the heartache of suspicion and exile. In short, Crisparkle, the muscular Christian of cheerful manner, with his warm welcome and defence of the Landless twins, was the clear hero of the first three instalments, thus justifying his mention alongside Rosa as the heroine. But how to explain Honeythunder? Even at this early stage his contribution to the book's plot was minimal. It is his contribution to the book's humour that justifies his inclusion here. Like Durdles, he was a funny character. Dickens' contemporary reviewers were predominately keen to champion such comic work and question his social satire.

But these responses in June were already fighting against the tide, for Dickens' death that month changed the novel from his latest work to his last one, and the way it was read was irrevocably changed. In the light of Dickens' death, readers returned to the *Drood* instalments with a different perspective. Increasingly, readers searched for significance in the book as it existed before them, in only three instalments, as in this letter to *the Daily News*:

> *Sir, – A short paragraph in the current number of 'The Mystery of Edwin Drood' has acquired a painful significance from the sad event of the 9th. Saddened as Mr Dickens must have been by the loss of so many old friends, notably by the very recent and sudden death of Maclise; the tone of thought, which dictated the few lines referred to is easily accounted for, but his own lamented departure points the moral with more than ordinary force. The few lines may be interesting to your readers. They are from a description of a stonecutter's yard: – 'The two journeymen have left their two great saws sticking in their blocks of stone; and two skeleton journeymen out of the Dance of Death might be grinning in the shadow of their sheltering sentry-boxes, about to slash away at cutting out the gravestones of the next two people destined to die at Cloisterham. Likely enough the two think little of that*

*now, being alive and perhaps merry. Curious to make a
guess at the two – or say, at one of the two.'
    I am, &c, R. S. June 11[19]*

Dickens wrote his instalments some time ahead of publication – hence
why he was working three months ahead on the sixth instalment at the
time of his death – so the attempt of R. S. to draw significance out of
the third instalment, which would have been written several months
before his death, seems even more absurd than our willingness to do so
with the sixth. The response of R. S. is emotional, rather than logical.
The extract quoted in his letter is from a scene set in a graveyard, and
the discussion of death therefore not such a remarkable occurrence
after all; but, ultimately, writer's intention was second-place to
readers' interpretation. Early responses to *Drood* were thus shaped
primarily by the precious quality the work inherited now it was known
to be Dickens' last. *Every Saturday* noted of the last instalment that
it 'will be read with mournful interest and lasting regret', but the
same can be said of the two preceding instalments, all read in the
knowledge of the author's death.[20] The *Illustrated London News* had
reviewed No. 3 before the loss of Dickens, and the change in tone in
its subsequent review of No. 4 is evident, as it opens with a disclaimer
that: 'The recent calamity sustained alike by letters and society must
be felt to exempt this latest production of Mr Dickens from minute
criticism.'[21] *Drood*, for the time-being, was being given a free pass in
respect of the author's death, swept up in a national wave of mourning
and commemoration.

In the days immediately following his death many obituaries,
having covered Dickens' life and previous writings, closed with a
look ahead to the end of *Drood*. The *Pall Mall Gazette* noted:

*For the best part of a year Mr Dickens had been hard at
work on 'Edwin Drood', and was at least several numbers
in advance of the published part of the story. He himself
has somewhere mentioned that his plan of composition*

was to begin, not at the beginning, but the end – to adjust
the final combination of the plot, and then set himself to
work up to it. It is possible, therefore, that the "Mystery
of Edwin Drood" may yet be solved.[22]

The objective tone of this comment was contrasted by the *Daily Telegraph*'s more passionate response:

His unfinished and scarcely yet begun 'Mystery of Edwin
Drood' has given promise of a tale so ingenious and
captivating that the public, after the first shock which the
tidings of his death will bring, may be pardoned a hope
that posterity will not lose the whole of this work, but
that the author had made such advances in it as to afford
some indication of its close.[23]

Despite only a quarter of the planned novel being published and available to the public at the time of Dickens' death, *Drood* was already being considered in the light of posterity as a tale 'so ingenious and captivating' – hardly in line with some of the criticism it would later receive from the likes of Wilkie Collins as 'the melancholy work of a worn-out brain'.[24]

The promise of infinite more words to come was now reduced into a finite measurement of text: every surviving word from Dickens' pen became something precious to savour. John Forster, who was bequeathed all of Dickens' manuscripts in his will and charged with overseeing the publication of the last instalments, undid the cuts Dickens had made. Lines Dickens would otherwise have edited out of the story were now reinstated. The emphasis was on quantity, not quality, and with a limited amount of words of the inimitable left on this earth, Forster opted to give them all to Dickens' readers. With the publication of the sixth instalment in September 1870, a short paragraph by the publishers Chapman and Hall explained that the well had now, at last, run dry:

All that was left in manuscript of EDWIN DROOD is contained in the Number now published – the sixth. Its last entire page had not been written two hours when the event occurred which one very touching passage in it (grave and sad but also cheerful and reassuring) might seem almost to have anticipated. The only notes in reference to the story that have since been found concern that portion of it exclusively, which is treated in the earlier Numbers. Beyond the clues therein afforded to its conduct or catastrophe, nothing whatever remains; and it is believed that what the author himself would have most desired is done, in placing before the reader without further note or suggestion the fragment of THE MYSTERY OF EDWIN DROOD.

Three months after his body had been interred at Westminster Abbey, the closing of the book meant Dickens was now truly gone. As one contemporary review noted, 'The sudden breaking off of the story tells us again with more emphasis than any words could convey that Charles Dickens is dead.'[25] Some bemoaned Chapman and Hall's decision. A review in *The Spectator* commented:

Though we agree with the publishers that any attempt to complete the tale by a different hand would have been an insult to Mr Dickens, and altogether unwelcome to the public, we do think that any authentic indications which may exists of the turn he intended to give to the story, ought to have been furnished to the readers of the fragment.[26]

This argument carries more weight given that Chapman and Hall's explanation was not correct. There *were* notes, albeit verbal notes, left to a handful of Dickens' friends, colleagues and family – Charles Dickens Jnr, Charles Alston Collins, Luke Fildes and John Forster – from which it was possible to construct a sense of how the story should end, but these would not appear in public for a few years yet.

CHAPTER ONE

It is a mystery in itself that Forster would later publish the comments made to him by Dickens in his biography but, as the editor of the final three instalments, did not think to mention any of it to Chapman and Hall. Possibly he did, and they simply decided to finish the book where Dickens had stopped. This would have involved some saving on their part, as the original contract for *Drood* involved payment to the author in instalments at the end of the first part, sixth part and final part. So stopping at part six allowed them to legally pay only half the agreed author's fee to Dickens' family. However, realistically, an authorised completion by the publishers would almost certainly have produced enough profit, so I find it hard to believe Chapman and Hall would decline on economic grounds. Whatever the reasoning, the publishers' decision to stop the story midway with no attempt at resolution left a vacuum among the readers that would swiftly be filled by the first of many solutions to the mystery. Despite the reverence of the early reviews, the early completions would ultimately capitalise on Dickens' death, often introducing tones of parody or making extraordinary claims bordering on libel.

Parody

The early completions to which this chapter will now turn to have frequently been regarded, or disregarded, as oddities in the history of *Drood* solutions, which is a gross unfairness as they have had the misfortune to be judged by the different standards of subsequent generations. These completions are doing something quite unlike what would follow them. What sets them apart is their lack of concern with uncovering Dickens' intentions and presenting a theory based on the facts buried in the text. Instead the novels, which appeared in the 1870s and 1880s, took Dickens' text as a starting point from which to launch entirely new tales, deviating from the original quite quickly and exhibiting a breathtaking freedom barely seen since in solutions. The first solution to *Drood* never even intended to be one. The American writer Robert Henry Newell, writing under his popular pseudonym of Orpheus C. Kerr (literally, Office Seeker), whose regular articles satirising the Civil War had been appearing in the American press since 1862, had already begun writing a parody of *Drood* shortly after the publication of the first instalment in April 1870 when Dickens was still alive, though the first weekly instalment of *The Cloven Foot* would not be published until 11 June 1870 in *Punchinello*. By the time the fourth instalment was published on 2 July 1870, a tribute to Dickens acknowledged the author's death, and soon after Kerr was left to complete his adaptation on his own initiative. *The Cloven Foot* is a very broad-humoured parody, Kerr explaining his motives as an attempt to show how ill-fitting British literature was to American culture. The old world had history, mythology and ethics, in contrast to the new world's obsession with commerce, progress and money:

> *Our American higher society, originating almost wholly as it does from the tendency of fluctuating wealth to spasmodic sensational luxury, and not from hereditary privilege or aesthetic aspiration, is informed much more by the logic of trade and the pride of financial energy than by the obligations of illustrious ancestry and the fine egotism of conscious superiority in class cultivation.*[27]

Cloisterham became Bumsteadville, Neville Landless becomes Montgomery, a Southerner, while Sapsea becomes Judge Sweeney – Kerr explaining that 'The present Adaptor can think of no nearer American equivalent [to an auctioneer], in the way of a person at once resident in a suburb and who sells to the highest bidder, than a supposed member of the New York judiciary'.[28] Thus, by setting a tale of England in the land of the free, Kerr's intention, apparently, was not to parody Dickens, but America itself. That said, whatever his plan, Kerr's book nonetheless tears into Dickens too. The changing of Rosa Bud's name to Flora Potts has nothing to do with American satire and everything to do with mocking Dickens' choice of names. Most damningly, John Jasper becomes John Bumstead, a drunken buffoon with a perpetual stink about him of cloves and a double vision frequently used to comic effect, such as his mourning for his *nephews.*

Nor was Kerr alone in parodying *Drood* at this time. In the same month that the *Athenaeum*, *Times* and *Illustrated London News* were singing the praises of *Drood*'s first instalment for its nostalgic echoes of Dickens' earlier work, *Judy* was attacking it for precisely the same reason. 'The Mystery of Rude Dedwin' is a one-page satire of the first instalment, which tears into the story for rehashing old characters (fig. 7). It pulls no punches, reducing the artistry of Fildes' illustrations to caricatures with ridiculous titles: 'Higgledy Piggledy' and 'Spoony Moony'. [29] The main attack is on what is felt to be repetitive Dickensian traits. Sapsea explains he is 'not Pecksniff, as you might imagine, but Papsy. I chose it because it was funny. I married a woman of the name of Ethelinda for the same reason.' [30] The piece simultaneously accuses Dickens not only of plagiarising his own works, but relying on silly names for his characters (it is a hard criticism to dispute of the creator of Mr M'Choakumchild, the Cheeryble brothers and – ahem – Dick Swiveller). The piece concludes its attack on *Drood* by arguing that 'the mystery is – *how it sells*'. [31]

In comparison to 'Rude Dedwin' then, Kerr's parody is positively sympathetic, though the obscurity of the *Judy* piece has left *The Cloven Foot* to face alone the full wrath of subsequent Dickensians who didn't get the joke: 'It is greatly to be regretted that the first sequel to *The Mystery of Edwin Drood* was of a burlesque character, even riotously burlesque,' sniffed J. C. Walters in 1912. [32] Of all the early completions, *The Cloven Foot* in particular has been consciously overlooked by subsequent Droodists for being too silly, the only point of merit being Kerr's theory that Datchery was Bazzard in disguise, which has since become a popular idea. But to dismiss it on these grounds is less a commentary on the merit of Kerr's book and more an indication of later Droodist priorities on plot and the mystery over style and character.

Kerr was positive in his praise of Dickens. He included an apology when the series was collected and published as a book, and while most of this consists of tongue-in-cheek negotiation of the book's attacks on contemporary America, the passages relating to Dickens are more careful to express admiration of 'the great Master of modern English Fiction'.[33] Not that this praise is absolute. In seeming to champion the significance of *Drood* 'as a revelation of the tired Worker in the Work never to be finished', Kerr characteristically insults through ironic deference:[34]

> *The Story, opening with an elaboration of masterly purpose in which the strength of intense concentration for a moment counterfeits the strength of spontaneity, soon halts with the halting power of the Story-teller so near his rest; then turns intractable and prone to break beneath the relaxing hand uncertain of its former cunning; a little later, shows the indomitable mind, constrained almost convulsively to a greater light because of the approaching shadow of the body's dissolution, and in its darkening premonitions throwing a shadow of that shade, and even a defined portion of the physical struggle against it, upon the wavering mimic scene; and, at last, breaks off, half told, to remain the tenderest of all its Master's stories – the story of his Death![35]*

It needs to be remembered that this is Newell writing in the character of Kerr, and that there is, therefore, a great deal of affect in the writing above. It is intended first and foremost to raise a smile rather than be a critical piece on Dickens. Ironically, the paragraph foreshadows a great number of interpretations of *Drood*, both in its insistence upon the weariness of Dickens, as though he were aware of his own approaching death, and the unevenness of his last work. But the dismissal of Kerr's book by later critics as a nonsense work, or worse, an attack on Dickens, does it a great disservice. Imitation is the sincerest form of flattery, after all, and for all of Kerr's linguistic acrobatics in his opening apology, his deference to Dickens shines through in the work itself. *The Cloven Foot* is remarkable for the close similarity it maintains to the original, parodying it not only chapter by chapter, but almost line by line. As one example, consider the discussion between Jasper/Bumstead and Edwin in Chapter Two of both novels:

A Dean, and a Chapter Also (Dickens)	A Dean and a Chap or Two (Kerr)
At length the cloth is drawn, and a dish of walnuts and a decanter of rich sherry are placed upon the table.	At length the cloth is drawn, Edwin produces some peanuts from his pocket, and passes some to Mr Bumstead, and the latter, with a wet towel pinned about his head, drinks a great deal of water.
…	…
Crack. On Edwin Drood's part. Crack. On Mr Jasper's part.	Crack. On Mr Edwin's part. Hic. On Mr Bumstead's part.
…	…
'Isn't it unsatisfactory to be cut off from choice in such a matter? There Jack! I tell you! If I could choose, I would choose Pussy from all the pretty girls in the world. My dead and gone father and Pussy's dead and gone father must needs marry us together by anticipation. Why the – Devil, I was going to say, if it had been respectful to their memory – couldn't they leave us alone?'	'And, if our respective respected parents didn't bound us by will to marry, I'd be mad after her.'
…	…
'Yes Jack, it's all very well for you. You can take it easily. You have no uncomfortable suspicion that you are forced upon anybody, nor has anybody an uncomfortable suspicion that she is forced upon you, or that you are forced upon her. You can choose for yourself. Life for you is a plum with the natural bloom on; it hasn't been over-carefully wiped off for you –'	'Nobody's dictated a marriage for you Jack. You can choose for yourself. Life for you is still fraught with freedom's intoxicating –'
…	…
'Don't stop dear fellow. Go on.' 'Can I anyhow have hurt your feelings Jack?	'Good Heavens Jack! I haven't hurt your feelings?'

A Dean, and a Chapter Also (Dickens)	A Dean and a Chap or Two (Kerr)
…	…
'I have been taking opium for a pain – an agony – that sometimes overcomes me. The effects of the medicine steal over me like a blight or a cloud, and pass. You see them in the act of passing; they will be gone directly.'	'Don't mind me, my dear boys. It's cloves; you may notice them on my breath. I take them for my nerv'shness.'
…	…
'Take it as a warning then'	'Lem me be a mis'able warning to you, Edwin'
…	…
'Shall we go and walk in the churchyard?'	You want cheering up,' says Edwin Drood kindly. 'Yeah – cheering up. Let's go and walk in the graveyard'.

Kerr not only presumed his readers knew Dickens' original, but was counting on it in order for much of the humour to work. Imagine then Kerr's reaction when Dickens died and he too, by consequence, was left without an end to his work. But – and here again is another point that singles *The Cloven Foot* out as remarkable among *Drood* solutions – come the finale, there is a complete lack of self-congratulation of solving the mystery. Unlike his successors, Kerr does not write his introduction to the sound of trumpet fanfare as he expounds on his difficult quest to continue Dickens' prose, nor does he bewail the long hours spent poring over the clues in the text. Instead he simply and swiftly announces:

> *The design of representing a man with a dual existence,*
> *in one phase of which he intends to, and thinks he does,*
> *commit murder, while in the other he confounds the deed*
> *and doer with a personality distinct from his own, is kept*
> *so nervously apparent at the beginning, as a justification*
> *of the plotted dénouement that any reader fairly skilled*

*in the necessary artistic relations of one part of a story to
another, must derive therefore a premature knowledge of
what the designer supposedly wishes to conceal for the
time being.*[36]

While later Droodists might disagree with Kerr's interpretation of
the end, the primary interest in the statement is not the proposed
resolution but the author's confidence in it. Put simply, for Kerr there
was no mystery, the ending was obvious: Jasper's memory of the
fateful night was confused, Edwin was not dead, and Datchery was
Bazzard in disguise.

A year after *The Cloven Foot* was completed it was republished in
England under the title *The Mystery of Edwin Drood* with the character
and place names changed back to their Dickensian originals. What had
started as a parody rhapsodising upon Dickens' text was transformed
in the process of Dickens' death into a substitution for the original.
The first completion had been submitted to the world, immediately
after Dickens' death, and appearing in such close proximity it carried
the same appreciation of Dickens' humour as the early reviews, and
it is this that would be Kerr's downfall. When other theories were
picked apart and analysed in later decades, Kerr's work would be
swiftly tossed aside without consideration for its crime of failing to
take the job seriously.

It's not what you say, it's who you pretend to be when saying it

In 1871, the same year that Kerr's novel was being repackaged with
legitimate character names, the next sequel, *John Jasper's Secret*,
appeared with equal recognition for the benefits of an authoritative
context. The name of the author, Henry Morford, did not appear
on the book, and this shadowy figure has been at times claimed as
American by British critics, and British by American critics, each
seemingly eager to pin the blame upon the other, primarily because of

the extraordinary claim by the publishers that the work was written by none other than Wilkie Collins, in collaboration with Charles Dickens Jnr.[37] It is not clear where this rumour began, although it certainly benefitted the publishers, as the false attribution of these authors gave the work far greater credibility as a solution than it deserved, and for many years after the work continued to appear with Collins and Dickens Jnr's names on the front. (At the time of writing, the work is still credited as one of Charley's on his Wikipedia page.)

The book itself, while enjoyable, is quite a departure from Dickens' text. The end itself of Morford's tale is relatively uncontroversial: Datchery is Bazzard in disguise, Edwin is alive and beloved by Helena, while Rosa marries Tartar and Jasper dies for his sin of trying to murder his nephew. A number of these ideas would be teased out and repeated by later solutionists, but it is Morford's cavalier introduction of new characters and subplots that makes this completion unusual compared to the solutions of the twentieth century and beyond. There is Dr Chippercoyne, 'a short old man, with a good face, and white hair and whiskers, who took snuff and grimaced like a Frenchman.'[38] He assists Mr Grewgious and Helena in concocting a truth serum that can be administered to Jasper on his next visit to the opium den, and his Dickensian pedigree is vouched for by his ludicrous name. But Morford goes beyond mimicking Dickens' styles of names with the Crawshe family, who live by the river and operate as a who's who of Dickens' past novels: Mr Crawshe 'with a heart as brave and a spirit as indomitable as they may exist in bosoms much better clothed' is Dan Peggoty reborn; his young daughter Exty, who has 'been wronged, dishonoured, cast out [...] working her penance', shares the tragic back-story of Little Emily; while his poor crippled yet 'patient, uncomplaining' son, known only as Little Crawshe, is Tiny Tim in all but name.[39]

The freedom with which Morford deviates from the cast provided in Dickens' text is a marked contrast to the claustrophobic restrictiveness of later solutions, as is the disregard for trying to justify the text through reference back to the first half. Morford is not trying to justify the solution to himself, as later Droodists would do. Nor is he trying to prove that his ending is the only logical one to follow

Dickens' beginning. Instead, his primary intention is on convincing the paying public. It is the packaging that argues for its authenticity. Morford's attempt at gaining authority for his novel comes from the emulation of Dickensian character names, assimilation of Dickensian types like the Crawshe family into the tale, and the subsequent claim to Collins and Dickens Jnr as authors. Furthermore, Morford's tale was published in monthly instalments just like the original, and with illustrations strikingly evocative of Fildes' engravings for Dickens. Not only characters but their surroundings are copied and assimilated, as seen if comparing 'Sleeping it Off' (fig. 8) with 'Wringing a Secret from Death' (fig. 9), or 'Mr Grewgious Experiences a New Sensation' (fig. 10) with 'Supper and Music for Four' (fig. 11). The anonymous artist for Morford's completion was clearly doing his or her utmost to continue the visual interpretation of Dickens' first half.

The fidelity of appearances contradicts the deviation of content: the pitiful tale of the Crawshes, Chippercoyne's assistance in unmasking Jasper's crime, and the unique revelation that Deputy, the raggedy scoundrel of the streets, is none other than Mr Honeythunder's abandoned son. All these take the story in a different direction away from Dickens. Style trumps content, and as long as the audience believed the work to be written by Dickens' friend and son, it carried more weight of authority than the slew of heavily researched solutions by strangers to Dickens personally.

This preference of readers for solutions by those who knew Dickens would cause issues for later solutions as living connections to Dickens became in shorter supply. So soon after Dickens' death, however, the authors of solutions were far more confident in claiming their proximity to Dickens. In 1873, one year later after Morford's work (and only three after Dickens' death), the same approach was used but with a far more audacious statement – indeed, it is without doubt the most audacious that would ever be made. Thomas Power James' *The Mystery of Edwin Drood Complete* was not, James insisted, his own work, but rather his crude attempt to transcribe what had been told to him by the ghost of Charles Dickens himself.

Unsurprisingly, this claim met with some criticism. Prior to the publication of the full work, James released extracts 'to gratify public curiosity', and he discussed the subsequent reaction in the 'Medium's Preface' to the finished book:

> *Some could identify those characteristics which stamped it as the production of Mr. Dickens' pen, while others could not perceive anything about it that bore the least resemblance to the great author's writings.*[40]

Worse still, poor innocent Mr James found himself under personal attack:

> *[A] very small class, in every sense of the word, I am glad to say [...] who finding nothing of any importance to exist in those extracts which would warrant a just condemnation, conceived the brilliant idea that, by attacking me, public attention would be directed from the book, and in that way they could "kill it."*[41]

Some did believe it to be by Dickens (although we have mostly James' word for this), but to explain the phenomena they argued, said James, 'that the manuscript of this Second Part was left completed by Mr Dickens at the time of his decease, and that one of his heirs, with a view to creating a sensation, thought it would be a capital plan to send it to this country and have it published this way'. But the most popular theory, apparently, 'was that the Evil One was at the bottom of the whole business; and it was said that, at a certain hour every night, his Satanic Majesty could be seen emerging from the chimney of my house and flying away into space, leaving behind him such a strong odor [sic] of brimstone that one could smell it for an hour afterwards.'[42]

Suffice to say, I do not propose that this work was actually produced by Dickens' ghost and, as such, James' apparent offence at such ideas should be best read as part of the showman's rhetoric in steering his audience towards the desired viewpoint, that this work can only be explained as being the work of Dickens' ghost. His mocking of other ideas, especially the gleeful detail he includes of the brimstone-smelling chimney, is a mere smokescreen to make his own outlandish explanation seem somehow more rational by contrast. As much as we can smirk at the cheek and audacity of James in the Medium's Preface, the Author's Preface that follows treads upon rockier ground. In it James speaks as though he were Dickens and argues for the reality of spiritualism. In doing so, he not only contradicts the real Dickens' known scepticism and frequent ridicule of the phenomena during his lifetime, but tries to convince Dickens' friends that all this is true:

> *I would be glad, however, if my personal friends on earth would seek to investigate the truths which this science – religious science, I should say, perhaps – contains, for I feel confident that they would be the happier for it in the end.*

The preface is rather ghoulish and in bad taste for the way it attempts to go beyond convincing the general reader, and instead attempts to dupe Dickens' friends and family that he is speaking to them now from beyond the grave.

The shame of this is that for all the questionable aspects of the framework, the completion itself is rather an enjoyable romp. As with Morford, the claim to authority through authorship allowed James the freedom to then deviate entirely from Dickens' plot, though he took this to a degree that far surpassed Morford. In James' completion, Jasper has a daughter, Betsy Traddles, granddaughter of Princess Puffer, whose daughter had been seduced by Jasper in her youth, leading to the younger woman's death. Datchery is the brother of the deceased woman, son of Puffer and uncle of Betsy, returning to Cloisterham not to investigate the mystery of Drood so much as to seek vengeance for his sister. Throughout James' solution, the tragedy of Betsy supplants the mystery of Edwin, who is alive and well and forgives Jasper for his attempted murder. Jasper himself takes the return of his nephew relatively well. It is the subsequent death of his neglected daughter that drives him mad and has him committed to an asylum. The book ends five years later when Jasper escapes from the asylum to return to Cloisterham, not to see Edwin, Rosa or any of Dickens' characters, but to visit the grave of Betsy, where he begs forgiveness:

> *The vision told me to kneel upon your grave, dear child, and ask you to intercede for the wretched man, who is not fit to live, and is not fit to die! You forgave me ere you died, Bess. I remember that – oh, how well! Ask God to forgive me, Bess, and take my spirit hence to dwell with you. You are an angel now, Bess, and can read my heart, and can behold how full of repentance it is for my misdeeds! While you are asking forgiveness for me, dear Bess, I'll lay me down to rest upon your grave. I'm very cold. Don't be long, dear child![43]*

Jasper dies with an arm around the headstone, his sins absolved at last by merit of his angelic child. There is more of Lady Dedlock in this than John Jasper. Needless to say, there is nothing in Dickens' text to support or suggest this ending is the correct one, but James, like Morford, is not seeking it. Rather than present *the* Drood solution, they both present a Dickensian soup of past plots. James does present himself with a greater problem than other completionists, in that not only did he have to produce a work that was suggestive of Dickens, but specifically had to be indistinguishable from the inimitable's style. For this, he had a cunning plan on hand to explain any perceived failings:

> *Concerning the merits of this book, it would ill-become me to speak. I can say this, however, that it is given to the public, word for word, as it came to me. An uneducated man myself, I am not qualified to deny or admit the existence of grammatical errors in its composition [...] it will be easily understood that the first production of a spirit pen would be very liable to contain some imperfections.[44]*

In other words, blame it on a faulty connection on the line from the spirit world. Spying further opportunities for sales, James was keen to point out that, with further practice and experience, 'future works, which are to come from the spirit-pen of Mr. Dickens, will be entirely free from imperfections', but sadly the promised next work – *The Life and Adventures of Bockley Wickleheap* – has failed to materialise.[45] James' work is one so wrapped in its own audacity that it is little surprise to see subsequent scholars choosing to pay it little heed. Aubrey Boyd summed it up best when he said: 'Over the results of this undertaking we had best draw a decorous veil.'[46] James' ideas for the ending of *Drood* are best taken with a pinch of salt, but the novel itself and what it represents should not be disregarded. It is a remarkable work, overconfident in its claims but utterly telling in its cavalier treatment of Dickens and his novel, and a necessary antithesis to the intensity of serious, overly reverent readings of *Drood* that would emerge in the early twentieth century.

After the horse has bolted

In 1874, the year after Dickens' ghost was speaking to the public courtesy of James, Dickens once again spoke from the grave, through the third volume of the biography penned by his close friend John Forster. The big reveal of this biography so far had been in its first volume when Forster disclosed Dickens' dubious time as a child working in Warren's blacking factory. And now a revelation that would have an equally long-lasting impact arrived in the final volume with Forster's account of Dickens' plans for the end of the *Drood*:

> *The story, I learnt immediately afterward, was to be that of the murder of a nephew by his uncle; the originality of which was to consist in the review of the murderer's career by himself at the close, when its temptations were to be dwelt upon as if he, not the culprit, but some other man, were the tempted. The last chapters were to be*

23

written in the condemned cell, to which his wickedness, all elaborately elicited from him as if told of another, had brought him [...] all discovery of the murderer was to baffled till towards the close, when, by means of a gold ring which had resisted the corrosive effects of the lime into which he had thrown the body, not only the person murdered was to be identified but the locality and the man who committed it [...] Rosa was to marry Tartar, and Crisparkle the sister of Landless, who was himself I think, to have perished in assisting Tartar finally to unmask and seize the murderer.[47]

The summary is quite explicit. Save for the identity of Datchery, it wraps the plot up rather well. But it was too late. Had this summary been included by Chapman and Hall at the end of the sixth number in 1870, it would have been a closed case. But appearing as it did in 1874, it allowed for four years of speculation. Discussion of *Drood* and its end was in full flow, and Forster's account was, frankly, an anti-climax. By suggesting the obvious end that anyone might guess – namely Jasper's guilt of Edwin's murder – it was a disappointment after so much discussion of what might happen. The result was that Forster's biography did nothing to stem the tide of *Drood* theories.

Not only were these theories appearing in print, but on stage as well. In America, there were several dramatic productions from the moment the book first appeared. In 1870, Fred Stinson's adaptation performed in Philadelphia, while T. C. De Leon's performed in Chicago and Baltimore, while a further adaptation written that year by Augustin Daly in New York was never performed. The American stage's fascination with *Drood* continued with further productions in 1873 by Robert Belmont and William Young, both in New York. In London, there were productions staged in 1871 (Walter Stephen's *Lost* at the Surrey Theatre), 1872 (by G. H. Macdermott for the Britannia Theatre) and 1876 (Robert Hall's *Alive or Dead?* at St George's Theatre).

The most intriguing playscript of the time was not staged. Dickens' son, Charles Jnr, collaborated in 1880 with Joseph Hatton on a four-act dramatisation, which takes several liberties in streamlining and adapting the story for the stage, but ending in the fourth act where Jasper's cell confession and reflections are replaced with a vision scene in the opium den where the murder of Edwin, by Jasper, is re-enacted for the benefit of the audience. Though the location is changed, the actual details of Charles Dickens Jnr's solution agrees with Forster's account, but the fact that it was not staged robbed Forster of a weighty ally in his argument for Dickens' plans – given the popularity of Morford's falsely credited novel, a work that was genuinely written by Dickens' son could have had a great impact at this time. That said, any credibility that Dickens Jnr's solution carries as a consequence of the author's relation to Dickens is tempered by the necessary changes inflicted to make that story viable for the stage. The binding factor of the stage adaptations was brevity and swiftness in purpose, retelling the existing text for the most part and providing a solution in the last act, they are more akin to Kerr's *Cloven Foot* in providing an end that seeks to tie up the plot of the first half rather than expand it and add new characters, as Morford and James chose to do. But their approach of widening the plot was as nothing compared to the behemoth solution produced by Gillian Vase in 1878.

A Great Mystery Solved was the most extravagant of all completions before or since, and certainly the lengthiest. Gillian Vase (real name Elizabeth Newton) produced a three-volume novel totalling nearly 1,000 pages – far surpassing the length of Dickens' proposed original. Vase opens it with a lengthy account of her own unworthiness in doing so:

> *I am well aware that this ambitious attempt of mine, to finish a work commenced by one of England's most illustrious writers, will be almost sure to meet with opposition; and, very likely, my audacious venture may be punished either by having to run the gauntlet of sharpest criticism or – a thousand times worse – being passed over in contemptuous silence.*[48]

Vase insists that at first she 'had only written a few chapters, just for [her] own amusement', but hers is one of many tales of a Droodist who gets sucked in beyond their original intentions:

> *I had idly entered on a road from which there is no turning back, even though only the grisly hag disappointment should be in waiting at the end. I had raised a monster which took possession of my body and soul.*[49]

For all her timid pleas of 'trembling hope, full of fear', the finished book she has produced, as one might expect from a work of such size, is greatly indulgent.[50] We are once again introduced to new characters with their own back-stories that threaten to engulf those from Dickens' text. The titular mystery is swiftly resolved. Edwin has survived Jasper's murderous attempt and is revealed to be in hiding as Grewgious' new assistant Robert Brand. Both he and Rosa struggle with their consciences when they meet new lovers, Madge and Tartar respectively, who ultimately are to be spurned as the pair realise they are meant for one another and none else.

Along the way there comes a moment of pure sensationalism as Jasper, long-known by this position in the novel to be a villain, ambushes Rosa by the river. After threats on his side, and pleas on hers, he grabs her and she faints, just as the sound of Crisparkle and Tartar fast approaching is heard to them both. Jasper, we are told, 'would have wrestled with Mr Crisparkle, or any two men even, in his present state of passion and strong nervous excitement; but numbers must overpower him in the end, and tear away his precious prize, now that he possessed it.'[51] He lifts Rosa aloft and begins to run, but his strength fails him. He curses 'the master whom he had served so long', and decides 'if she could not be his in life, she should be his in death':

> *With sudden impulse, he sprang up the bank of the river, and standing upon its brink, looked back towards his pursuers, and then down upon the lovely face resting on his shoulder.*

CHAPTER ONE

He had never seen it so beautiful, he fancied. No, not even when flushed with health and happiness. Her bright luxuriant hair hung dishevelled over his arm and framed in a face, pale as death, and chaste and pure as marble.

Tenderly, almost reverently, he stroked back the soft, clinging curls, and let his eyes feast for the last time in contemplation of her beauty – beauty which had brought them both to this – to this.

Then he bowed his head, and pressed convulsively his burning, passionate lips on her pure cold ones; raised her high in the air in full sight of his pursuers, who stood still, paralysed with terror; clasped her to his heart again; and with a wild cry of defiance and exultation, sprang with her into the river.[52]

And that's just the end of the second volume. It's a remarkable moment of Gothic drama, reminiscent more of a Brontë novel, or Victor Hugo's *Notre Dame de Paris*. Ultimately, the magnitude of the mystery is really to be found in its length, and there is a pleasing commentary to be found in the sheer size of Vase's solution. In his early career, Dickens himself had so eagerly wished to write a prestigious three-volume novel, or triple-decker, such as that which the great novelists such as Scott wrote. Shortly after *The Pickwick Papers*, he secured a contract to write *Barnaby Rudge* in just such a format, but other obligations got in the way leading to Dickens' continuation, and eventual embracement, of being a serial novelist. That Vase should, eight years after his death, present her solution as a triple-decker, with the grandiose title of *A Great Mystery Solved*, is in every respect, then, a reflection of how far Dickens had come in terms of prestige. The indulgence and magnitude of Vase's continuation is a direct commentary on the willingness of Dickens' readers to wallow in his world as much as the confidence of publishers that they could capitalise on this desire. Though Vase was a pseudonym, thankfully it was not one pertaining to be Dickens or any of his associates, and while *A Great Mystery Solved* still takes liberties with the plot, it does at least have a more respectful approach to the author, which perhaps explains why it receives less withering remarks from later generations (William Robertson Nicoll wrote in 1912 that 'It is the only continuation worth looking at').[53] Equally, however, the fact that such a lengthy response to *Drood* could appear after the publication of Forster's biography shows how little impact Forster had upon closing speculation.

One more novel requires discussion in this chapter. In 1885 Georgie Sheldon – actually Sarah Elizabeth Downs, wife of George Sheldon Downs – had her continuation published in serial form from 21 February to 18 July. *The Welfleet Mystery (An Outgrowth of Dickens' Last Work)* started the whole story from scratch, assigning new names to Dickens' characters and retelling his plot as well as her own conclusion. Like her predecessors, Sheldon's work can be viewed either as a celebration or an exploitation of Dickens' text, rather than an attempt to show his intended solution. Her reason for retelling the early part of the story is 'to vary the characters, incidents and conversations, so that they may not seem simply a tame repetition to those who have read the great master's work'.[54] This can be read in two ways. On the one hand, like Kerr before her, Sheldon assumes her readers have already read Dickens' original text and do not need to have it presented before them again. On the other hand, the fact that this solution, unlike those of Morford, James and Vase, does present the original story alongside that of the continuation, argues the opposite point that it is catering for an audience who are not automatically familiar with the mystery. Either way, the change of character names and rewriting of the first section is a simple way to have the complete story without infringing on copyright, and whatever the reason for having done so, it does allow Sheldon to re-examine the focus of Dickens' text.

The Welfleet of the title is not a person but the new name for Cloisterham, with the shift in focus from one character to the whole town. While many characters are similar to their Dickensian alter-egos, Sheldon does make a radical change to Princess Puffer. Renamed as Sylvia Houghton, she is much younger than the original and ultimately revealed to be the first love of John Jasper/Knight who was first put on to the slippery slope of drug addiction by her lover. Puffer/Sylvia will ultimately be saved by the redeeming love of Tartar, here called Edward Stuart, while Rosa/Theodora Lander marries the resurrected Edwin/Herbert Knight. Like the many dramatisations that would arise for stage and screen, Sheldon's advantage in *The Welfleet Mystery* lies in not only writing the end of the book, but rewriting the beginning as well, allowing her to change the first half to suit her projection into the second, and consequently ensuring greater cohesion across the whole. Edwin's ring – a lynchpin for many solutions in identifying the body – is given greater emphasis upon its introduction in Sheldon's work than it receives in the original. Edwin/Bert, after breaking the engagement with Rosa/Theo, places the ring in his pocket absent-mindedly, from where it drops to the floor unnoticed by him and discovered by Rosa/Theo after he has left:

> *She picked [the ring] up and carried it to her room, thinking that she would give it to him the next time she saw him, yet never dreaming how important – how vital that trifling incident was to prove, when, after long, dark months of suffering and trial, it should be remembered and related.*[55]

The Welfleet Mystery belongs to the early group of continuations for not attempting to be Dickens' planned solution. The aim is simply to continue the story, not to solve the mystery in a definitive way. This is why I describe them as opportunistic, not as an inherent criticism, but as a recognition that each work is capitalising on the opportunity afforded by Dickens' recent death to launch a work of their own. These first solutions lack the elaborate cross-referencing back to clues in Dickens' text as support for their own theories that would become a commonplace feature of later theories, articles and stories.

Instead, where these stories attempt to gain authority is either through the cloak of admiration for the master, as in Kerr and Sheldon, in indulgent celebration and wallowing as in the remarkably long continuation of Vase, or in the more direct and audacious attempts at borrowed authority by Morford and James under the pseudonyms of Collins, Dickens Jnr and Dickens.

The comparatively free manner in which these early solutions treat the mystery is indicative of the response to Dickens himself who, though enormously popular, was not yet at the heights of literary reputation he would achieve in his afterlife. And as living memory of the man was replaced by the lasting reputation of the works, the manner in which writers responded to *Drood* changed also. Aubrey Boyd notes of the early completions that:

> [W]hile all of them assumed the dramatic guise of sequels
> to the unfinished story, the illusion ceased at its outset;
> in style and content they proclaimed from the first their
> own absurdity.[56]

Boyd's commentary is relatively objective – it is true that the completions of these Opportunists are absurd, and true that their concerns in being a sequel do not extend very far beyond the title-page. But for this to be a failing is something that only the next generation would determine. John Cumming Walters – who will come to feature heavily in the next chapter – judged the works harshly by his own standards, stating that 'no conclusion can be held to be good and justified which departs from Dickens' own lines'.[57] Attitudes to the sanctity of Dickens' texts were changing. Sheldon's completion may have looked back to those of the 1870s, but she was already writing in a time at which the responses to *Drood* were heading in an entirely new and more earnest direction. The early responses had prepared no defence against the new wave of veneration of Dickens' original intentions, and their legacy would be trampled underfoot by the next generation of *Drood* solutions.

CHAPTER ONE

Princess Puffer:
Unintelligible

> What visions can she have?' the waking man muses, as he turns her face towards him, and stands looking down at it. 'Visions of many butchers' shops, and public-houses, and much credit? Of an increase of hideous customers, and this horrible bedstead set upright again, and this horrible court swept clean? What can she rise to, under any quantity of opium, higher than that! – Eh?

All just a dream, deary, all just a dream...quite a confused dream, if I'm honest with you deary. Here I am, trying to make a living – and it's hard, deary, so hard, especially what with Jack Chinaman down the road trying to steal my customers, but he don't make it the same as like I do – and all the while trying to sort out this mystery. The only mystery.

Oh him! I know that one, deary, course I do. Comes in not so often, but when he does he's always surly, thinking he's better than me, whoever I am. Taking his opium and going on and on about Ned and a journey...but I'll have him. I followed him you see, and now I knows who he is – Mr Jasper of Cloisterham, no less. Oh yes, I know who he is. But knowing who me is – well, that's the problem deary.

Princess Puffer, some call me. Others call me Mother Combs, Old Sal, Mrs Tranders, or Sylvia Houghton. What's in a name, eh? It all comes down to the same thing. Call me Puffer then, owner of this here haven from the world, from reality itself. They comes here, they do, to escape you see? To forget about the daily grind and wake up somewhere new, somewhere...ek sotik. Sometimes it seems the dreams they have make more sense than the waking world.

Still, Mr Jasper, I've got you now. Only, I don't know why I've got him, deary. Sometimes I think it's to squeeze money out of a customer who got a little too big for his boots. Other times I worry about me daughter, and how he done her wrong. Other times I'm not even sure I have a daughter. Maybe it's me he did wrong. Awkward that, deary, when you're not sure if a man is a lover or a son-in-law. Still, makes Christmas interesting, eh?

They all comes here, you know. Not just him, and my customers, but the others who want to trap him, Oh yes, use the opium they figure, get it out of him while he's dreaming. They all loves that idea. It seems I barely get a moment's peace without yet another person coming in, 'Can I use this special mix?', 'Can I hide behind the curtain?'… well it's not good for business if this gets about is it deary? And that Datchery fella – if he is a fella – well he's the worst of them. Seems he keeps popping up to ask questions or set traps. One time I thought he was my long-lost son back from the wars. Another times it was this woman from Ceylon in a costume – and there was me thinking I was confused, deary.

No, if you ask Old Sal – I mean, Sylvia – I mean, Mother Combs, if you ask me, *whoever I am, it's got to such a point where what's real don't make all that much sense no more. Better off in dreams, you see? Dreams have colour and shape, but out here it's all blurred and changing. Better to just have a taste of the pipe, eh deary. Finest you can get, you see, not cheap, but smooth. I'll get that Jasper, or not, soon as I know who I am, and who I am is in the pipe, that's what I am. Princess Puffer. Just one small taste and it'll all make more sense deary…*

CHAPTER TWO

Clues and Conspiracies: The Drood Detectives 1878-1939

A new direction

In 1878, a twenty-page article appeared in *Belgravia* which, though shorter than any of the completions published at this time, heralded the new wave of *Drood* solutions that would eventually outnumber and consume the work of the Opportunists, to represent how many would forever categorise Droodism. The article, simply titled 'The Mystery of Edwin Drood', was attributed to a Thomas Foster, actually an alias for Richard Proctor, whose name would become well-known to subsequent Droodists. Proctor (as Foster) argued that Edwin is alive, not dead as Forster would have us think, and returns to Cloisterham in disguise as Datchery. The idea itself is not so removed from that which the completions were selling. The real difference comes in presentation. This was not a fictional second half designed to sell numbers, but a carefully argued article, with the emphasis on proving the end to be true, rather than entertaining the reader. Proctor had an agenda, writing in his conclusion that:

> *I would venture to express my strong dissent from the opinion which I have heard expressed by one of the ablest living novelists, that 'The Mystery of Edwin Drood' was far below what Dickens had before written. It seems to me, on the contrary, far above the average of his other writings, and, if inferior to any, inferior only to one or at the most two of his leading works.*[58]

This was not about creating a new novel. This was an earnest attempt to champion what the author believed to be the true complete *Drood*. He was not alone. In 1884, a year before Sheldon's *Welfleet Mystery*, a short anonymous article appeared in *The Cornhill Magazine* in which:

> *The writer has merely endeavoured to do in the form of a short article, what every reader of 'Edwin Drood' endeavours to do in his head, viz. to deduce a correct conclusion from somewhat incomplete premises.*[59]

The key phrase here is a *correct* conclusion. Any solution would not do. The desire of the public was for an authenticity beyond the smoke and mirrors of Morford and James' assumed aliases. The flights of fancy encapsulated in the early fictional completions were now to give way to a deluge of dogged attempts to determine precisely what Dickens intended to happen next. Hitherto, such an approach had been limited to brief musings only, such as the *Saturday Review*'s condescending forecast that 'we may guess pretty safely how the schemes of the bad characters would have been defeated, and all the good people portioned off with comfortable incomes and abundance of olive-branches", or Edith Simcox's short and empty prediction that 'the solution of this problem was evidently reserved for the sagacity of Mr Datchery, agent doubtless of Mr Grewgious, seconded by the still unexplained animosity of the opium-seller'.[60]

The *Cornhill*'s writer proposed, uncontroversially, that Jasper kills Edwin and buries him in Mrs Sapsea's tomb, and that the ring is the key to identifying the body. Tartar and Rosa marry, and Helena and Crisparkle marry, while Neville 'begins the world anew' (in contrast to Forster's earlier statement of 1874 that Neville would die while in pursuit of Jasper). Finally, on the subject of Datchery, of which Forster was so frustratingly silent, the writer proposes him to be a new character, and certainly not Bazzard who is instead working for Jasper. Like Proctor/Foster's article, its significance is not to be found in its size or specific content but rather for being at the head of the queue. The *Belgravia* and *Cornhill's* articles were the first to offer an extended discussion on a Dickensian ending for *Drood*. They are the earliest Detectives, offering the first of a multitude of carefully argued solutions keen to ground themselves as the true solution, picking over passages in Dickens' text for clues and evidence much as investigative sleuths – real and fictional – would attempt to read and solve their own mysteries.

What would turn this small spark into an incendiary of ideas was the argument and counter-argument each article provoked. Proctor wrote another article, still under the pseudonym of Foster, this time for *Knowledge* in June 1884, where he attacked the *Cornhill's* conclusions. This was countered by a replying letter in *Knowledge* the following July attacking Proctor's ideas, to which he then counter-argued yet again over the course of ten instalments, resulting in yet another reply. [61] The *Cornhill* article thus prompted thirteen more in quick succession, thanks to this quarrelling tendency. The letter pages of journals afforded response and counter-response to build up a dialogue of *Drood* theories, sharpening each writer's ideas and provoking them on to produce more. Over the coming decades this literary dispute would not only continue through newspaper correspondences, but find a new battleground for extended arguments with the eventual formation of the Dickens Fellowship and its associated journal *The Dickensian*. Disagreement would prove to be the key aspect of generating such a deluge of *Drood* theories in the early twentieth century, as factions were formed and arguments grew heated over precisely who Datchery might be, and the current state of Edwin himself. The one thing they could all agree on was that some great twist must exist within the plot, primarily on the subjective basis that their faith in Dickens' mastery as a writer meant his work must have an ending that would elude the casual reader and not be so patently obvious as Forster had suggested. Instead, the Detectives insisted:

> *It is literary clockwork, scrupulously designed and fashioned, every particle of mechanism perfect and*

polished, every adjustment made; and it is set going and proceeds with regularity; but the designer alone had the key to its secret operation, its marvel of movement to an appointed and fateful stroke.[62]

Proctor and Walters' volley

Fuelled by the growing number of articles he had written on *Drood*'s ending, in 1887 Proctor stepped out from his pseudonym and published a full book on his theory under his own name. Despite its length, *Watched By the Dead* was not, as the books discussed in the previous chapter had been, a fictional completion, but a monograph with academic pretensions that interrogated Dickens' text and argued for the veracity of its own assumptions. Great length was thus devoted to one person's argument on the ending of *Drood*. In short, this book formed the blueprint for much of what would follow over the ensuing decades. B. W. Matz, writing in 1905, called it 'hitherto the most valuable book the story inspired', while Montagu Saunders recognised it as 'the first to examine *Edwin Drood* in a quasi-scientific way'.[63] In writing this, Saunders either ignores the earlier articles or is unaware of them. It is fair to say that the greater prominence of Proctor's book arises from its format as much as its argument. Its presence as a book allowed it to have a longer duration than Proctor's preceding articles, though the ideas presented corroborate with his earlier writing. The result of his extended account is as much a manifesto as a solution, putting in place ideas that would be echoed by many more.

Proctor's book thus continued his argument that Edwin Drood did *not* die, but returns in disguise as Datchery. As proof of his theory, he refers to the back-catalogue of Dickens' works to highlight what he considers to be a recurring theme, namely that of one character being watched unknowingly by another (often a wicked man being watched by a good one): in *Barnaby Rudge* Haredale watching Rudge senior; Brooker watching Ralph Nickleby, the marchioness watching the Brasses in *The Old Curiosity Shop*; Nadget watching Jonas *and* old

Martin watching Pecksniff in *Martin Chuzzlewit*; Carker in *Dombey and Son* watched by old Mother Brown; *David Copperfield*'s Uriah Heep watched by Micawber and Littimer by Miss Mowcher; Hortense watched by her fellow lodger in *Bleak House*; Rigaud watched by Caveletto in *Little Dorrit*; the aristocrats watched by the peasants in *A Tale of Two Cities*; Pip watched by Magwitch, who is watched by Compeyson in *Great Expectations*, while both Pip and Mrs Gargery are watched by Orlick; finally, Rokesmith watching pretty much everyone else in *Our Mutual Friend*. Thus, Proctor argues, there is a clear heritage of the unknown watcher, which he feels can only be fulfilled in *Drood* by the miraculous survival and subsequent disguising of Edwin.

The argument is intriguing, the conclusion nonetheless a leap – and therein lies the criticism that can be levelled at most of the works to follow in this chapter. After a lengthy surmise of how the final chapters will resolve the tale, and who will marry who (Rosa gets Tartar), Proctor deferentially adds that 'Very little of this suggested close of Dickens's half-story is invented'. [64] This is a worrying statement in its lack of self-awareness, but all too typical of the solutions that will follow in the author's unwavering belief that they have merely reported what Dickens planned to do, rather than proposing their own ideas. Another worrying precedent for future solutions is set in his claim, regarding his discovery of the watching theme, that:

> *Regarded as a story turning on the murder of a light-hearted lad by a jealous villain of diseased mind, the 'Mystery of Edwin Drood' has scarcely any interest in its main plot; while the accessory details have little meaning. But so soon as we recognise in the novel the working out of Dickens's favourite theme, and in such a way that the finished story would have been his master-plot, every line is seen to be full of life and light.*[65]

In other words, Proctor maintains that the simple solution proposed by Forster and repeatedly signposted in Dickens' text does not merit our attention. What this means is that his eagerness to promote his solution comes at the expense of any respect for the original story. If we were to read it as Forster (and Dickens) intends, it is a terrible story. Only once we accept Proctor's solution can we appreciate it as genius. This is an argument whose concern lies in reconfirming Dickens' last tale as 'his master-plot'. If Forster was to be believed, and *if* the story was to be read as a mystery, then for Proctor and those who followed, this was a mystery story where the solution is all too evident, and that was something they simply could not accept. Proctor's book raised the standard for the many attempts that followed that would all, like him, reinvent the tale by showing how Dickens instead planned to fox his readers. Proctor's 'loving study' was subjective, a love-letter to the Dickens he wanted rather than the Dickens he got, and one that was determined to repackage his final story as the greatest mystery in literature.

Proctor's book might well have followed the path of so many works of literary criticism and slipped away unnoticed had it not been subjected to an equal bout of condemnation and commendation in the press. In particular, John Cumming Walters, a subsequent heavyweight in *Drood* debates, was a constant presence in the letters pages as he made his attacks on Proctor's theory. Like Proctor, he too made the leap from newspaper correspondence to full monograph with *Clues to Dickens's 'Mystery of Edwin Drood'* in 1905. In it, he pulled no punches in dismissing Proctor's idea of Datchery as Edwin in disguise as 'so very commonplace, melodramatic, and even amateurish, that we could but assume Dickens had deceived himself as to the "incommunicable idea"'.[66] Walters' thesis stood directly opposed to Proctor – he argued emphatically that Drood was dead and, more controversially, that Datchery 'the avenger was Helena Landless'.[67] And yet while their conclusions differed, Proctor and Walters' approach to *Drood* was remarkably similar. Walters too lamented the loss of the whole, while commending the book on condition of its completion as envisioned by him.

> *'Edwin Drood' is a torso, and as we contemplate the unfinished masterpiece we are led to realise how cunning*

was the hand of the craftsman who shaped it, how superb the sovereign intellect that conceived it, and how majestic would have been its proportions had he completed it.[68]

Proctor and Walters both insisted upon the potential of the book so strongly as to implicitly argue the deficiency of the fragment. Their passionate argument for the twists in the tale, taking the form of an attack on the original, were actually prompted by the desire to defend Dickens and champion his last work as a great mystery. Not only does Walters' description of the book's 'labyrinthine plot' champion its complexity, it also qualifies the need for him act as our guide in solving it.[69] In arguing that they had discovered Dickens' true intentions, both Proctor and Walters defended Dickens and promoted themselves in the bargain. Each claimed to offer the true solution, each boasted a better understanding of Dickens' intentions than any other, including his friends and family. The discussion of *Drood's* ending became a tale in itself. Matz's review of *Clues* commends the 'masterly and convincing manner' of the argument, which makes 'the reading of it almost as absorbing as a well-told story'.[70] These lengthy arguments of Proctor and Walters proved the merits of both the writer of the mystery *and* the writer of the solution. Dickens' reputation was raised to become a scaffold on which others could stand, and the debate of *Drood's* ending became a battle for the title of most insightful Dickensian.

Proctor himself kept relatively quiet after the publication of his book, with Andrew Lang leaping into the ring to defend his view against Walters'. Lang eventually published *The Puzzle of Dickens's Last Plot* in 1905, after frequent appearances in articles, book reviews and letters to the national press.[71] Indeed, regular disputes erupted in the letter pages, with lengthy correspondences going back and forth, occasionally mediated by bemused editors wondering what they had let themselves in for after publishing the initial missive of each volley. In a letter from 'H. H. F.' to *The Academy* titled 'Bazzard v Helena Landless', the writer surmised that 'There is only a choice of absurdities, and opinion will vary as to which is the least absurd.'[72]

G. K. Chesteron was one of many others to weigh-in, in his tellingly titled article 'Mr Lang Detecting *Again*' (my emphasis), in which he supported Lang (and Proctor) and rubbished Walters' Datchery theory.[73] Lang's continual referral back to Proctor's book ensured the earlier work maintained its presence in *Drood* criticism, without which it could easily have slipped quietly away. The debate thus swung on Edwin's status – dead or alive – and Datchery's identity, with the latter being the grounds on which Walters most frequently had to defend himself in supposing it to be Helena in disguise. Resurrected heroes were a thing of little surprise to readers, but the suggestion that Dickens might write of a cross-dressing heroine was a step too far for many. Lang accordingly lampooned the idea, but to do so he called in backup from the highest authority in the land – Sherlock Holmes.

The employment of Holmes in the case would prove to be yet another precedent that many later solutions would follow. In this first instance, Lang was as ardent a Doyle enthusiast as he was a *Drood* fan, so the merging of his two passions is little surprise. He twice wrote pieces involving Holmes in the mystery: the first, in 1905, 'At the Sign of the Ship', imagined Holmes and Watson discussing Dickens' final book and the theories proposed by Proctor and Walters (a slow day on Baker Street, that the world's greatest detective should turn to literary criticism); the second in 1911, 'About Edwin Drood: A Dialogue' descended further into parody with 'Sheerot' and 'Whatson' discussing the book in response to Henry Jackson's book *About Edwin Drood* published that year.[74] Such wrapping of fiction within other fiction was not unique to Lang. A similar technique was also used at this time by his friend and ghost story writer M. R. James. James' 1905 spoof 'The Edwin Drood Syndicate' for *The Cambridge Review* uses his familiar trope of a fictionalised discovery of papers, in this case the reports of several members of the university gathering to share their thoughts on a *Drood* report, to which the responses are typically frustrating of an academic board:

Mr E said he should like to ask the Syndics one plain question. Had they taken the elementary step, as he might call it, of consulting Mr Dickens himself as to the solution of this so-called mystery? He could not see from the Report that they had. If they had not, he thought most emphatically that the Report should be referred back to them.

The Vice-Chancellor interposed with a word of explanation. Mr Dickens was dead.

Mr E said that of course that might be taken in some measure as a reply to his question.[75]

James used his metafiction device to further confound and mock the very solution he was presenting, leaving less certainty than was there to begin with. In contrast Lang's use of Holmes was an implicit endorsement of the mystery itself. Not only did it confirm the idea at the time that *Drood* was a mystery story, but moreover suggested what an unfathomable mystery story it must be for the world's greatest detective to take an interest. Furthermore having Holmes present an opinion also gave authority to the given solution. Lang inadvertently does what Morford and T. P. James did before him – in the absence of an actual manuscript by Dickens he invents a new form of authority, though here it is grounded in another fiction rather than trying to find reliability through Dickens' friends or ghost. When Holmes argues Proctor to be right, fictional though he may be, his reputation and fanbase as the world's greatest detective carries more weight than Lang's personal commendation ever could. Lang sees the joke in this and ensure that Holmes has little praise for him, the detective judging Lang as 'that pedant' and 'the idiot'.[76] Lang's dialogue may have dismissed *Drood* as an afternoon's diversion for Holmes, but the detective would be called upon many more times by subsequent writers to solve *Drood*, not only reading Dickens' book as Lang had him do, but directly interacting with the residents of Cloisterham in person.[77] Holmes' afterlife has been frequently split between endlessly solving

Drood and finding Jack the Ripper. In both cases the employment of Doyle's creation shows a yearning for a definite answer and the associated embedding of each mystery as the greatest of their age. It is no coincidence that the new direction in solving *Drood* synchronises with the golden age of detective fiction. The popularity of the genre radically affected the way we read Dickens' final novel, taking the 'mystery' of the title literally and distorting it into a whodunit.

The Fellowship (or: Lord of the Cataloguings)

By far the greatest impact on Droodism and the wider discussion of Dickens at this time was the establishment in 1902 of the international Dickens Fellowship, and its associated journal *The Dickensian*, launched three years later and edited by Matz. The Fellowship came at a time when Dickens' work was seen as outdated by literary critics. He was an author to be enjoyed, but not studied. Even in the midst of writing in defence of Dickens as an author of a previous romantic age, G. K. Chesterton wrote of the 'great and splendid' Dickens that 'we are bound to find a considerable amount of Dickens's work, especially the pathetic and heroic passages, artificial and pompous'.[78] Chesterton and his co-author, Frederick Kitton, were among the few men of letters to come forward in open praise of Dickens at a time when he was generally under critical attack. But this minority among men of letters did not extend to the general public, where the majority were still very much enamoured with Dickens. Writing in 1970 and looking back on this time, Tomlin writes:

> If the critical estimate of Dickens reached its lowest point in the early years of this century, it may seem a paradox that in 1902 the Dickens Fellowship should have been founded. This was not a desperate move to salvage Dickens's works from popular neglect. There was no popular neglect.[79]

Despite any critical maulings, Dickens remained popular with the general public. Yet the origins of the Fellowship and its journal betray an underlying tension in how to remember Dickens, and who had the right to do so. It was certainly not the first club to be formed in celebration of Dickens, but it was the first to truly establish itself as a literary society. In doing so it was in opposition to The Boz Club, which had been formed in the immediate aftermath of Dickens' death, and consisted of friends and family only. These men (and it was only men) would meet to talk about the man they knew, but as those with primary knowledge of Dickens passed away themselves, the shift in Dickensian discussion focused away from those who understood the man to those who were better versed in discussion of his works. Against this battleground for Dickensian ownership, the Fellowship emerged in triumph, and its journal *The Dickensian* allowed a space for lovers of Dickens to pour forth their ideas to an equally willing audience. Here then was both a ready community of Dickens enthusiasts and a platform for them to present their ideas to one another beyond the limitations of the newspaper letters pages.

Though the general feeling towards Dickens' works was enthusiastic, popular sentiment of the time still favoured the earlier novels over the later ones. Chesterton asks of Dickens' last works: 'His later characters were more like men, but were not his earlier characters more like immortals?'[80] Of *Drood* he notes how the comic side of Dickens 'alive to the end [...] makes one splendid and staggering appearance' in *Drood* by inserting in 'this otherwise reasonable and rather melancholy book [...] the frantic and inconceivable epitaph of Mrs Sapsea'.[81] George Gissing, though suggesting that '*Edwin Drood* would probably have been [Dickens'] best-constructed book', nonetheless expresses deep regret at the tone and subject of the final work in comparison to all that had come before:[82]

One cannot help wishing that Dickens had chosen
another subject – one in which there was neither mystery

> *nor murder, both so irresistibly attractive to him, yet so far from being the true material of his art. Surely it is unfortunate that the last work of a great writer should have for its theme nothing more human than a trivial mystery woven about a vulgar deed of blood.*[83]

The energy and joy of the earlier novels certainly encapsulated much of what Dickens' readers were first drawn to in the early twentieth century, but the enticing possibility of *Drood's* open-endedness allowed it to buck the trend and capture the imagination of Dickens' readers at this time. Within the pages of *The Dickensian* especially, lengthy correspondences and a deluge of reader theories resulted, prompting the editors to ban any further discussion of *Drood* in its pages on three separate occasions, in 1911, 1915 and 1928, all of which were overturned by the inexhaustible tide of new publications and theories. Whatever the exasperation of the editors, the readers and contributors wanted to talk about *Drood*. In addition to ushering in new ideas, *The Dickensian* also afforded the opportunity to reflect and consolidate on what had been said so far. As early as September 1905, in its first year of publication, an article appeared offering 'The History of a Mystery: A Review of The Solutions to "Edwin Drood".'[84] The article would extend over the following two months' instalments, and does in that early stage what this book proposes to do now: present an overview of the solutions thus far and summarise the main points they contain. In doing so it recognised and confirmed Droodism as an entity, no longer just individual theories but part of a larger and ongoing dialogue. The cataloguing of *Drood* solutions and the attempt therein to establish a bibliography of Dickensian criticism was both a reaction and prompt of the movement away from knowledge of Dickens as a person and towards knowledge of Dickens as a writer. True Dickensians no longer needed to have known him personally. Instead they proved their credentials through awareness of the subsequent discussion of the books. Walters had previously argued in *Clues* that the multitude of solutions was in itself a testament to the genius of *Drood*:

The fact that the mystery has been 'solved' a dozen times in a dozen different ways, that there is divergence of opinion as to the whole scheme of the work, that Richard Proctor believed the story would end 'pleasantly,' and that others are equally convinced it would close in blackest tragedy – surely all this indicates that the mystery was a very real one after all.[85]

Drood studies had gone meta. The book's merits were no longer to be found in its own pages but in the far greater volume of pages written by others trying to solve it. The Dickensians had set themselves not only above Dickens' friends, but even Dickens himself.

The continued disregarding of Forster's account is a case in point of this movement towards text over testimony. Rather than trust the words of Dickens' friend, many chose to place their faith in their interpretation of the book. As a material object, *Drood*'s cover provided one of the strongest arguments for dismissing Forster. It had been drawn by Charles Alston Collins, younger brother of Wilkie, who had been intended to illustrate all of the work till ill health made him step back. Collins' cover followed the pattern used for other Dickens novels by presenting various vignettes of scenes from the book, some of which would not feature until later numbers. Droodists have accordingly slaved over each panel looking to identify not only scenes that had occurred, but those vital scenes that were yet to occur (see fig. 12). Who was the young man in the bottom centre vignette? Could it be Drood himself? Or someone dressed to appear as Drood's ghost? Or could it be Datchery, and thus a clue to his identity? The book itself thus became a counter-witness to Forster: text over testimony.

The movement away from those who knew Dickens towards those who studied his works prompted a backlash, and justifiably so, in the matter of *Drood*'s ending and Dickens's intentions. Whatever sway the critics might have elsewhere in their reading of a text, surely here at least, with the book unfinished and no text present to analyse, was one area where those who actually knew Dickens could, and should, claim authority over the critics? Consequently, as the critics attacked Forster, so others stepped forward to corroborate and defend him. *Drood*'s primary illustrator Sir Luke Fildes wrote to *The Times Literary Supplement* on 3 November 1905 to counter the dismissal of Forster and the faith placed in Collins' cover, confiding that 'Collins told me he did not in the least know the significance of the various groups in the design'.[86] But the greater bombshell came in his revelation regarding Edwin's fate. Having asked Dickens whether Jasper's neckerchief was to be included in illustrations, Dickens gave, in Fildes words, this dramatic reply:

> *He, Dickens, appeared for a moment to be disconcerted by my remark, and said something meaning he was afraid he was 'getting on too fast' and revealing more than he meant at that early stage, and after a short silence, cogitating, he suddenly said, 'Can you keep a secret?' I assured him he could rely on me. He then said, 'I must have the double necktie! It is necessary, for Jasper strangles Edwin Drood with it.'[87]*

Kate Peruginni, Dickens' daughter and widow of Charles Alston Collins, came forward the following year to give a more robust defence of Forster. In a 1906 article for *Pall Mall Magazine* she pointed out the rampant hypocrisy of the increasing number of people who were choosing to disregard the biographer's word in favour of wilder and more exotic theories:

> *It is very often those who most doubt Mr Forster's accuracy on this point who are in the habit of turning to his book when they are in search of facts to establish some theory of their own; and they do not hesitate to do this, because they know that whatever views they may hold upon the work itself, or the manner in which it is written, absolute truth is to be found in its pages.[88]*

In private correspondence to George Gadd, Dickens' son Henry corroborated this idea that the Droodists were veering away from Dickens: 'I need hardly tell you that any solutions which have appeared are purely efforts of imagination on the part of the writers.'[89] All of this seemed rather damning evidence against the wilder theories and speculation, but once a conspiracy begins, no amount of evidence can erase it.

The persistent presence of *Drood* discussion in *The Dickensian* meant that new authors now had a large body of work to react against, amongst which Peruginni, Fildes and Forster were just three pieces of many. Subsequent *Drood* theories would become increasingly conscious of all the ideas that had come before, either to champion them, or demolish them, and the sheer length and breadth of *Drood* theories became a subject of discussion in itself. By 1912, the romance of *Drood* was being replaced by weariness of the enduring discussion, as evidenced in the pseudonymous Dak's sardonic verse:

> *THAT MYSTERY*
> *A beardless youth had disappeared,*
> *A beardless youth, without a beard.*
> *He went away but left behind*
> *A note for – well now, never mind.*
> *What's that? 'Decoyed!' 'Abducted!' No Sir –*
> *But left for reasons quite sub Rosa,*
> *But tired at last of Egypt went*
> *By easy stages back to Kent, –*
> *Got home (his ring a fine carbuncle),*
> *Met that prophetic soul his uncle.*
> *For reasons, more or less, sub-lime*
> *The sight knocked Jasper out of time, –*
> *J. climbed to marconi police*
> *But fell from fright, hence J's decease.*
> *Remember if you think this droll*
> *J. had a fine prophetic soul, –*
> *The sort of soul that looks ahead,*
> *(He'd seen himself when lying dead),*

A soul inflamed by love (not rum)
Plus opium theologicum.
(What things they see, what things they suffer,
Who won't walk wide of Princess Puffer!)
There's never been so great a stir
Since then in cloistered Rochester.
That's why we see the picture people
All clambering up the crumbling steeple.
(The steps that Mr Ovey drew
Showed where J. went, though drawn askew
A CRASH! A SMASH! – well anyhow
They've got another steeple now.
The towerless town felt far from gay
(They hanged poor D. for killing J.)
When your best tower has tumbled low
You must hang somebody you know.
A lovely lady Cingalee
Long grieved for D. a single she
(I'd like to see her portrait printed
In The Dickensian, Matzotinted.)
But there – enough of mystery summing
With Nicoll come and Cuming coming
It's time to stop this Drood debating –
The Mystery's grown ex(j)asperating.[90]

There is an atmosphere of a boys' club in this poem, thanks to its many in-jokes and the patronising dismissal of Helena. To so cavalierly reduce this remarkable character to 'a lovely lady Cingalee', someone to admire as a portrait rather than as a character, identifies the issues Walters faced in championing her as his detective hero. Between the groaning puns and joyful nonsense of the proposed plot lies a plethora of references to contemporary *Drood* theories. There is the name-checking of John Cuming Walters, W. Roberston Nicoll and Augustus Ovey, or the pun on the *Dickensian* editor's name in 'Matzotinted'.[91] Dak expected his readers to get the joke, he was writing for an audience well-versed in the endless torrent of 'Drood debating'. And a torrent it was – beyond the ongoing debate and plethora of smaller articles in *The Dickensian*, new monographs continued to appear as well, themselves prompting new avenues of discussion in *The Dickensian* – and more bibliographies. By 1911, B. W. Matz's catalogue would span four pages of the journal, testifying both to the amount being written already, and implicitly inviting readers to catch up on all that had been said. [92] Droodism was no longer a debate for someone to just wander into with their own ideas, but a separate scholarly field that newcomers were expected to be read-up on. Accordingly, Nicoll's 1912 book *The Problem of Edwin Drood* is steeped in references to the theories of his predecessors. In the chapter 'Who Was Datchery', Nicoll works through the ideas of Proctor, Walters, Lang, Gadd, Jackson and several others before siding with Walters, rather than approaching the question as though fresh. Discussion of *Drood* was no longer a matter of reading the book and making your own end, but reading the other theories and selecting the one you wanted from the menu: *Drood* à la carte. The book even closes with a reprint of Matz's short bibliography to allow readers themselves to select their own three-course ending from the available options.

Unsurprisingly then, a fuller review of theories past was soon published: *The Complete Mystery of Edwin Drood: The history, continuation, and solution 1870-1912*, compiled by *Drood* stalwart John Cuming Walters in 1913. Walters sought to establish what had been said and present to his readers the complete tale, albeit through the prism of his own views of what was, and was not, proper Droodism. The early completions of the 1870s did not fare well:

> *Continuations and sequels must be sharply distinguished from theories and solutions. It must not be supposed that an attempt to continue the story necessarily involves a careful or scientific attempt to master the problem.*[93]

Those early completions had failed to take the task seriously enough for Walters' liking – 'the writers of sequels cut the Gordian knot rather than untied it'.[94] Walters was not only reporting on what had been said, but directing new readers on what he felt was worth reading, and what was not. The past was reshaped to conform to the sensibilities of the present. *The Cloven Foot* and its ilk was to be regretted not for lack of merit but for failing to meet Walters' definition of a *Drood* solution. The cataloguing of *Drood* solutions has already been noted for its implicit self-congratulation of Dickensian criticism, this now extended to selective dismissal of unsuitable works.

Drood on stage, screen – and trial

As *Drood* solutions became increasingly self-referential, new theories became more reactionary and convoluted, such as Wilmot Corfield's 1913 theory that Datchery is not one person in disguise, but three (Neville, Helena and Mrs Crisparkle's brother-in-law, communicating to each other via the chalk marks on the wall), and Jasper does not kill Edwin, at first, but then does later on at the end of the novel.[95] Solutions were increasingly becoming a race to say whatever had not already been said, to find a twist upon a twist. Yet it must be noted that while scholarship on *Drood* became increasingly insular and intensive, dramatisations of the novel still continued with significantly less anxiety over unimaginable endings. J. Comyn Carr's 1907 adaptation proved a significant hit on the stage when it was performed the following year by Sir Herbert Beerbohm Tree's company, with Beerbohm Tree himself playing Jasper. In it, Edwin returns from the dead to marry Rosa, while Jasper dies of a guilt-induced seizure. The controversy of Datchery's identity was sidestepped by the total absence of the character in the play. Carr's adaptation carried no explanation of how the ending was deduced, nor justification for it being in line with Dickens' intentions: such concerns were for the scholars, not the playwrights. Yet the play did cross over into literature thanks to an accompanying edition of the book, which included the programme and a photograph of Beerbohm Tree in the role (fig. 13 and 14). Theatregoers could thus obtain a copy of *Drood* endorsed by the Beerbohm Tree production, stamping the authority of Carr's solution upon Dickens' novel.

Carr's production was followed by two further adaptations in 1908 (Charles A. Clarke and S. B. Rogerson's adaptation in Manchester, and Henry Doughty's script for Bedford Music Hall), and another in 1911 in Stratford, featuring Oswald Clay as Jasper. But a wider audience was being reached on the silver screen. Silent movie adaptations of the story were released in 1909, 1912 and 1914. Not one of the films has survived to the present day, so we are reliant on contemporary reviews for any information. Arthur Gilbert directed the 1909 film, for Gaumont studios, 'in thirteen scenes', and was said to follow Dickens 'fairly closely in the opening scenes' before Gilbert 'supplied his own solution to the story':

> *The body is disposed under the floor, and the murderer throws the cloak and hat of his victim into the river. Datchery, the Bow Street runner, gets on the trail, and at a stile by the roadside Jasper attempts to incriminate Neville Landless; Datchery watches the scene and is suspicious. He follows Jasper to an opium den; this is a fine dramatic act, with the ghost of Edwin Drood appearing. The end is the accusation and sudden death of John Jasper, and in the last scene Landless and Rosa Bud are quietly married in a little country church.*[96]

We only know the casting for three parts: Cooper Willis as Edwin, Nancy Bevington as Rosa, and James Annand as Neville. We are left to fill in assumptions in the gaps to work out the story of this adaptation (much as we do with the original novel): the marriage of Rosa to Neville suggests, as in later movies, that Tartar may have been cut. The suggestion that Datchery follows Jasper to the opium den immediately after Neville is accused further suggests that the flight of Rosa to London, and therefore the Billickin, Tartar *et al*, are cut. Referring to Datchery as the Bow Street runner implies he is a new character, and a detective to boot.

Even less is known about the 1912 movie. Made in France by Film d'Art, there is no record of its director or cast. While silent movies have a certain universality, the review reveals changes in names – Neville is changed for the continental Nevil, but Rosa's transformation to Pussy has no such justification, though it does result in Edwin's pet name for her becoming everybody's name for the character. We are told that after Edwin and Nevil go for a walk by the river, Nevil returns home while Edwin sits down, falls asleep 'and is surprised by Jasper and murdered, his hat and stick being flung into the river in the hope that suspicion will fall on Nevil'.[97] The body is dragged to the crypt where it is hidden thanks to the keys taken from Durdles (in line with the original text). After Nevil is arrested, Datchery, 'his master' in this film, suspects Jasper and 'conceals himself in the choirmaster's room, and listens to the mutterings of the murderer whilst he is under the influence of opium', leading to the dramatic finale:

> *Jasper wakes up and realises he has betrayed himself.*
> *Jasper is forced into signing a confession of his guilt,*
> *after which he succeeds in making good his escape. He*
> *reaches the cathedral, and, entering the crypt, takes his*
> *life close to the spot where he had concealed the body of*
> *his former pupil.*[98]

Again, we are left to infer further details from absence of information. The swiftness of the action once more implies the absence of Tartar, Billickin and even possibly Grewgious and Crisparkle. Furthermore, the review constantly refers to Edwin as Jasper's pupil, suggesting either that the film explicitly changed the relationship of the pair, or else made so little of it as for the reviewer to not realise a familial connection.

There is (slightly) more detail to be found on the 1914 silent film, directed, written by and starring Tom Terriss for the World Film Corporation. The film features an entirely different place of murder than had been considered previously or since. Jasper kills Edwin and hides the body not in the crypt, or anywhere mentioned in Dickens' text, but in 'a quiet pond'.[99] It might be presumed here, as perhaps with the river murder in the 1912 film, that the location has less to do with a grand vision of Dickens' concept and a lot more to do with the opportunistic nature of early cinema to adapt to whatever locations were available, but Terriss' film does include scenes in the crypt later on. The second hypothesis must be that a river, or pond, provided a more dramatic backdrop, or simply better lighting. Either way, the practical considerations of film-making that inform the direction of the plot result in movie adaptations being a curious antithesis to the trend in print towards ever more exacting reconstructions of Dickens' vision. Instead, the films draw back more on the fascination the early completions had for telling a good story to turn a profit. Accordingly, Terriss' film comes under criticism most when it favours sensation over sense. *The New York Dramatic Mirror* called it 'interesting' and 'exciting melodrama', but found it difficult to accept the absurdity of the pond and Edwin's subsequent resurrection:

> *For some time we see no more of Drood, but the plot of the picture requiring his return, Mr Terriss asks us to believe that Drood retained the breath of life until picked up by fishermen. Many hours must have elapsed between the evening that Drood was thrown unconscious into the pond, and the day he was rescued, still unconscious but alive. This is not plausible.*[100]

Another review in *The Bioscope* provides further details on what happened next. Neville is arrested, but we see 'his escape from prison, in which he is aided by Rose', after which 'Helena, disguised and calling herself Datchery' keeps an eye on Jasper who is in turn confronted by Edwin.[101] Jasper attacks Edwin again and takes him to the crypt, while Helena enlists the help of Princess Puffer 'the woman whom Jasper had many years ago reduced' and rescues Edwin while Jasper is gone.[102] On finding the body missing once again, Jasper goes into shock, 'his drug-sodden brain' reeling 'under the strain, and the gibbering, raving man staggers back to his home, whither he is followed by the wretched woman [Puffer], who deliberately sets fire to the house, and perishes with him in the flames'.[103]

The identity of Datchery shows that clearly Terriss has read his Walters, and this is seen to be to his credit. The same review that attacks Terriss for the implausibility of Edwin's survival in the pond commends the director for having 'a better right than most people to guess at a solution […] for his knowledge of Dickens is unusually thorough'.[104] Both criticism and praise of the film focused on its authenticity and scholarship as much as the quality of the film itself. *The Bioscope*'s review praised Terriss' performance of Jasper even as it found faults in its credibility:

> *Jasper, as played by Mr Terriss, is a mean, cringing, hound, whose fawning oily manner […] would have betrayed him to even the egregious Mr Sapsea, had that gentleman been deemed of sufficient importance to warrant his inclusion in the film […] and the result is not, perhaps, as effective as it might have been.*[105]

Dramatic performance played second fiddle here to believability. The reviews of the 1914 film show a different perspective than the earlier reviews in 1909 and 1912, one that recognises the critical heritage and betrays a preference for unpicking the clues of Dickens' text and presenting a valid solution. All three films show evidence of cuts and changes made for practical purposes. Expendable parts are removed and locations altered. As much as screen and stage adaptations felt able to dismiss the scholarly heritage, nonetheless any such awareness of the labyrinthine debates reflected well in the eyes of Droodist. In Terriss's film at least, there was some conscious attempt to reflect the debate dominating elsewhere.

Meanwhile the debate was also reflecting back on to the stage. On the evening of 7 January 1914, the Dickens Fellowship held a public trial of John Jasper (see figs. 15-19). Actors were employed to play the parts of the characters, with several Dickensians and authors present to prosecute, defend and judge. The event was widely anticipated in both national and international press, with the *Daily Sketch* noting how the trial 'appears to be exciting considerable interest', for proof of which the writer cites his own attempts to buy a copy of *Drood* in preparation only to find it sold out in the various booksellers he visited.[106] The *Dickensian* offered the 'advice […] that no time should be lost in making application for the tickets that remain'.[107] The anticipation was caused not least by the touted involvement of various literary celebrities. One paper stated 'It is probable that the jury will include Jerome K. Jerome, Sir James Barrie, Sir Edward Russell, Mr Percy Fitzgerald, Mr W. W. Jacobs, Mr William de Morgan, Mr Coulson Kernahan and Sir Frank Burnand, all of whom are interested in the production.'[108] In the event, neither Jerome, Barrie nor Fitzgerald took part, with G. K. Chesterton instead presiding as judge, while the jury of thirteen was extended beyond the usual dozen by the late appearance of George Bernard Shaw, who had previously declined when invited by Matz:

> *If I were to serve on the jury it would probably disagree, as the only verdict I could conscientiously arrive at is one of Not Guilty on the ground that if Jasper did not kill Drood he was clearly not guilty of murder, and if he did, there is no guilt in killing an insufferable bore, even when the slayer is almost as great a bore as the slain.*[109]

His reasons for declining stood as a warning against the likely tone of his contribution (a warning that prove to be utterly true). His unexpected arrival on the night threw a last-minute spanner in the works. Standing against the cavalier frivolity of Shaw, the barristers were Dickensians familiar to any who had been following the debate: Walters was Council for Prosecution, assisted by Matz, while Cecil Chesterton and W. Walter Crotch were for the defence. Of course, in defending or prosecuting Jasper the combatants also sought to address other related and non-related issues, such as Edwin's fate and Datchery's identity.

The excitement before the event betrayed the different expectations everyone had. While the *Midland Evening News* proclaimed that 'a body of prominent literary men are to solemnly "try" the case', others were more wary about the possible sensationalism of the event. J. Levett, the verger of Rochester Cathedral at the time of the trial, offered a very cautious response to Matz's invitation to attend:[110]

> *In reference to your kind invitation for tomorrow I write to say that I hope to be at stage-door well before six-thirty, but have been thinking since you were here yesterday that if it is at all possible for me to get a seat somewhere out of the way, and not on the stage that I should prefer it. If not possible then I must come on the stage, but I would much rather that the Verger of Rochester Cathedral was not mentioned as I don't want it to appear in the Press at all. I am looking forward to coming tomorrow and hoping you will understand why I don't want to be mentioned.[111]*

The verger's concern of being associated with the event, along with his reference twice to the stage, betrayed the theatrical undertone to what the *Midland Evening News* was confident would be a solemn, literary event. The trial had potential to be either a serious literary debate, or an entertaining piece of fiction, but with no rehearsals or coherent plan overseeing the various participants, it ended up trying to be both and failing to be either. The result was an evening too chaotic to please those who wanted a serious discussion, and too long-winded for those seeking light relief. 'Somehow or another the Dickensian fantasy trial to-night was rather a tame sequel to the fascinating story of Edwin Drood,' lamented one reviewer, 'They promised a richer feast of fun than they could possible provide.'[112] While 'eleven of the twelve [sic] good men and true said never a word, and looked unutterably bored', Shaw compensated for this with several interruptions of idiosyncratic pieces of witticism for their own sake.[113] William de Morgan wrote cattily afterwards to Matz that while, on reflection, 'the farcical element was inevitable […] if it had been kept solemn and bonafide [sic] as my ideal, we should have lost Chesterton's Judge, and I should have been the poorer by a resource for sleepless nights'.[114] Chesterton bore as much of the brunt of the Dickensians' wrath as Shaw, if not more so, for after the verdict of 'Guilty', he closed proceedings (too late for some) in the most controversial event of the night, with a complete dismissal of all present:

> *My decision is that everybody here, except myself, be committed for Contempt of Court. Off you all go to prison without any trial whatever!*[115]

There was outrage. Droodists who had turned up expecting the matter to be taken seriously had seen their field ridiculed. Nor was it only the audience who were upset. Crotch complained that the verdict 'was typically Shavian, and therefore totally farcical and unsatisfactory'.[116] More damningly, for Droodists of the time and their strict adherence to discovering Dickens' intentions, the verdict was 'absolutely untrue, for the other jurors were not consulted as to its terms'.[117] Shaw himself responded to this irreverently, of course, stating that Edwin's disappearance from the plot was 'evidence, not of murder, but of common sanity'.[118] The trial was a mismatch of devoted Droodists and bemused authors, the one group wanting to take the entire thing utterly seriously and the others perplexed by the over-reading of a work of fiction. The majority of reviews found sympathy with the former. 'If Dickens were alive today,' *The Independent* raved, 'we can imagine how he would have scoffed at a performance which, from beginning to end, was an elaborate piece of absurd and childish fooling.'[119] *Drood* was no laughing matter, but a subject demanding deadly earnestness. As a result of the misjudged tone of the evening, two further trials took place in America, with actual members of the judiciary standing in place of scholars and writers.[120] Again, no verdict was reached as they felt there was insufficient evidence. All three events proved to be futile exercises in which the legal system or reality was mismatched against a mystery of fiction. Those seeking a definitive ending, in spite of the testimonies of Dickens' friends and family, were frustrated by the simple truth, however arrived at, that the end of Dickens' book could never truly be presented.

From fatigue to fictional forensics

Though the trial failed to give an answer, it nonetheless recognised the community of Droodists. Between this, the bibliographies and the consistent public correspondence, discussion of *Drood* was becoming increasingly self-referential, as scholars pored over the solutions of their predecessors as part of the course of formulating their own. In the same year as the trial, a new completion was published, the first since *The Welfleet Mystery* but very different in approach. It was written by W. E. Crisp and released, as Dickens' original had been, in monthly instalments, beginning with the six written by Dickens before continuing seamlessly into Crisp's six parts. Even the cover was the same (see fig. 20). In doing so it tried to give a sense of cohesion between the original first half and Crisp's continuation, as does the subsequent illustration 'Jasper sees what is left of his victim' (fig. 21), which clearly depicts Jasper in the same pose seen on the monthly cover, holding a lantern above his head and peering through the gloom. At other times the illustrator, Zoffany Oldfeld, has been less authentic. The overall style of illustration is more twentieth century than nineteenth, as is especially evident in the dress of the characters, most conspicuous in 'Rosa sees her reflection' (fig. 22), where the hero of an 1870 novel set in the 1840s is decked out in the latest fashion of the 1910s. *Drood* and its cast existed across time, from Dickens' through to Crisp's. As for the actual plot, the identity of Datchery is revealed just two chapters in to Crisp's work when he whips off the wig to reveal brown tousled hair underneath: not Bazzard, but a detective employed by Grewgious. Whether intentional or not, Crisp immediately undercuts the Datchery controversy to focus instead on the main plot, most of which follows Forster. Edwin is decidedly dead, but Neville managed to escape the mortal fate described by Forster and instead marries Rosa. It is not nearly so wild as the early continuations, nor so controversial as some of the theories put forward by Walters and his fellow Droodists, instead taking a cautious middle road to try and complete Dickens without upsetting anyone. As the first completion to have been published since the formation of the Fellowship, it differs wildly from the earlier completions of the nineteenth century in trying to offer a solution that will not fall foul of close scrutiny and counter-evidence. As a work, it is thus neither sensational for the sake of sales figures, nor original for the sake of pushing a new theory, but conciliatory in such a way as to offer readers a chance to read a complete tale instead of Dickens' half one. As the method of publication suggests, it is a pleasant illusion that readers are asked to place themselves under, to dream of what might have been had Dickens lived.

The return of a fictional completion in print was soon followed by another in 1920 when Percy Carden released *The Murder of Edwin Drood recounted by John Jasper*. But in Carden's work, the focus had shifted from fully fictionalised completion to a basic summary of the projected plot, with little attempt at dramatic style. Rather than offering a diverting read as the early completions had done, this was offering readers a fleshed-out synopsis. It offered closure rather than sensation. Matz's guest introduction to the piece echoes the words of the *Cornhill Magazine* back in 1884, yet sounds rather weary and bewildered as he writes 'I suppose every reader of *Edwin Drood* laments bitterly that it comes to so abrupt an end, and few lay it aside without some thought as to how it was to terminate had Dickens lived to finish it'. This is not, as the *Cornhill* article was doing, prompting a new direction, but rather retreading a familiar, well-worn path – Carden's ending replicates the suggestions of Forster to the letter without attempting to replicate the style or format of Dickens, resulting in an odd work that falls between an extended discussion of the plot and a minimalised dramatisation of it.

It is greatly contrasted to the work of Mary Kavangah the previous year in 1919, whose work *A New Solution on the Mystery of Edwin Drood* certainly delivers what the title promises. She opens by stating 'it will be generally admitted that no very happy elucidation of that always fascinating problem has hitherto been offered to the public' before offering an idea quite unlike the ones published so far.[121] She dismissed Walters' Helena theory on the grounds that 'Datchery is distinctly uncompromisingly masculine', and adds further that 'The weight of evidence is greatly in favour of Edwin's escape', for which she draws attention to the monthly cover as 'really incontestable proof.'[122] So far, so overconfident, so similar to previous solutions. Then comes Kavanagh's own theory. Edwin returns, not as Datchery, but as Tartar. For this she steps out of the book and into topography, relying in part on the connection of Cloisterham and Rochester, and taking the latter not as inspiration for a fictional city but an absolute blueprint for it:

> *No: an explanation of the mystery is only to be found in the circumstance that Cloisterham was a seaport town (it stands for Rochester, which is within a short distance of Chatham docks) and that Edwin got taken out to sea, either by his own devices, or by being smuggled on board with the help of others [...] What more natural then, than that he should return to England in the character of a sailor? And what more likely than that Lieutenant Tartar and Edwin Drood are identical?*[123]

There is an interesting tendency of Droodists to use rhetorical questions in confident ignorance of the abundancy of contrary answers available. Thus, Kavanagh, argues, what more likely than that Lieutenant Tartar and Edwin Drood are identical? Well, this causes its own issue in that Crisparkle recognises Tartar as an old schoolfriend, explained by Kavanagh as a deliberate ruse suggested by Grewgious to prevent Rosa being overwhelmed by the discovery of Edwin's return (who is of course unrecognisable having got a suntan and bought a wig). But her ideas don't end here. Having argued that Tartar is Edwin, she then proceeds to show that Jasper is not Jasper, but Jasper's older brother who has murdered the real Jasper the year before and now masquerades as the choirmaster while plotting Edwin's downfall. For Kavanagh, the evil brother is some mixed-race stepchild: 'The Asiatic stain in him is suggestive of illegitimacy.'[124] Though all those who have known Jasper for some time are fooled, remarkably Helena is not and discloses her fears to Grewgious who then sends Bazzard abroad to find a member of the Jasper family who can corroborate. Thus, *another* brother of Jasper emerges, who turns out to be none other than Helena and Neville's father. This is vital as the happy presence of a father renders Helena legitimate and makes her marriage to Crisparkle respectable, allowing for a happy ending which fulfils Kavanagh's idea of the Dickensian:

> *We may all imagine as we like best that happy concluding Christmas Day, when all secrets are made known, and all wrongs set right [...] We may picture them set on the high road to happiness and prosperity, in the good old style, and in Dickens' own best manner.*[125]

Jasper has already died in the chase, as 'All the iniquity of his life meets and overwhelms him', and Neville too dies, but happy in the knowledge that he has a father and his sister is getting married. Rosa, meanwhile, marries Edwin who she has fallen in love with as Tartar. If this solution is convoluted – and it is – its purpose lies, like so many of this time, in confirming Dickens' genius as a writer, in particular against charges of having tried to mimic Wilkie Collins:

> *The story, had he lived to complete it, would have been a finer work from an artistic point of view than Wilkie Collins' masterpiece [The Moonstone]; and the fact that he undertook to write it, chapter by chapter, without aid from notes or rough copy, is enough of itself to show that he was indeed a past master in the art of construction.*[126]

The unsubtle insistence here that the apparent lack of planning is actually a sign of genius, not a fault, plays into the tendencies at the time to read Dickens as infallible, and consequently that very insistence in the perfection of the author invites the modern reader to counter it.

For all the boldness of her theory, and the certainty in the conclusion of establishing Dickens' genius, Kavanagh's opening statement is curiously cautious:

> *It now remains to be seen whether the attempt set forth in the following pages shall be consigned to oblivion as*

*unsatisfactory with its many predecessors, or shall be so
fortunate as to carry off, by general consent, the palm of
victory, as being the true solution at last.*[127]

What Kavanagh does not state is *how* the solution is to be determined
as the true one. Who gets to judge? It would appear that popularity
was presumed to harbour truth. If enough people believe it, it would
become true 'by general consent'. Nonetheless, the cautionary note in
Kavanagh's statement recognises the insecurity of theories in a time
when solutions were abundant. In 1914, Montagu Saunders published
his book *The Mystery in the Drood Family* and, like Kavanagh, he
strikes a less assuming tone in his own assessment of his solution
(that Datchery is a new character, and Edwin is dead), claiming that
'if only one of the several suggestions which I have advanced should
meet with general acceptance, I shall esteem myself amply repaid for
the labour which I have expended upon it'.[128] Once Droodists heralded
their solutions as a shining light and the one that would undeniably
be accepted as the true ending. Now they were grateful simply to be
noticed in the crowd. Saunders' hope that just one of his ideas might
be agreed with is both timid and weary. The abundance of *Drood*
writing was turning out to be its downfall, as it started to seem that
all had been said, and many Droodists such as Saunders were looking
not so much to redefine the field as simply to get a word in edgewise.
After the hectic hullabaloo caused by the print debates of Walters,
Lang and others, interest began to dwindle in the lack of new ideas,
and the start of the First World War provided more pressing matters
to focus on in the national press than the squabbles of literary critics.

But the ideology of the Droodists writing in this time did not end,
and would soon erupt again. Already in 1922 Aubrey Boyd published
'A New Angle on the Drood Mystery', a work that would prove to be of
later significance. Unusually, he supported Forster's statement, arguing
that 'There seems to be no cause, beyond the caprice of theorists, for
questioning it'.[129] As a result, drawing particularly on Forster's note of a
new and incommunicable idea in the novel, Boyd dismissed both Proctor
and Walters' theories, on the grounds that repetition of a Dickensian theme

(along the lines of Proctor) hardly constituted something new, while Helena as Datchery was really rather communicable. Instead he insisted that Edwin was dead, and favoured Tartar for Datchery, but this was not where Boyd's interest lay. For him, the great incommunicable idea at the heart of *Drood* was the theory that Jasper might be a mesmerist. The evidence for the theory was both external and internal. Not only did the fame of Dr Elliotson mean the concept of mesmerism was well-known to Victorian readers, but Dickens himself was a practicing mesmerist. Boyd then looked within the novel at Rosa's confession to Helena that she felt Jasper's eyes upon her, also pointing out that Crisparkle's inexplicable trip to the Weir in which he coincidentally finds Edwin's watch and pin may itself be a result of hypnotic suggestion, the good reverend unknowingly carrying out the choirmaster's sinister plot. Boyd extends the theory to a tantalising possibility, that Jasper does not commit the murder himself, but hypnotises Neville and makes him do it:

> *It might also be possible to prove that Jasper actually forced Neville to murder Drood and dispose of the body. He had previously roused young Landless to fury of resentment against Drood that ended in a threat to kill him; his scheme may well have been not only to direct suspicion against Neville after the crime, but to make him the actual instrument in committing it.*[130]

Boyd's all-important 'might' at the beginning of the conjecture is important here. Like Saunders before him, he shows an increasing awareness of the dangers in over-confidence when it comes to *Drood* theories. Boyd noted the 'doom of so many investigators' and the difficulty in maintaining 'an unwavering sanity while picking his way through the labyrinth' of the mystery.[131] He also notes the difficulty of exclusion in writing an article for a readership that will most likely be read by a dedicated group rather than the wider public:

> *I have included in the introductory pages certain data familiar to every student of the Drood problem, with the*

object of making the subsequent discussion immediately clear to the general reader, and of emphasising the facts that are particularly relevant to the theory I have set forth in conclusion. Since, however, it is the mark of the true Droodist, (as of the literary enthusiast in every other field), that such rehearsals are rather welcome than otherwise, the explanation is perhaps unnecessary.[132]

To summarise, the data is familiar but repeated nonetheless because true Droodists enjoy poring over the problem repeatedly anyway. It's self-critical, with Boyd including himself among the group and laughing at his own folly as much as anyone else's. But also included in there is the awareness that *maybe* somebody new to the *Drood* theories is reading the article. That all-elusive general reader could equally be scared off or encouraged by the definition of *Drood* studies as a field in itself. The disputes of the earlier decades were now the set-texts and reading material for the next generation. Nobody was pretending this was new anymore, and the necessary tone was one of self-deprecating humour and careful framing of any new offering. That said, the issue of multiple solutions was treated more harshly by Felix Aylmer, who wrote:

From the regularity with which fresh attempts are made to divine the 'very curious and new idea' which Dickens told Forster he adopted for his last story [...] it may be concluded that none of those hitherto put forward have created any widespread impression of finality. And the reason, I think, is clear [...] whereas Dickens speaks of an idea for a book, they offer us an idea for an episode.[133]

If Aylmer's confidence stands out at this moment, that is nothing to the contrast his work would offer when it appeared in full several decades later. For the time-being, he wrote two articles, both for *The Dickensian*, in 1924 and 1925. In the first he lays out his idea that 'Jasper is entirely innocent of any attempt on the life of Edwin Drood', leaving the second article to posit that the mystery lies somewhere in the past dealing with Jasper's heritage: 'Jasper was not to be given a surname because he had no right to one. He was illegitimate.'[134] Understandably, Aylmer's idea of Jasper's innocence was the one to create the most discussion, with several responses appearing in a subsequent issue, and while most of these were finding fault with the idea, one voice alone praised it. Katherine Kelly had herself published a short piece in *The Dickensian* in 1923 where she waxed lyrical of Jasper as a tortured soul and lamented the vicious labelling of him by other critics:

> *Wicked he, and I have no wish to minimize his crimes; but the 'Monster,' 'Vampire' and 'black-hearted villain,' etc., of my fellow theorists hurt me as much as the opium woman's striking him in the face. When the opium devil is cast out, I see Jasper, deeply repentant, facing his death unshrinkingly, even eagerly, as 'lawful and right,' and looking across the ruin of his earthly hopes, to the Resurrection and the Life.*[135]

For Kelly, Jasper's cell confession was to be more reminiscent of Magwitch than Fagin. Accordingly, she was delighted to see Aylmer go one further and completely exonerate the choirmaster:

> *As I believe I may claim to be the first Droodist to see good in Jasper – you allowed me to explain my view of his character in The Dickensian of January, 1923 – it was with delighted excitement that I read Mr Felix Aylmer's article this October. He goes one better: "Jasper is entirely innocent of any attempt on the life of Edwin Drood."*[136]

Her 'hope it will not be another ten years before I have the pleasure of buying his book' would not be realised as Aylmer would not return to *Drood* until 1964, but her feeling that 'Any fresh study of the Mystery throws some new light upon it' offers a counterpoint to the downbeat tone of Saunders and Kavanagh.[137] New solutions were possible, but to be new they had to completely upturn the story. The volume of *Drood* solutions inspired weariness or wackiness.

On cue, in 1924 Sherlock Holmes returned once more to 'the most fascinating of all literary puzzles' in an article written by Harry B. Smith.[138] If the employment of Holmes had been done before, so had his conclusion: Edwin was alive, Holmes deduced, and Bazzard was Datchery. If you are wondering what Arthur Conan Doyle thought of his creation's regular moonlighting in Cloisterham, the truth, stranger than fiction as it may be, is that he himself was at around this same time on the case of *Drood* himself. A firm believer in spiritualism, Doyle attended a séance held by his friend Florizel Von Reuter, in which he quizzed Dickens' ghost to discover that 'Edwin is alive and Cris[parkle] is hiding him'.[139] Though the ghost, on this occasion, disavowed any knowledge of Thomas Power James and his 1874 completion, the desire of Doyle to ask Dickens himself is both a welcome look back to the wilder solutions of the nineteenth century, and further confirmation of the early twentieth century's fixation with authorial approval.

As if ghostly voices were not enough, H. R. Leaver self-published a book in 1925 where several more voices were heard as the characters from *Drood* presented monologues on their life and the mystery. What really makes the work stand out is that all of this is in verse. Why? It is a question well asked, and anticipated by Leaver himself, who states in his introduction that 'No writer could copy Dickens' style' and 'Any other prose style would lack the true attachment'.[140] Instead, 'Metrical form involves an elevation of the subject, and whether such elevation has been achieved is a matter for the reader to judge'.[141] *Drood* was not just any text, but one requiring elevation of subject: Dickens the Bard of Gads Hill. The book presents, in order, poems titled 'Jasper', 'The Minor Canon', 'Grewgious', 'Sapsea', 'Rosa', 'Bazzard', with the inclusion of the latter explained by Leaver's belief that Bazzard is Datchery. Each poem spans several pages, and the full impact of the work can only be appreciated in its entirety, but as a short example take the excerpt below from 'Jasper':

But to my story ere the hangman comes.
Within this cell I write it for the priest
The Minor Canon, who devoted, calls
To fan the ashes of my sullen soul
With mention of the better world to come;
But this I tell him having learned it here
That there can be no better world for me
If Rosa be not mine both here and there.[142]

In Leaver's own words, 'whether such elevation has been achieved is a matter for the reader to judge': judge away. Leaver's aim is to flesh out the backstory of characters, thus giving us Rosa's recollection of a time in her childhood when the young Edwin presents her with a bird and the young Jasper, already jealous, destroys it and then savagely explains his actions to his nephew:

'My fingers have been formed for this,
For strangling what you would with her enjoy.'
At this he burst into a flood of tears,
And fell upon the turf beside the hawk.[143]

Jasper becomes another Heathcliff. Rosa herself is something of a cipher in Leaver's hands. Despite recounting her flight from Jasper and her assistance from Grewgious, no mention is made of Tartar, and with Edwin dead she is left alone, 'happy in the bliss of Helena', who is to marry Crisparkle, but with no hints as to what her own plans might be. Everything about Rosa's dialogue focuses on what has been, on the tragedy of Edwin and the machinations of Jasper. Leaver's work is one that invites ridicule for its poetical pretensions, but like all completions begs recognition for the courage of the author. It stands as yet another testament to the variety of solutions and the devotion of the *Droodists*. Meanwhile, contributions had begun *again* to *The Dickensian* leading in time to the third and final (and once again short-lived) moratorium on contributions. But it was in America where a new player was at work who would rival Proctor, Lang and Walters for significance in Droodism: Howard Duffield.

Duffield is primarily famous among Droodists for one article in particular, 'John Jasper – Strangler'. In it he argues that Jasper, in strangling Edwin then hiding the body, is following the rituals of the thuggees of India. For this idea to work he is required not only to convince of Dickens' awareness of the thugs, but moreover of why Jasper should be following this cult. The result drew upon the oriental themes of the novel. Jasper's opium addiction is a self-destructive absorption of exotic culture that highlights his deviant nature. Boyd had already noted 'the Oriental matter with which the tale is so thickly strewn', but it was Duffield's article that really raised the profile of the idea of orientalism shaping the tone of the novel.[144] As much as Jasper appears to be an upstanding citizen, he carries this secret of a non-British culture. For Duffield, this was more than just an addiction but a wider devotion to the cult of Kali, the goddess who the thugs worshipped and who Jasper in turn is led by as he destroys his nephew as tribute to her. It held remarkable sway over later critics for this blending of orientalism and exoticism into the reading of Jasper's villainy. Duffield's article would come to influence those who were apparently denouncing the wilder theories of Droodism, not least among them Edmund Wilson (who will be discussed in full in the next chapter). Wilson's championing of Duffield gave the work a longer legacy and respectability that in turn prompted other critics to take it as read that the thuggee theory was correct. In 1945, Una Pope-Hennesy would write of the theory as almost a given, noting 'broad hints of thuggery' throughout the novel, though qualifying it with her own judgment that 'the murder has not, it seems, been carried out by an initiated Thug but by a man dreaming of being a Thug.'[145] Later still in 1956, Mario Praz would, while writing on a separate area of Dickens, mention quite casually in passing of *Drood* that it 'seems certain, Edwin Drood was the victim of a ritual sacrifice by an initiate of the fierce cult of Kali'.[146] Lilian Nayder approaches it more cautiously in 2010, when she notes 'Whether or not Dickens intended to unmask Jasper as a thug, he connects the choirmaster to the Orient', but even though it is objective she does nonetheless still discuss it.[147] Duffield's thuggee theory was one

Fig 1. Summary of *The Mystery of Edwin Drood* No. 1 by Alys Jones

Fig 2. Summary of *The Mystery of Edwin Drood* No. 2 by Alys Jones

Fig 5. Summary of *The Mystery of Edwin Drood* No. 5 by Alys Jones

Fig 6. Summary of *The Mystery of Edwin Drood* No. 6 by Alys Jones

THE MYSTERIOUS MYSTERY OF RUDE DEDWIN.

[*Intended for the perusal of those only who have been able to read what is published of* Mr. DICKENS's *new Work.*]

PROLOGUE.

THE other day a great author called upon JUDY, to read the proof-sheets of a forthcoming work, and to ask her opinion on its merits. "By all means," said JUDY; "pray begin." And he commenced as follows:—

CHAPTER I.—FOUR IN A BED.

"The clock tower with its eye out! But how can the clock tower be upside down! The well-known clock at Bestminster standing on its head with its feet in hot water! But then you know what the bear said. Why did he want the soap! Therein lies the mystery. Won't fifty billion dancing dervishes do as well; if not, let's go in for white elephants. Confound the clock! why won't it stand the right end up! Why don't it strike? I'll strike it if it don't. Aha! it isn't a clock after all, but an old woman in a frilled nightcap; and I m lying one of four in bed, and feel very particularly jolly uncomfortable."

"But ain't that rather disconnected?" asked JUDY.

"Isn't it powerful, though?" said the great author.

"Very," said JUDY.

And the great author proceeded:—

The man who has these fantastic imaginings arises from the bed, and knocks his head against the wall to settle his senses.

"Have another pipe," says an indistinct female, in a querulous rattling whisper. "Deary, dear! the Lascar gentleman whose toes is in the air is a reg'lar customer, and so 's John Chinaman, here, twisted up like a pair of lazytongs struck by lightning. We're opium-eaters, we is. I got drunk on gin for sixteen year, and now I've took to opium. It 's generally allowed I've a good constitution."

"Get out," says the man of the fantastic imaginings. "I play the organ in Bestminster Cathedral, and they 're waiting for me to begin evening service. It 's a way they have."

CHAPTER II.—A DEAN AND A CHAPTER TOO.

WHOSOEVER has observed that extremely useful, though homely, vegetable, the potato, may have noticed, in a sackful, how like each bulb is to its brother. In like fashion there is a sort of semblance 'twixt the Dorrits, Dombeys, Micawbers, and Pecksniffs of other days, and the Rapsers, Tokes, and Crisparkles of to-day. But what does it matter?

"Mr. Rasper is late to-night," says the Dean.

"Oncommon," says the person addressed. (You must read it over once or twice, and you may, perhaps, find out whom it is.)

"Say uncommonly," says the Dean blandly; "and is he ill?"

"*Un* — common," says the other.

"—ly," adds the Dean, with increased blandness; as who should ssy, If you don't mind your terminations, where will you end?

* * * * *

Crack, crack.

"I have these sorts of fits," says Mr. RASPER, "but don 't mind me, RUDE TEDDY. If you were boxed up in an opium-loft all day long (with a comprehensive glance including the clock tower and a large portion of the Thames Embankment) you 'd almost like them, even, for a change. Have a nut!"

Crack.

"It 's a bad 'un, but never mind," says RUDE TEDDY; "I 'm going to be married, you know, to the girl I was betrothed to by my parents. You may remember a similar state of things in several old farces, also in a novel called 'Our Mutual Friend.'"

HIGGLEDY PIGGLEDY.   [*See* CHAP. I.]

SPOONY MOONY. (*See* CHAP. V.)

"I do," replies Mr. RASPER, with a comprehensive glance, including all SMITH's Library and the greater part of the railway bookstalls. "Wait till I have another fit. Take another nut while I do so."

Crack, crack.

"Thank you."

Then Mr. RASPER dissolves his attitude with a little hot water, and takes it without sugar.

"Thank you kindly," says JUDY, "It seems, so far, extremely amusing, and very easy to follow."

CHAPTER III.—"STICKY."

SUPPOSE, for the fun of the thing, we go on calling Westminster Bestminster. It 's an awful lark, looked at one way. In Barleysugarment Street (there 's a fantastic imagining for you) is situate Miss TINKLETON's "Young Ladies' School." It is an old house repainted, and naturally puts the most unimaginative persons in mind of a withered coquette who has been Rachelized.

Miss TINKLETON's pet pupil's name is PITT: they called her POPPIT, as a matter of course. She is the young lady RUDE TEDDY is engaged to,

She doesn't love him very particularly, but she has a fine taste for bulls-eyes. When he comes to call on her they buy them together.

Then they make love, and she looks very pretty with her mouth full.

"Don't," cried POPPIT, "I 'm all sticky."

CHAPTER IV.—PAPSY.

THERE was a jackass of the name of Papsy. He carried on the trade of auctioneer, and in his leisure hours wrote comic tombstone inscriptions.

"My own name," said the auctioneer, with his legs stretched out, and solemnly enjoying himself, "is not PECKSNIFF, as at first you might imagine, but PAPSY. I chose it because it was funny. I married a woman of the name of ETHELINDA, for the same reason. I also knock off little things of this sort (poetry to comic tombstone), which occur to me quite naturally on reading over a book of epitaphs. But here comes MURDLES."

MURDLES is a sexton. He has a way of getting drunk. He also carries his dinner in a bundle. When he taps the cathedral floor, he can tell directly whether there is a vault underneath. If there is, he breaks it open, and stirs up the ashes of the illustrious departed with his pickaxe.

The cathedral authorities are much pleased at his so doing.

When he is drunk enough to go home to sleep, and yet can't go of his own accord, he hires a street Arab to fling stones at him at a halfpenny per evening.

The street Arab does so, and very frequently knocks his brains out; but MURDLES don't mind that. He rather likes it.

CHAPTER V.—GOOD NIGHT.

MR. RASPER goes home to bed. RUDE DEDWIN is already slumbering. Mr. RASPER contemplates him, as he sleeps, with one of those comprehensive glances before alluded to. Then with great care he steals, thief-like, to his room, and summons up, beneath the potent demon's influence, the weird spectres of the previous night.

Again the eyeless tower.

Again the dancing dervishes.

Again the bear who wanted soap.

Chaos! —— Oblivion!! —— Crack!!!

"Sweetly pretty!" said JUDY, when the great author had finished; "but what 's the Mystery?"

"It must go no further, if I tell you," the great author said.

"I swear!" said JUDY.

"The MYSTERY is, then," whispered the great author—"*the Mystery is——How it sells!*"

Fig 7. 'Rude Dedwin', *Judy*, 13 April 1870 (Courtesy of ProQuest)

Fig 8. 'Sleeping it Off' by Luke Fildes for *The Mystery of Edwin Drood*

Fig 9. 'Wringing a Secret from Death' by unknown artist for Henry Morford's *John Jasper's Secret*

Fig 10. 'Mr Grewgious Experiences a New Sensation' by Luke Fildes for *The Mystery of Edwin Drood*

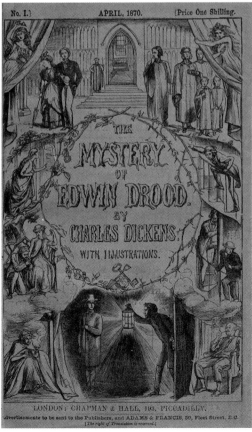

Above: Fig 11. 'Supper and Music for Four' by unknown artist for Henry Morford's *John Jasper's Secret*

Left: Fig 12. Original Monthly Cover for *The Mystery of Edwin Drood* by Charles Alston Collins

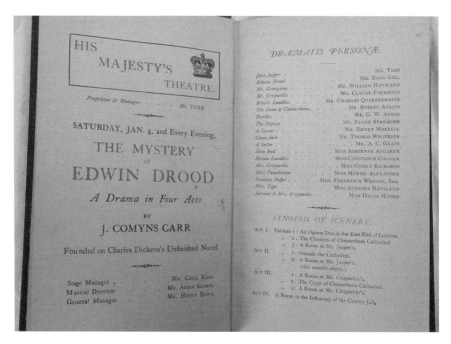

Fig 13. Cast list for Herbert Beerbohm-Tree's production of *The Mystery of Edwin Drood*, 1908

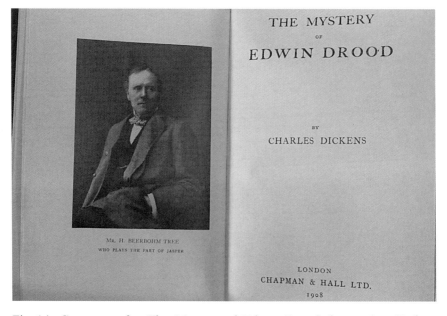

Fig 14. Coverpage for *The Mystery of Edwin Drood* showcasing Herbert Beerbohm-Tree in the role of John Jasper, 1908

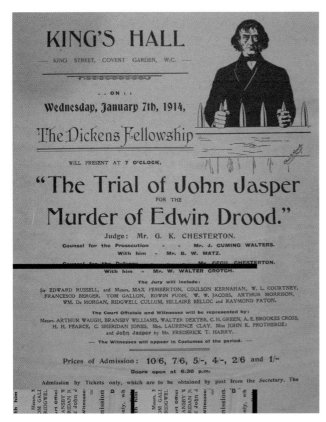

Fig 15. Poster advertising The Trial of John Jasper, 7 January 1914

Fig 16. G. K. Chesterton as Judge, The Trial of John Jasper

Fig 17. Defence and Prosecution, The Trial of John Jasper (L-R: Walter Dexter, John Cuming Walters (sitting), A. E. Brookes Cross, B. W. Matz, Cecil Chesterton, Walter Crotch)

Fig 18. The Jury, The Trial of John Jasper (Back row, L-R: Coulson Kernahan, Ridgwell Cullum, William de Morgan, Huntly McCarthy, William Archer, Thomas Secombe; Front row, L-R: Edward Russell, W. W. Jacobs, Pett Ridge, Arthur Morrison, Francesco Berger, Tom Gallon, George Bernard Shaw)

 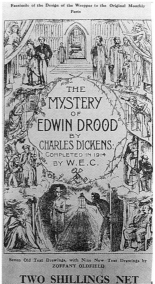

Above left: Fig 19. Sketch of the Trial of John Jasper, *The Sphere,* 17 January 1914

Above right: Fig 20. Amended Monthly Cover for *The Mystery of Edwin Drood* continued by W. E. Crisp

Below left: Fig 21. 'Jasper Sees What is Left of His Victim' by Zoffany Oldfield for Crisp's continuation

Below right: Fig 22. 'Rosa Sees Her Reflection' by Zoffany Oldfield for Crisp's continuation

Above left: Fig 23. Claude Rains' Jasper leers over Neville and Rosa, *Universal Weekly*, Vol. 37, No. 1, 20th April 1935

Above right: Fig 24. Poster for Broadway production of *The Mystery of Edwin Drood* by Rupert Holmes

Below: Fig 25. Poster for *The Mystery of Edwin Drood*, directed by Timothy Forder

THE D. CASE

OR THE TRUTH ABOUT THE MYSTERY OF EDWIN DROOD

CHARLES DICKENS
CARLO FRUTTERO & FRANCO LUCENTINI

"A singular achievement not to be missed." —BOOKLIST

Victorian Popular Fiction Association

Left: Fig 26. Coverpage for *The D Case* by Carlo Fruterri and Franco Lucentini

Below: Fig 27. Programme for 'The Mystery of Edwin Drood: Solutions and Resolutions', conference held at Senate House, London, September 2014

THE UNIVERSITY OF BUCKINGHAM

The Mystery of Edwin Drood: Solutions and Resolutions

Programme

9:30-10:00	Registration
10:00-10:45	**Introduction: The Heritage of *Edwin Drood*** *Chair: Dr Pete Orford, University of Buckingham*
	Keynote: Reflections on past and present *Drood* scholarship — Professor Don Richard Cox, *University of Tennessee*
10:45-11:35	**Panel 1: The Solutions of *Edwin Drood*** *Chair: Dr Pete Orford, University of Buckingham*
	Imitating the inimitable: attempts to complete Edwin Drood — Dr Camilla Ulleland Hoel and Dr Tor Nordam, *Norwegian University of Science and Technology*
	M R James and the *Edwin Drood* Syndicate — Jane Piddock, *University of Aberystwyth*
11.35-11.45	Coffee break
11:45-12:30	**Q&A: Finishing *Edwin Drood*** Discussion session with David Madden, author of *The Mystery of Edwin Drood* (2012) and Gwyneth Hughes, screenwriter of the BBC adaptation (2012)
12:30-13:30	LUNCH (provided)
13:30-14:45	**Panel 2: The Appropriation of *Edwin Drood*** *Chair: Professor John Drew, University of Buckingham*
	Premonition of the End: Fictionality in Dickens' *Edwin Drood* and Gissing's *Henry Ryecroft* — Tom Ue, *University of Birkbeck*
	Another kind of immortality, more essential and more strange': Dick-ensian hauntings, in the works of Susan Howe and Jean-Pierre Ohl — Clemence Follea, *Université Paris Diderot*
	Evidence, storytelling, and the resistance of closure in Dan Simmons's *Drood* — Dr Anne-Marie Beller, *University of Loughborough*
14:45:-15:00	Coffee break
15:00-16:15	**Panel 3: The Characters of *Edwin Drood*** *Chair: Professor David Paroissien, University of Buckingham*
	From 'universal terrorist' to 'tragic anti-hero': John Jasper as a villain of the times — Dr Jonathan Buckmaster, *Royal Holloway*
	The Identification of Sapsea — Sven Karsten, *Independent*
	The Mystery of Heads in *Drood* — Emma Curry, *University of Birkbeck*
16:15-16:25	Coffee break
16:25-17:15	**Panel 4: The Locations of *Edwin Drood*** *Chair: Dr Hazel Mackenzie, University of Buckingham*
	The great black city cast its shadow on the waters': Jasper's London in *The Mystery of Edwin Drood* — Hadas Elber-Aviram, *University College London*
	Venerable, Architectural and Inconvenient': The Rented Spaces of Edwin Drood — Ushashi Dasgupta, *University of Oxford*
17:15-18:00	**Round table: The Digitalisation of *Edwin Drood*** *Chair: Dr Hazel Mackenzie, University of Buckingham*
	Discussion from the Drood Inquiry team on digitising Drood — Dr Pete Orford, Alys Jones, *University of Buckingham*

Fig 28. Publicity photo for 'A Dickensian Whodunnit: Solving The Mystery of Edwin Drood, exhibition at Charles Dickens Museum, London, 2015

Fig 29. Matthew Rhys as John Jasper in *The Mystery of Edwin Drood*, adapted by Gwyneth Hughes, BBC, 2012 (Copyright © BBC Photo Library)

of the few from the Detective era that would manage to curry favour with the next wave of Droodists.

This acceptance of Duffield's idea is the more remarkable for the extraordinary methods behind his theory. The area of his article that has been less discussed, but is to my mind far more fascinating, is Duffield's bibliography for his argument. It is listed below in full and as presented in Duffield's article:

> *The Thugs or Phansigars of India;* by Sir W. H. Sleeman. *CAREY & HART, Philadelphia, 1839.*
>
> *Confessions of a Thug,* by Meadows Taylor. *R. BENTLEY, London, 1839.*
>
> *The Wandering Jew,* by Eugene Sue. *RICHARDS. 1845.*
>
> *The Woman in White*, by Wilkie Collins. *HARPERS, 1860.*
>
> *Cord and Creese,* by James de Mille. *HARPERS, 1869.*
>
> *The Moonstone,* by Wilkie Collins. *HARPERS, 1873.*
>
> *Following the Equator,* by Mark Twain. *HARPERS, 1897.*
>
> *At the House of Dree,* by Gordon Gardiner. *HOUGHTON MIFFLIN, 1928.*
>
> *The Bagshot Mystery,* by Oscar Gray. *MACAULEY, 1929.*[148]

The bibliography is remarkable because not one of these books is either by Dickens or about Dickens. Wilkie Collins and Eugene Sue are the only authors to have known him, and Taylor's *Confessions of a Thug* was first published in *All the Year Round*, but that is as far as a tangible link extends. Aside from the first two on the list, they are all works of fiction, and the last four even postdate Dickens' death. Yet Duffield drew on them all to explain the plot of *Drood*, with no attempt to suggest that Collins, Twain, Gardiner or Gray were privy to *Drood*'s projected plan and utilised that in their own works. In fact, many of the works are not even cited in the main article, but simply presented at the end without explanation. Furthermore, he fails to mention *A Strange Story*, by Dickens' friend Edward Bulwer-Lytton, which was published in Dickens' journal in 1860-61 and in which a hypnotic strangler is said 'to belong to that murderous sect of fanatics whose existence as a community has only recently been made to Europe, and who strangle their unsuspecting victim in the firm belief that they thereby propitiate the favour of the goddess they serve'.[149] Clearly, Duffield's interest does not lie in tracing literary influences on the author. What then are these books, with little to no direct link to Dickens, doing in the bibliography of an article about *Drood*?

The remarkable answer to this becomes clearer when consulting Duffield's remarkable collection of Droodiana. As president of the New York branch of the Dickens Fellowship, Duffield had acquired first editions of several solutions, many of which are now the sole surviving copies that continue to inform *Drood* studies, thanks to the donation of the Duffield Collection to the Charles Dickens Museum in London. His work as a collector makes him invaluable to anyone studying *Drood*, thanks to the rare items he preserved, resulting in 'what is easily the largest and most complete collection of *Drood* materials in the world'.[150] But his marginalia on some of the less obvious works in the collection are eye-opening as an insight into the mind of a Detective Droodist. Gordon Gardiner's *At The House of Dree*, listed in his bibliography for 'John Jasper – Strangler', is a book with no tangible connection to *Drood* or Dickens, but closer inspection reveals a passage in the book detailing a storm, which is adorned with annotations by Duffield. He underlines one sentence during the storm that states 'overhead a full moon was fleeing in and out', and writes in the margin that it 'shows that on Xmas Eve in Cloisterham in that fierce storm of wind there was bright moonlight'.[151] To clarify: Duffield uses Gardiner's book because it describes a scene like the storm in *Drood* and therefore assumes it must shed light on the events in Dickens' book. Nor does he limit himself to fictional parallels. His collection also includes newspaper clippings of strangling cases from twentieth-century America. Duffield conducts his investigation of the murder of Edwin in the same manner as one would conduct a real-life murder case. He looks for parallel cases and assumes they must hold bearing on this case. It is one of the most extraordinary cases of separating a book from its author.

Duffield approaches the plot of *Drood* as though it must necessarily obey the rules of real life. He presumes there to be an objectivity across different fictional worlds, believing that one scene described in one book must be true of a similar scene in another book. He fails to consider that the book begins and ends in Dickens' mind, and instead adorns it with a life of its own, allowing for the plot to be considered separately from the intentions of Dickens. It is incredibly audacious, and makes the subsequent acceptance of his thuggee theory by the later Academic movement all the more wondrous. Yet it cannot be denied that, as questionable as his methods may have been, Duffield's theory had a major impact on the field.

Droodism in the 1930s

While it may have lacked the intensity of the pre-war years, the fundamental ideas of the Detective Droodists persevered through the 1930s. Duffield's rabbit-hole of fiction within fiction was followed by Edwin Harris's completion *John Jasper's Gatehouse*. It harkens back to the early completions of the 1870s in Harris's attempt to assume authority by his position, rather than his prose. While the earlier completions were contemporary enough to pretend to be written by Dickens' friends, family or ghost, Harris – writing sixty years later – was one of the last to be able to make a direct connection to the original author. The book cover thus proudly proclaims that 'Mr Edwin Harris, as a small boy, knew Dickens', implying therein that Harris, an author in his own right, was best-placed of all to pick up the gauntlet.[152] In reality the link is more tenuous than James' ghost. Closer reading reveals that Harris's contact with Dickens was limited to the time when, as a boy, he got his head stuck between the railings of a fence, and Dickens happening to pass by, pushed the boy's head out. And that is as far as their time together extends. It is hardly an act of heroism on the lines of Dickens' much-reported involvement helping out after the Staplehurst crash, nor is it an instance of tutor and pupil to rival Merlin and Arthur. I sincerely doubt Dickens felt compelled whilst pushing the boy's head out of a railing to hurriedly whisper the ending of the book he was currently writing. Instead, Harris's story takes several cues from Forster (Rosa marries Tartar, Helena marries Crisparkle, and Edwin is dead), a few from Droodist predecessors (Bazzard is Datchery), and a few more variations of his own, taking the trope from the 1870s of Jasper being a man who has previously seduced other women, and identifying Princess Puffer as the mother of the unfortunate Mary, led astray by the choirmaster and dying after giving birth to their child, who emerges as none other than Deputy. For all his posturing of a connection to Dickens, in reality his debt is to the Detective Droodists.

Meanwhile, a far more removed solution arrived when *Drood* emerged on the big screen once more, with similar results to its earlier forays into the medium. Stuart Walker's 1935 film for MGM starred Claude Rains as Jasper, and just like its predecessors cut the part of Tartar to streamline the plot for movie length. In his absence, Neville assumed the hero's role, not only being a love-interest for Rosa, but also returning to Cloisterham in disguise as Datchery. The death, not resurrection, of Edwin was the sole thing to represent Forster's account, while Jasper himself was played admirably by Rains as a conflicted but ultimately demonic choirmaster (see fig. 23). His end, chased to the top of the cathedral by an angry pursuing mob, before toppling to his death, is reminiscent of any number of Gothic horror movies from *Frankenstein* to *The Hunchback of Notre Dame* or, indeed, James Cagney in *White Heat*. Rains had been cast by the studio in the role fresh from his great success as the eponymous protagonist of *The Invisible Man* in 1933, for which Jasper served as a continuation of the tortured, insane outsider. While Droodists were attempting to expand the tale in print, on screen the focus was on simplification. Jasper was obviously a villain from the start, and the mystery was really non-existent. The beauty of the film lies in its simplicity and clarity, and lack of apprehension over authority and justification of every decision.

CHAPTER TWO

But the Hollywood treatment was one rogue element against a tide of carefully argued conspiracies. Discussion of *Drood* continued in print with ever more awareness of the precedence of previous arguments. While chapter one of this book had only to consider five texts, this chapter has had to cover a plethora of theories, and even then, there are many more articles and discussions that have not been covered. The sheer bulk of *Drood* theories and arguments occurring at this time cannot be overstated, and the inevitable result was a suffocation of the subject through over-exhausting the topic. Subsequent critics would come to offer terms and categories to retrospectively organise the cacophony of voices into specific groups. In 1956, Gavin Brend termed those who believed Edwin was dead as the undertakers, and those who believed him to be alive as the resurrectionists. Later still, Carlo Fruterro and Franco Lucentini would dub the entire group as 'Agathists' as a nod to their adoption of a murder mystery framework in their search for the great twist they all felt sure to exist in Dickens' final story. And, of course, I myself have opted for the broader term of Detectives. Such terminology is simultaneously helpful and self-defeating. It attempts to make sense of a great wealth of ideas, but in creating special jargon only exacerbates the sense of a closed discussion of *Drood*. In the 1930s, the field was becoming increasingly insular. Rather than being an open puzzle that anyone could offer their ideas on, it had become an area of study in itself that required expertise of trends and ideas. Increasingly, *Drood* was being left to those with the passion to jump into the wealth of previous theories, leaving others discouraged by the sound and fury of squabbling scholars.

In all this time, discussion continued apace in *The Dickensian*. Where once in 1908 an article had appeared with 'Last Words on the Drood Mystery', by 1937 the title of articles had changed tone completely with 'Edwin Drood again'. [153] Gone was the optimism of a final word to be replaced by a weariness of a never-ending discussion. The book had become a familiar, almost dreaded, topic of conversation among Dickensians. Those who did discuss it either began with an apology, or a fervent insistence that they were different from other Droodists. The field had acquired an air of embarrassment or exhaustion. As Dickens' works became increasingly considered in more scholarly terms, so

Droodism was cast as the slightly embarrassing uncle, impossible to ignore but preferable not to acknowledge. For decades *Drood* solutions had been one of the major themes of Dickens discussions, providing a field for scholars to flex their intellectual muscles within his work. Now that attention was shifting towards a general praise of Dickens as an intellectual and not merely a popular writer, the old vanguard of Droodism seemed rather quaint and redundant. Where once Droodism had been the mainstay of Dickensian discussion, now it was becoming a hobby-horse only for the most devoted and most obsessed of his fans. There is a tragic irony in reading the Detective's dismissal of the Opportunists, unaware that that same condemnation will one day be poured on them. Even in 1922 Boyd, looking at the contrast of American and English critics, pointed out that the scorn poured on the early American completions worked both ways:

> [T]he proximity of Dickens' fellow-Englishman to the circumstance affecting his art has by no means prevented them from writing their full share of nonsense on the subject of the Drood mystery. Their extravagance has never been as impetuous and complete as ours, but the difference is largely attributable to a national trait of moderation; they have been idiotic in a formal and quiet way, escaping our wilder fantasies through a racial antipathy for the vehement, and remaining dazedly circumspect where with us the lunacy has been ardent, whole-hearted, and unrestrained.[154]

Like the Cheshire cat says, we're all mad here. *Drood* studies was a glasshouse and stone-throwing was ill-advised. In 1955, George Ford wrote retrospectively that 'the number of books and articles provoked by that tantalising fragment is breathtaking', adding the proviso:

> With some valuable but rare exceptions, most of these publications have been the work of amateurs whose enthusiasm is equalled only by their critical and scholarly innocence.[155]

Ford himself tempers this dismissal of enthusiastic amateurs by noting that: 'To satirize the activities of the organised readers of Dickens is too easy and also presupposes that there must be only one way of reading his novels.' But others around him would be less considerate in their attack on the glut of conspiracies that the Detectives had produced.[156]

Ford is quite right, though. Looking back, it is very easy to scoff or mock the *Drood* theorists of the early twentieth century, and it may be that such ridicule is warranted, to a degree. However, this needs qualifying with a recognition that for all the temptation to dismiss these theories out of hand, they did keep the Dickens discourse alive, and events such as the trial of 1914, though failing to solve the mystery, succeeded in promoting Dickens and his work and encouraging further exploration of both. The scholars that follow in the next chapter, though demolishing much of what was said before, could not have been in a position to do so without the precedent of Proctor, Walters, Lang, Matz and Duffield. They provided a framework of scholarship and, while the conclusions can be disagreed with, their devotion to Dickens and the level of conversation they generated around his works should be respected.

Helena Landless:
A Slumbering Gleam of Fire

> The lustrous gipsy-face drooped over the clinging arms
> and bosom, and the wild black hair fell down protectingly
> over the childish form. There was a slumbering gleam
> of fire in the intense dark eyes, though they were
> then softened with compassion and admiration. Let
> whomsoever it most concerned look well to it!

*It was a Tuesday, with the rain lashing down in the city outside my
window, when this dame comes knocking at my door. She was tall,
dark-haired, of ambiguous ethnicity. Said her name was Landless,
and asked me if I'd heard about the Edwin Drood case.*

*'Sure,' I said. Crazy dame, there wasn't a private eye in the world
who didn't know all about that case. The real question was, who hadn't
heard of it? But turns out the dame had theories. Yeah – her, everyone
else and their dog too. (Come to think of it, did the dog do it?)*

*'The case is really quite elementary,' she said. 'I've been applying
my little grey cells to it, and I'm sure I know whodunit.'*

*I poured myself a bourbon and let her talk on. Turns out she
was quite the amateur detective down in Cloisterham. Been asking
questions and poking her nose around for some time. I figured she
had maybe a personal stake in all this.*

'What's a nice girl like you doing in a case like this? You got a fella?'

'I don't see that as relevant, detective.'

*'Sure it's relevant. You gonna marry this Edwin guy like they say?
What about Crisparkle – maybe even Jasper?'*

*Her eyes glowed fire at me. I figured it was a good time to move the
conversation on.*

*'I hear there's another dick been asking questions down there in
Cloisterham – new guy, name of Datchery. You ever bump into him on
your rounds?'*

*'I haven't yet met him face to face, as it were, but the name is
known to me.'*

CHAPTER TWO

This tigress was playing it cool all right.

'So,' I said, lighting my cigar, 'you got Jasper pegged for this like everyone else?'

'He seems the most likely suspect, save for the orangutan... – IF you think it's murder we're accusing him of.'

I sat up. 'Wait – you saying Drood's not dead?'

'I say nothing,' she replied, 'I merely observe, and eliminate all options till the last one, however unlikely, remains.'

'But you think Jasper's guilty of something?'

'Jasper will show his true colours soon enough. Criminals are a superstitious and cowardly lot,' she noted, running her hands along a utility belt I ain't noticed before. This dame took her sleuthing too serious for the likes of me. I pulled out my file and pointed to the Forster statement.

'See this guy, Forster. He already spoke to the boys in blue some time back – laid out the whole case from start to finish. Seems to me the whole thing is pretty open and shut. No need for another detective to get involved.'

She leapt up, eyes blazing.

'You'd trust that man over me? This is not any case. This is THE case. And it's more complicated than anyone knows. A victim alive and dead. A murderer who hasn't murdered. And a detective who could be anyone. I won't rest till it's solved.'

She ran out the door and I breathed a sigh of relief. Then a knock, and she was back in again.

'There's just one more thing that bothers me,' she said, smoothing out the crumples in her raincoat.

'Is it who Rosa's gonna marry? I hear that dame has options.'

'No you fool. It's how to catch him. I need truth serum, a sidekick, and the entire cast of characters rounded up in one room for no reason while I explain everything to them.'

'Lady, you got yourself a bag of troubles there, and I ain't looking to be your porter. You best be on your way.'

'You're right, there's much to do, and I can't sit here all day. The game's afoot!'

She pounced out the door and back to Cloisterham. I didn't know if I'd ever see that crazy dame again. I wondered about that other guy Datchery and what theories he was cooking up, and what would happen if the two of them ever got their heads together somehow. One thing's for sure, when they did get together, it would be moider!

CHAPTER THREE

Academics vs Enthusiasts: Taking Drood Seriously 1939-1985

Taking Dickens seriously

What comes to categorise the new wave of ideas coming through in the mid- to late-twentieth century is the desire to firmly locate Dickens within the wider canon of literary writers. Identifying this coming group as Academics, and the critics that went before as Detectives, is problematic. Many of the Detectives would want themselves to be thought of as scholars, while assigning 'Academic' as an umbrella title for the more cautious responses that follow has the negative connotation of implying all academics were lacking the enthusiasm of their forebears. Yet loosely speaking, the terminology holds water. Discussion of *Drood* at this time falls into a larger framework of establishing Dickens as a suitable area of study for the academic institution. The writers who we will see in the next few pages are frequently more concerned with reputation and respectability rather than putting a daring new theory forward. They were trying to prove that Dickens deserved to be studied academically on his own terms, staying much closer to the parameters suggested by Forster and showing less enthusiasm for arguing previously unforeseen twists. The wilder days of Droodism were now to be placed under threat by a mature approach. Speaking objectively this is neither good nor bad, simply different. The rationalism that the Academics introduced certainly restored credibility to *Drood*, and Dickens, but equally there is a great deal of fun and energy in the volatile debating of the Detectives that gives a vitality in itself to discussion of *Drood*.

At any rate, the introduction of a new faction shifted the balance of power. The Detectives were about to be hoist by their own petard and subjected to the same scorn and derision they had levelled at the Opportunists before them. This lay not only in demolition of the *Drood* conspiracies, but equally in the growing awareness, and acceptance, of Dickens' relationship with Ellen Ternan. The death of Henry Dickens, his father's last surviving child, in 1933 removed any need for delicacy and opened the floodgates for increased investigation and speculation of the great author's relationship with the young actress.[157] The fascination the literary world had with these revelations offered a real-life mystery to rival and even overwhelm the case in Cloisterham. Many felt it necessary to clarify that, while some readers might be taking a scurrilous interest in the unfolding details, they themselves of course did not have an interest quite so base. George Ford wrote:

> *The importance of the Ellen Ternan story [...] is important not so much in itself as a morsel of gossip but because it leads to fresh evaluation of the complexities behind Dickens' work.* [158]

It may sound like an excuse (it may even be one), but Ford is accurate in identifying a deeper purpose behind the scandal. This was the opportunity many had been seeking to seize Dickens from the nostalgic readings of Chesterton and reinvent the author as an edgy, tortured writer. Contrary to destroying Dickens' reputation, the scandal proved the making of him. It resulted in splitting Dickensians into those who preferred to ignore or disbelieve the rumours and keep the idea of the jolly, family-friendly Dickens, and those who relished this new darker aspect of Dickens as a way into more mature and nuanced readings of his work. Philip Collins, a respected Dickens scholar whose work on *Drood* will be shown to be of great import, noted of the Ternan divide how it galvanised either faction of Dickensians:

> *The wrath of the more orthodox Dickensians at these imputations against their hero's character and conduct*

*gave the iconoclasts a happy sensation of being champions
of Enlightenment. Neither spirit was conducive to a quiet
stock-taking.*[159]

Controversy bred conversation. Where *Drood*'s end had previously
prompted intense discussion, now Jasper had to fight the scandals of
his author for the reader's attention. As will be seen, Collins' summary,
writing within the time of this conflict and regretting the inability of
compromise from either side, is unintentionally ironic given his own
barbed and derisive comments made against earlier interpretations of
Drood. As much as the Academics attempted to be more level-headed
in their interpretations of *Drood*, there was still a passionate debate
occurring over ownership of Dickens. In this chapter, we will trace
the origins of a new way of reading *Drood* as a tortured narrative of a
tortured man written by a tortured man. It was not quite a re-invention,
but a reclaiming of Forster's summary of the plot and an acceptance of
Drood on its own terms. But the Detectives did not go down without
a fight, and while their golden age might be over, several still carried
on the battle, no longer worrying about internal division so much as
re-establishing authority over Forster and the new breed of Academics
who were championing his account of the conclusion.

Two Scrooges, two Jaspers

The paradigm shift in *Drood* studies occurred with Edmund Wilson's
seminal essay 'Dickens: The Two Scrooges'. First delivered as a
lecture in 1939, then produced in print as part of his collection of
essays *The Wound and the Bow* in 1941, Wilson's argument has been
seen as a major step forward not only for *Drood*, but for the academic
study of all of Dickens' work. Later, in the centenary of Dickens'
death, Denis Donoghue noted:

> *It is widely agreed that the account of Dickens which
> Edmund Wilson gave in The Wound and the Bow [...]*

has had remarkable success with academic readers. It is hardly too much to say that we think of Dickens very largely in Wilson's terms.[160]

Wilson sought to address what he saw as an absence of critical work on the author:

Of all the great English writers, Charles Dickens has received in his own country the scantiest serious attention from either biographers, scholars or critics.[161]

Setting aside honourable mentions for Gissing, Chesterton and Shaw, he provocatively dismissed the trend of criticism that had preceded him, claiming that 'The typical Dickens expert is an old duffer [...] primarily interested in proving that Mr Pickwick stopped at a certain inn and slept in a certain bed'.[162] Like several before (and after) him, Wilson sought to rescue Dickens from the interpretations of earlier critics and to recognise his genius anew. Specifically, his concern was to move away from the idea of Dickens as a popular and cheery writer best read nostalgically and lovingly, and instead to highlight the darker elements of his writing to recognise and celebrate the complexity of Dickens' work. 'It is the purpose of this essay,' he writes, 'to show that we may find in Dickens' work today a complexity and a depth to which even Gissing and Shaw have hardly, it seems to me, done justice.'[163] Drawing heavily on Dickens' misery, either in the blacking factory or the unhappy termination of his marriage, Wilson explodes the idea of Dickens as the ever-cheerful Boz, using the wreckage to build a new portrait of a serious, haunted, deep and insightful artist. In the course of his essay he works chronologically through the novels, offering indications of how we can better appreciate the serious tones within, so that by the time he reaches *Drood* at the end, it is no surprise to see a more solemn interpretation directly contrasting the wilder work of the Detective Droodists.

This is not to say, however, for all his self-positioning as a new voice, that Wilson does not draw upon those who have followed him. Quite aside from recognising Gissing, Chesterton and Shaw for their comments on Dickens in general, he also builds his view of *Drood* on the specific foundations of four before him: Forster, Walters, Duffield and Boyd, albeit with some implicit (or explicit) criticism. While he bemoans 'Forster's elaborate memoir, which even in the supplemented edition of Ley has never been a real biography', he nonetheless builds on the 'certain hints supplied by Forster' for the ending to *Drood*.[164] His speculation of plot, where it occurs, lies solely outside of Forster's account, such as the identity of Datchery, for which he turns to Walters' Helena theory:

> *It had already been established by Cuming Walters – it was the first of the important discoveries about Drood – that Datchery, the mysterious character who comes to Cloisterham to spy on Jasper, is Helena in disguise. We have been told that Helena used to masquerade and pass herself off as a boy; and Dickens' alterations in his text, both the amplifications of the written copy and the later excisions from the proofs, indicate very clearly that he was aiming in dealing with such details as Helena's wig and her attempts to conceal her feminine hands to insinuate evidences of her real identity without allowing the reader to find it out too soon.[165]*

Like Forster, Walters is taken on trust. Yet Wilson's main debt is to Duffield and Boyd for their work on thuggism and mesmerism respectively:

> *It has remained for two American scholars to hit upon the cardinal secrets that explain the personality of Jasper [...] so far as I know, up to the present time, nobody who has written about Dickens has been in a position to combine these ideas. Yet what happens when one puts them together is startling: the old novel acquires a sudden new value. As one can revive invisible ink by*

holding it over a lamp or bring out three dimensions in a photograph by looking at it through certain lenses, so it is possible to recall to life the character of John Jasper as he must have been conceived by Dickens.[166]

Pulling the two works together, Wilson conceives a Jasper with mesmeric powers who is following the ways of the thuggee cult in killing his nephew and hiding the body. Written like that, it sounds every bit as outrageous as some of the earlier solutions. The significant shift here is that Wilson is not attempting to rewrite the book, nor look for a surprise ending. His comments on the plot itself are mostly incidental. He is taking Forster's summary on trust, assuming without doubt that Edwin is dead and Jasper is guilty.

Wilson's interest in plot is minimal, stating the most likely case as 'established' and moving swiftly on instead to look at the implications. While this abrupt attitude lays him open to challenge and contradiction, ultimately Wilson's concern does not lie in arguing over the different possibilities for *Drood*. For Wilson, the interest of the end lies not in *what* happens, but *why* and *how*:

For though it is true that Edwin Drood has been enormously written about, it has been always from the point of view of trying to find out what Dickens intended to do with the plot. None of the more serious critics of Dickens has ever been able to take the novel very seriously. They persist in dismissing it as a detective story with good touches and promising characters, but of no interest in the development of Dickens' genius. Bernard Shaw, who is interested in the social side of Dickens, declares that it is 'only a gesture by a man three quarters dead'; and it is true, as Forster remarked, that The Mystery of Edwin Drood seems quite free from the social criticism which had grown more biting as Dickens grew older; but what Forster and Shaw do not see is that the psychological interest which had been a feature of

84

Dickens' later period is carried farther in Edwin Drood.
Like all the books that Dickens wrote under the strain
of his later years, it has behind it bitter judgments and
desperate emotions.[167]

Wilson's great contribution to the direction of *Drood* studies lies in this, his re-imagination of the story not as a detective novel, but a psychological study. It was not a story about what happened to Edwin, but what is happening to Jasper before our eyes. The focus of the tale and the key to holding the reader's interest lies not in the crypts of Cloisterham but rather in the recesses of the choirmaster's mind. 'Dickens, so far as we can see,' Wilson argues, 'is exclusively concerned with a psychological problem.' Amidst the 'fairy tale' setting of Cloisterham, the novel's 'realest figure is Mr Jasper'.[168]

Wilson identifies Jasper as a man of contradictions, both a vicious murderer but equally a 'good and faithful servant' to his cult, arguing that 'it is at the command of his imaginative *alter ego* and acting in the name of his goddess that Jasper has committed his crime'.[169] Jasper thus becomes, in Wilson's hands, 'a man who is both innocent and wicked', with the final scene in the condemned cell offering an insight into the clash between these two personalities.[170] In arguing for this exploration of the psychology of the murder, Wilson repositioned Dickens' last work, moving it out of the detective genre and into a new canon:

[Dickens] is to explore the deep entanglement and conflict
of the bad and the good in one man. The subject of Edwin
Drood is the subject of Poe's William Wilson, the subject
of Dr Jekyll and Mr Hyde, the subject of Dorian Gray. It
is also the subject of that greater work than any of these,
Dostoevsky's Crime and Punishment.[171]

Wilson lifts *Drood* up, away from the popular and into the literary. His comparison in particular to Dostoevsky is massively significant as much for its commentary on Dickens as on *Drood*. Though he had dismissed the figure of the 'old duffer' for his enthusiastic but facile interpretations of Dickens, he was equally derisive of scholars who had unfairly overlooked the writer altogether: 'The Bloomsbury that talked about Dostoevsky ignored Dostoevsky's master, Dickens.'[172] There is certainly an element of trying to making Dickens cool by association occurring here as Wilson attempts to justify Dickens' suitability for literary criticism by likening him to an author already prone to such readings. But for *Drood* it offered a much-needed new way of reading the book. Instead of arguing that the 'curious and new idea' described to Forster lies in a mystery twist designed to save the book from being mediocre, it encouraged readers to see the story as an exploration of the interior world of Jasper's mind as much as the exterior world of his actions.[173]

As much as Wilson draws on Dostoevsky, he also justifies his judgment by looking back across Dickens' own work for precedents, unwittingly echoing the approach of Proctor before him. Where Proctor saw patterns of the innocent man watching the wicked, Wilson notes a recurring motif of contrasts: 'This dualism runs all through Dickens. There has always to be a good and a bad of everything.'[174] He recognises a specific precursor for Jasper in Bradly Headstone of *Our Mutual Friend*, with 'Jasper presenting, like Headstone, a gruesome travesty of the respectable Victorian', but another model for Jasper begins to show through Wilson's interpretation: Dickens himself.[175] He draws on the remarks of Dickens' daughter Kate that 'my father was a wicked man – a very wicked man', connecting it to the focus he has made throughout his essay on Dickens' hidden skeletons and tortured past, and ultimately ties these ideas together by painting the author as another Jasper:[176]

> *Mr. Jasper is, like Dickens, an artist: he is a musician, he has a beautiful voice. He smokes opium, and so, like Dickens, leads a life of the imagination apart from the life of men. Like Dickens, he is a skilful magician, whose power over his fellows may be dangerous. Like Dickens, he is an alien from another world; yet, like Dickens, he has made himself respected in the conventional English community.*[177]

Jasper joins Oliver Twist and David Copperfield as a channel for Dickens to exorcise his own demons. But where elsewhere biography focused on the abandoned child in the blacking factory, here it paid more heed to the adult, respectable figure attempting to maintain his reputation whilst hiding a notorious secret. Wilson's redrawing of Dickens may be seen as an attack on the man, but it is done as an attempt to celebrate the artist. The dark, brooding figure makes for a far more interesting and intellectual figure than the jolly crowd-pleaser and allowed academics of the time to get over their hang-ups of liking such a popular writer. Here at last was a direct challenge to those who had previously looked upon Dickens as fun, but unaccomplished, and many were now emboldened by Wilson's salvo. George Ford noted that:

> *Virginia Woolf affirmed haughtily in 1925 that she would not trouble to cross the street in order to meet Charles Dickens [...] Had Mrs Woolf lived to read Edmund Wilson's analysis of Dickens's character, it is possible that she might have found the novelist a more interesting and sympathetic figure.*[178]

In terms of *Drood* specifically, the final and most significant shift that Wilson thus introduced in his appraisal of it is an unashamed championing of the novel not for what it could be, but for what it is. Where Proctor and Walters had dismissed the surviving half as a poor fragment devoid of its crowning glory, Wilson argued that Dickens' genius could be seen throughout:

> *In this new novel, which is to be his last, Dickens has found a new intensity. The descriptions of Cloisterham are among the best written in all his fiction: they have a nervous (in the old sense) concentration and economy rather different from anything one remembers in the work of his previous phases.*[179]

Where previous scholars of *Drood* had sought to apologise for the work, Wilson came to celebrate it; where they had tried to add to it,

Wilson was content with it as it was; where they saw it as Dickens' last labouring effort, Wilson saw it as a work of new intensity. *The Two Scrooges* ushered in a new wave of scholars who sought to stop worrying about the half that was not written, and start focusing on the half that was.

Battle-lines are drawn

The early 1950s saw an array of new Dickens biographies appear – by Jack Lindsay in 1950, and both Julian Symons and Edgar Johnson in 1952 – and in all their readings of *Drood* we can trace the ripples of Wilson's work. Lindsay includes in his biography 'a special tribute to Edmund Wilson's essay', and Symons too praises it as 'one of the few illuminations in the morass of Dickensian criticism'.[180] Of *Drood*, Lindsay accordingly calls it 'a thorough exploration of the problem of divided consciousness in Jasper', while Symons, citing the 'phrase in Mr. Wilson's essay in which he suggests that the artist with whom Dickens has most in common is Dostoevsky', proclaims that 'No sooner has the comparison been made [...] than its justice is realised.'[181] Both biographies were overshadowed by Johnson's, which received a greater critical reception. His book also celebrates the darker Dickens of Wilson, claiming him as:

> *Dostoevski's [sic] master; for Crime and Punishment and the Brothers Karamazov, though far greater books than Barnaby Rudge and Martin Chuzzlewit, are tremendously indebted to their studies of murders and rebels against society.*[182]

Johnson then echoes Wilson in celebrating *Drood* as the next step forward in Dickens' supremacy over his Russian counterpart:

> *But with John Jasper, in 1870, Dickens was approaching those dark and tangled labyrinths of alienation that*

Dostoevski [sic] explored in Raskalnikov, whose very name means dissenter. And although there is a kind of twisted comedy in Dostoevski, he cannot come within measurable distance of Dickens's high-spirited and irresistible vivacity.[183]

Given this praise afforded to Wilson, and the influence his essay clearly held a decade after it had been published, it might appear that his ideas on *Drood* were proving triumphant, but it did not end the attempts of the Detectives to 'solve' *Drood*. Instead it drew a new line in the sand for Dickensians to choose their side. The ire previously conducted internally among the Detectives now extended to a wider battle as all of them squared up against the sneers of the Academics, who dismissed them – to repeat Ford's phrase – as 'Amateurs whose enthusiasm is equalled only by their critical and scholarly innocence.'[184] J. C. Walters had once mocked the early responses of the 1870s for their failure to adopt a thorough and rigorous method. Now fate had come full circle and he and his contemporaries were accused of precisely the same fault by their successors.

But the Detectives did not die. They simply become more resilient. Richard Baker wrote several articles for *Nineteenth Century Fiction*, which were eventually republished as a full book, in which he explored specifically the identity of Datchery, the guilt of Jasper, the fate of Edwin and the possible ending for the book. In other words, all the classic traits of the Detective Droodist.[185] Arguing for Grewgious as Datchery, Edwin dead, and Jasper as mesmerist, Baker was adamant in his continuation of detectivism: 'I cannot accept Forster's explanation of the fragment.'[186] Other Detective Droodists, post-Wilson, lived in denial. William W Bleifuss simultaneously attacked the methods of the Detectives while reaching similar conclusions as to *Drood*'s ending. Like Wilson, he bemoans the work of his predecessors, noting:

Unfortunately many of these writers see the novel as a detective story and fail to note how similar in theme, characterisation, and development it is to the other

Dickens novels. Instead of remaining faithful to their author, they follow a pattern of inquiry worthy of Sherlock Holmes himself.[187]

Again, like Wilson, he argues:

To examine Edwin Drood as though its author were Sir Arthur Conan Doyle and Dick Datchery were an early incarnation of Sherlock Holmes has been a common error. [Dickens] was not, as we shall see, writing a detective story.[188]

And again, like Wilson, he argues: 'What surprises there are in Dickens's novels arise not from the "what" but the "how"'.[189] However, where Wilson tried to restore faith in Forster, Bleifus goes on the attack:

There is good evidence [...] that Dickens by 1869-1870 no longer considered Forster so indispensable a friend. He wrote fewer and fewer letters to his literary advisor as the years passed.[190]

Having vigorously rubbished those who have gone before him, Bleifus changes track to argue that Edwin is alive after all. It is a bizarre contradiction, where at one moment he will happily conclude Datchery to be Bazzard, adding derisively that 'To accept Bazzard is the easiest way out, and therefore the most unsatisfactory to a Sherlock Droodian', the next he is attacking Forster and reclaiming a surprise ending for *Drood*.[191] It is little surprise that T. S. Blakeney, writing one year later, should state that Bleifuss was 'twisting his data to suit his theory'.[192] If Bleifuss was a Detective in denial, then Blakeney, like Baker before him, is out and proud, proclaiming that 'however much Mr Bleifuss may dislike' the idea of *Drood* as a crime story, it is 'such a story, and a detective story – a very successful one, too, since we have been trying to solve it for 85 years!'[193] This sort of commentary would not have been out of place in the debates of Proctor, Lang and Walters. To Blakeney, like them, the joy and wonder of *Drood* lies in the unintended mystery of its incompletion, not the skill of the remaining fragment, as Wilson had argued. That Blakeney's attack on Bleifuss proves prelude to his assertion that Datchery is Helena only further reminds us of the earlier controversies at the beginning of the twentieth century. It seems Wilson's essay was yet to convince everybody.

Bleifuss also came under fire from Gavin Brend, who introduced his credentials as 'one of Sherlock Holmes biographers', who accordingly felt compelled to comment given Bleifuss's frequent references to Holmesian attempts at solving *Drood*, countering:

> *Dick Datchery may be poles apart from Sherlock Holmes,*
> *but Dickens is not quite so remote from Conan Doyle [...]*
> *I think, therefore, that Dickens was quite capable of*
> *sending his readers off on a false trail.*[194]

The piece is a letter to the editor in direct response to Bleifuss's article, and it is worth noting that Bleifuss, Brend and Blakeney were all printing their ideas in the *Dickensian*. Just as the magazine had proved fertile ground for Droodists before, for the time-being it was a safe haven where solutions and theories could continue to be discussed. Brend's conclusion that Edwin is alive and Datchery, whosoever he might be, is *not* Bazzard, draws not on the text so much as popular opinion: 'I know of forty-one attempts to supply the answer. If Edwin is dead and Bazzard is Datchery seven of these are right and thirty-four are wrong.'[195] Brend, like Blakeney, is bedding down and restating the significance of the canon of *Drood* solutions. Intentionally or not, it is a direct contrast to the ideas of Wilson.

While Blakeney cried that 'we just go round and round in a circle', Brend was looking to move on from existing arguments only to focus on other aspects, as 'there are so many other problems to argue about in connection with *Edwin Drood*'.[196] Discussions of *Drood*'s ending were not over, and to prove the point, Brend returned to the case in 1956, in the *Dickensian* once more, where he launched the most extended attack on Forster yet. His article, '*Edwin Drood* and the four witnesses', systematically worked through the testaments of Forster, Charles Dickens Jnr, Charles Allston Collins and Luke Fildes to show how none of them could or should be trusted.[197] It is a further attempt to demolish the idea of *Drood*'s ending being clear and apparent, to open the door for re-interpretation of the stories' close. Of Charley Collins, Brend call the idea 'rather remarkable that Dickens should have disclosed the secret to a man whom he disliked so intensely'.[198] The same cannot, of course, be said for Dickens' son, so for Charles Dickens Jnr Brend has to take a different approach:

> *Charles tells us that during a walk at Gadshill he said to his father 'Of course Edwin Drood was murdered?' and Dickens with an expression of astonishment replied 'Of course; what else did you suppose?'*
>
> *Charles wrote this account many years later. I suggest that he may have been mistaken about the look of astonishment, that Dickens may never have uttered those first two words 'Of course' and that he evaded his son's question by asking him another question – 'What else did you suppose?' I see nothing improbable about this reconstruction.[199]*

Charley Collins was damned for being a fool and out of the loop, Charley Dickens was mistaken. Two down, two to go. The final refrain 'I see nothing improbable about this reconstruction' could be lifted directly from the pages of Proctor, Walters or Lang. Brend is applying his subjective argument with the veneer of detached objectivity. Fildes, like Dickens' son, is queried for having taken so long to come forward with notes on the conclusion of *Drood*, and again the words imparted to him by Dickens regarding Jasper's scarf – 'Jasper strangles Edwin Drood with it' – are broken apart and twisted by Brend:

> *I have my doubts as to whether these words were ever spoken, but, assuming that they were, what do they prove? Suppose that Jasper makes an unsuccessful attempt? Is*

not the word 'strangle' adequate in ordinary conversation?
Must Dickens add that the strangling is in fact ineffective?[200]

Another rhetorical question by a Droodist. I cannot help feeling that the answer to Brend's last question must be, in a word, yes. What Brend sees as an obvious interpretation is not obvious to others, not least those to whom these words were first addressed. But Brend is adamant in his rewriting of the witness statements, sketching each witness as missing the point of the person who was talking directly to them and assuming that he, writing eighty-six years after Dickens' death, better understands what he was saying to his friends and family. For sheer audacity, it is equal to Thomas Power James' employment of Dickens' ghost to end the tale. Of course, the greatest scorn is reserved for Forster. Brend draws on the popular idea growing in biographies that Forster and Dickens had grown apart, and therefore argues that Forster's awareness of *Drood*'s end is a false claim made by a man who 'may feel that his personal prestige is at stake'.[201] Worse yet, Forster does not give *enough* details:

> *I find it rather surprising that of the second great problem in Edwin Drood, the identity of Datchery, Forster seems to know little and care less. We are in fact asked to believe that Dickens found it essential to bring him into the picture so far as the fate of Edwin was concerned but quite unnecessary to do so in the case of Datchery. Surely this is hardly consistent.*[202]

Poor Forster was damned for saying too much and damned for saying too little. Brend's essay is more character assassination than literary analysis. He defends his critiquing of the witnesses, and his intense probing of their words, by magnifying the importance of *Drood* in the Dickens canon:

> *We must remember this is not just an ordinary incident in the life of Dickens about which there is no special significance or dispute. If it were, there would be no particular reason for doubt.*[203]

There were many works by Dickens where readers were uncertain of how it might end – whether Little Nell would live or die, or whether Pip and Estella would ever be united – while all the time Dickens was disclosing the book's conclusion with his close circle of friends (Bulwer Lytton famously proposed a new ending for *Great Expectations*, while Dickens persisted in sending updates on Little Nell to William Charles Macready in a remarkably insensitive act given that Macready's own daughter had recently died). *Drood* and its mysterious ending was not remarkable in Dickens' canon, and there is no reason to presume he would not discuss it with those close to him. Brend's pre-emptive defence against those who see 'any attempt to question John Forster's authority' as 'a desperate Resurrectionist manoeuvre to bolster up a tottering case' speaks volumes.[204] In the wake of Wilson, such attacks and attempts to rewrite the testimonies of Dickens' friends and family only seemed to become more desperate, but this in turn highlights the stepping up of the Detectives to defend themselves against a new foe. Brend's additional contribution to *Drood* studies was to coin the terms of undertakers and resurrectionists for those who believe Edwin to be dead or alive. Both names have been picked up by several subsequent critics, and has an interesting side-effect of re-establishing the great divide of *Drood* solutions as existing between the Detectives. The result of this is that it sidelines Wilson's view, not crediting it as an opponent, but instead seeing the Detectives as all-encompassing, with the main fight still being between the Detectives, and Wilson reduced to being just another undertaker, rather than an entirely new model of thinking outside the Detective approach.

At this time *Drood* appeared on television in two adaptations, one in 1952 and the other in 1960. Like the silent films before them, neither still exists, and the 1952 one particularly has very little surviving details recorded about it. It was performed as part of the American series *Suspense,* which presented different tales of danger each week. In the case of *Drood*, all we know is it took two weeks, on 18 and 25 March, and starred John Beregay, though we do not even know which part he played. The 1960s television series however has much more information left for us. The series writer, John Keir Cross, recalled the time he 'chatted with John Dickson-Carr', a detective writer in his own right, who gave Cross the idea for the series during a long discussion about Dickens' novel:

> *'But,' said Dickson-Carr, 'suppose Dickens was not going to be content with the obvious solution to which so many of those clues seem to point? Suppose he was keeping a trump card up his sleeve? He hinted as much in conversations about the book with his friends.'*[205]

Words like 'suppose', 'obvious solution' and 'trump card' identify the subsequent series as more informed by the Detectives than the Academics. Cross's series ran for eight weekly episodes, each half-an-hour long, in which the 'first five parts of the serial consist of a dramatic reconstruction of Dickens's own material, with all the clues fairly presented and even occasionally emphasised'.[206]The sixth episode would allow 'a brief interlude for outlining theories of celebrated writers and criminologists', after which Cross would 'in all humility' carry the story forward to show 'what, according to Dickson-Carr, might have happened on that macabre Christmas in old Cloisterham.'[207]

As the only documents surviving are from articles advertising the forthcoming show, the exact details of that ending are not clear, and we are left to work out what we can. The television guide's synopsis for the opening episode sets the tone pretty clearly for Jasper's guilt and intentions: 'The first episode contains a whiff of opium, a strangler's scarf, and a strange, half-empty tomb.'[208] John Jasper was played by Donald Sinden, who relished what he saw as a chance to step out of his usual role: 'I have been getting worried about being type-cast,' he noted. 'People have come to associate me with the wolf character,' (a wolf in this sense being a serial womaniser).[209] Accordingly, in this series he was said to step 'right out of character to portray the strange, hypocritical uncle, John Jasper.'[210] Jasper was not to be a man known for his luck with the ladies, but a strange figure instead: an outsider. Princess Puffer was referred to throughout simply as the old opium woman, and the synopsis for episode seven suggests a grisly end when 'At last Mrs Sapsea's tomb is opened, and someone finds a hideously effective way to silence a blackmailer'.[211] While the previous episodes had all contained in their cast-lists the elusive misinformation that Datchery was played by 'The unnamed player', by episode seven this had changed and his name instead was listed as 'Bazzard alias Datchery'.[212] As helpful as these are in laying out fairly plainly the major plot points, the final episode's synopsis is infuriatingly opaque:

> *The murderer confesses. Is there still, perhaps, another way to interpret the evening of the night when Edwin Drood mysteriously disappeared?*[213]

Edwin is listed among the cast for that final episode, but this could just as easily be for flashbacks of the murder. Fittingly, guessing the ending of Cross's serial has become as elusive as guessing the ending of the book it is based on.

What is clear is the overtones of Detective Droodism at work here. The hints of 'another way' still at the end, and the earlier comments from Cross on his conversation with Dickson-Carr, suggest some twist in the tale beyond Forster's statement. The interlude in the sixth episode involved a discussion between the series' presenter Michael Ingrams and his two guests: actor Raymond Francis, known for playing Chief-Superindent Lockhart on television, and crime-writer Ngaio Marsh, who was interviewed accordingly by the *TV Times*. Marsh, unsurprisingly, is definitely a Detective, though she betrays an unfamiliarity with the book, claiming it was 'about a third written' and referring to Datchery as 'Datchet'.[214] Her comments when interviewed indicate a predilection for twists and challenges to Forster's statement:

> *Apparently he told one of his sons that Edwin Drood was dead. But he could have been deliberately misleading, or he could have said it ambiguously.*
>
> *Anyway, one of Dickens' tentative titles for the story was "The Return of Edwin Drood," which seems to imply,*

as some people have suggested, that Datchet [sic], who
certainly seems to be wearing a wig, is Drood in disguise.[215]

Once she read the book, she 'just could not stop' thinking about a
solution, estimating that were she to write one it 'would take thousands
of words to explain in full'.[216] Given that her role was to present a
different theory to Cross and Dickson-Carr's solution, the result is not
consolidation of an agreed end but further opening up of Dickens'
novel to interpretation. Marsh's interviewer suggests that 'Viewers
will be able to compare the views in the following two weeks with the
ending devised by Dickson-Carr', while Cross himself admitted that
'It may be that, as the clues assemble, viewers will arrive at a different
solution'.[217] The series was deliberately prompting and provoking
discussion and different ideas for what Dickens had in mind for the end.
It was the antithesis of what Wilson had laid out in 'The Two Scrooges'.
Seminal as Wilson's essay may be considered for Dickens studies now,
his specific ideas for *Drood* were being buried thanks to the efforts of
the Detectives. What was needed now was another resurrection.

Collins joins the fray

Wilson's idea found an ally of sorts in Philip Collins' 1962 book
Dickens and Crime. Collins was unequivocally in favour of Forster's
summary and the idea of a no-surprises ending: 'Jasper has killed
Edwin and we are never intended to doubt it.'[218] Collins was writing
in an era where scholarly exploration of Dickens was growing, and
he had little time for those unwilling to take an intellectual approach
to *Drood*. Where Wilson had gently poked fun at 'the old duffer',
Collins went at them with barbed sword:

> *It would be a very stupid and inattentive reader who could*
> *fail to see that John Jasper is a wicked man, that he has*
> *'cause, and will, and strength, and means' to kill Edwin,*
> *that he makes careful preparation to do so and to throw*

suspicion elsewhere, that Edwin disappears permanently at the climax of these preparations, and that Jasper thereafter continues to act in a fashion compatible – to say the least – with his being a reasonably prudent murderer.[219]

Where once Dickensians had railed at each other in public over the minutiae of surprise twists in *Drood*'s end, now Collins dismissed the entire thing as ludicrous and pointless. Accordingly, when he does refer to earlier critics it is usually to attack or dismiss their work. While Wilson championed Duffield's thuggee theory, Collins regarded it as 'one of the many theories about *Edwin Drood* which deserve to be cut off by a literary Occam's Razor'.[220] But as much as Collins agreed with Wilson's fundamental principle that *Drood* was not a detective story, he still opened fire on many of Wilson's other ideas. He did not think, as Wilson did, that *Drood* was some of Dickens' finest writing:

Nor need we assume that everything in the fragment is perfect in its placing and relevance, or that Dickens was, for once, going to write the perfect plot. The completed novel might well have contained as many loose ends and imperfections as usual.[221]

This is not quite a return to the tactics of Proctor who would rubbish the original in order to justify and triumph the necessity of his solution, but nor is it the celebration of Dickens' writing that Wilson trumpets. Instead Collins begrudgingly states 'I wish that Dickens had been capable of writing the novel that Mr Wilson thinks up for him', in a manner simultaneously wistful and patronising. It relegates such thoughts of *Drood* as a great book to the realm of dreams. It is a pleasant, but untrue, idea for Collins, and to think it of *Drood* renders Wilson's work as subjective and emotional in Collins' eye, rather than objective and logical.

The second major deviation from Wilson's argument rests on Jasper himself. While Collins agrees he is the murderer, and the story to document his downfall, he cannot believe that Jasper should be the divided man that Wilson describes:

> *I find it difficult, indeed, to see any 'insoluble moral problem' in Jasper or in his creator. Jasper, I have insisted, is a wicked man who murders for lust; there is no evidence in the book about his moral processes, except his opium confession that he greatly enjoyed the act of murder.*[222]

To Collins the book was not a psychological study, but 'a better novel of the kind [Dickens] already knew how to write – a Sensation novel, but with a firmer plotline, and less hackneyed sensations'.[223] Collins did not see a great comparison to be made between Dickens and Dostoevsky save for 'superficial similarities'.[224]

Discussion of *Drood*'s plot was moving away from the what to the how. Collins and Wilson both agreed that Jasper killed Edwin, and neither sought to rewrite the book or challenge Forster. It was in the character of Jasper that disagreement now reigned. Collins read Jasper's feelings towards Edwin as 'alleged love for his nephew', taking it as fact that Jasper says he loves Edwin, but querying the interior monologue of the choirmaster. This is an area where Forster is no help, through no fault of his own. Like Charles Dickens Jnr, Charley Collins and Luke Fildes, the statement provided was for the benefit of Droodists of the time, whose concern was on the events that occur, not the manner in which they are described nor the characterisation of the principal figures in the story. Thus, while Collins and Wilson could both draw on these external witnesses as definitive proof that the Detectives were heading down a blind alley, they themselves were finding new cul-de-sacs of thought with no ready source to satisfy one or the other in their views. For Collins, the redefining of Jasper as a plain villain has a second purpose in rescuing Dickens from Wilson's portrayal of an equally wicked and innocent man. Recognising the need of Wilson to counteract 'the popular notion of the Inimitable Boz' with 'a thorough immersion in the destructive elements of his character and behaviour', Collins nonetheless seeks to rescue Dickens from the depths of despair and torment that Wilson would have him plunged in.[225] 'It was easy,' notes Collins, 'during the first flush of excitement about the newly-discover Ellen Ternan affair, to exaggerate his moral alienation from his age, and then to blow up the more aggressive and anti-social aspects of his behaviour until a thoroughly split personality, a manic-depressive victim, emerged.'[226]

Collins' work on *Drood* is of great significance, returning Wilson's arguments to the common consciousness two decades later, and stamping further down on the Brends and Blakeneys of the world who strived to market *Drood* as detective fiction. But, as much as it moves forward, there remains in it several elements common to Droodism. In particular, Collins draws heavily upon the idea of facts. Though Collins certainly aims to steer away from the solutions of the Detectives, this Gradgrindian fixation on what is provable is a direct descendant of their work. He attacks Wilson (again) for his vision of the tortured Jasper in the cell as a passage with 'a satisfying conclusiveness, which seems to me unwarranted by the facts', implicitly suggesting that Wilson's argument rests as much upon narrative potency as objective reasoning.[227] He then closes his analysis of *Drood* by stating:

> *Whether I am right or wrong, I have put forward the*
> *evidence, not all of it well-known, which should help*
> *other critics and historians to arrive at judgments more*
> *securely based upon the facts.*[228]

Objectivity appears to be Collins' watchword, but his occasional zeal in denouncing the subjectivity of those before him ironically points towards a certain subjectivity in himself. Collins has no time for the Detective Droodists, just as they had no time for the early solutions. Much as he noted the post-Ternan debate of iconoclasts vs orthodox Dickensians, his own dismissal of the latter as 'stupid and inattentive' readers hardly builds towards a ceasefire between the camps. Whatever was happening in the wider world of Dickens studies, *Drood* debates continued to be a place of name-calling and ire. Writing much later in 1990, Collins spoke deferentially of his earlier work:

> *I had my own say, briefly, about Drood in my Dickens and Crime (1962) and would, I think, still stand by what I then wrote in my (comparative) youth, though predictably none of my reviewers singled out that chapter as the one they most admired.*[229]

Collins' reviewers may not have seen the merit at the time, but scholars of *Drood* did. His book came at a necessary time where many Detectives were treading over Wilson's ideas. Collins in turn was shouting back at the Droodists, so that in the two decades since Wilson's work, his message was starting to gain dominance.

Aylmer's run; or: The Detectives Strike Back

So what does a Detective Droodist do when popular opinion shifts against the idea of hidden clues and twist endings? While the moderate Detectives quietened down, those with the most enthusiastically-held ideas continued to make their voices heard: re-enter Felix Aylmer. He had kept busy since his early *Dickensian* articles in 1924 and 1925. Though an actor by trade (he played Polonius in Laurence Olivier's film *Hamlet*), Aylmer had recently enjoyed great success with the publication of *Dickens Incognito* in 1959.[230] This book touched on the other great Dickens mystery of Ellen Ternan. Piecing together clues found in county rent books, Aylmer was able to identify Mr Tringham as a pseudonym for Dickens, and thus find the residence where the author lodged Ellen Ternan. The work is a genuinely important one for the developing awareness of Dickens' relationship with Ternan, though as Michael Slater notes Aylmer goes a step beyond the evidence in a quest for Dickens' lovechild, which was swiftly disproved leading Aylmer to ruefully withdraw the claim 'but still clinging on to his belief that there *was* a son'.[231] Emboldened by the success of his Dickensian investigation, Aylmer applied the same method of detection to *Drood,* for 'As the last work of our best loved novelist and one of the most famous puzzles in literature, it is better known, and has won more critical attention, than any comparable book that can be cited'.[232] It is almost as though Wilson and Collins' work did not exist: *Drood* was a puzzle once more, still to be solved. Like many Detective Droodists before him, Aylmer's interest lay less in the novel itself and more in the surrounding mythology of conspiracy and controversy. He confesses to having had little interest in the book until the Fellowship's trial of Jasper:

> *Although, as a boy, I had read all the other Dickens novels, I had shirked Drood on account of the frustration and disappointment to be foreseen at the point where the author's pen gave out. Reluctance, however, is seldom proof for long against curiosity, and when, in 1914, the Dickens Fellowship organised a mock trial, in which many of my most admired authors were to take part, I sat up and took notice.[233]*

Aylmer's statement reconfirms how far removed from Dickens' original text the argument had gone. Where his contemporary audience was reading a series eagerly, ignorant of the impending absence of an ending, Aylmer, like everyone else post-1870, could only ever approach the book as a fragment. And like so many Detectives, the fragment was intrinsically disappointing as a reading experience. Only as a puzzle could it be considered attractive. The more people argued over the ending, the more the mystique of the book's potency as an unsolvable riddle grew. Detectives like Aylmer read it not as a book to enjoy, but an enigma to solve. The claims of Wilson that it was a book of great intensity held no place in such a mindset – the end crowned all, and he who found that end could claim the crown.

Aylmer is not merely a Detective, but one of the arch-Detectives, for the sheer confidence he holds in his own conclusion to the absolute exclusion of all other possibilities. 'The success of this puzzle in remaining unsolved for the best part of a century is remarkable' he states, 'in that the bulk of the evidence is to hand, and much of it reasonably obvious'.[234] Once more then, in Aylmer's work we see that the familiar and confident assertion that all that followed could be directly evidenced beyond doubt in Dickens' work was made, and once more that confidence was wholly misplaced. Recalling his earlier argument of 1924, Aylmer went further than anyone before in re-imagining how *Drood* might end. It was no longer a question of whether Edwin was dead or alive. Aylmer challenged the one constant that no one but himself had dared question before: Jasper's guilt.

Like Collins, Aylmer dismisses Wilson's idea of Jasper being a man of two halves, but where Collins dismissed the innocent Jasper, Aylmer dismisses the wicked. Giving Jasper a dual personality, asserts Aylmer, 'is a last-ditch position forced upon Jasper's enemies by their determination to condemn him in spite of his acknowledged affection for his victim'.[235] The talk of 'Jasper's enemies', as though the character is a real-person, takes Duffield's fictional forensics to a new level as Aylmer seeks not to vindicate the book, or the author, but the choirmaster, freeing him from suspicion at last of false accusations of murder.

Given Collins' previous statement that 'we are never intended to doubt' Jasper has killed Edwin, how does Aylmer reverse the apparent trend of Dickens' novel to reinstate Jasper as an innocent man? For this reversal is not simply the idea that Edwin is alive – for such theories still insist that Jasper at least *tried* to kill him – but rather that Jasper is not only innocent of murder, but actively trying to save his nephew from those who would kill him. The key to Aylmer's argument, and Jasper's salvation, lies in Duffield's thuggee theory. Drawing upon this oriental interpretation of the novel, Aylmer imagines a backstory involving Edwin and Rosa's fathers. Drood Snr, while abroad, marries a local girl to the anger of her father. The alliance results in the birth of a child: Jasper, who is now no longer Edwin's uncle, but step-brother. Drood Snr's father-in-law challenges him, during which Drood Snr takes the upper hand too far and nearly threatens the older man's life, stopped only by Rosa's father. This results in two acts: a curse of death is placed upon the Drood family, and a blessing of protection on the Bud family, with both being inherited by the children upon the death of the parent. This, then, is why Edwin must marry Rosa, so that her blessing cancels out the curse upon him. Rosa, Edwin and the rest of Cloisterham are ignorant of this. Only Jasper, void of the curse thanks to his mother, knows of the threat against his beloved nephew. Jasper, in love with Rosa, thus must step aside for the sake of his nephew's life, mistrusted by many but ever faithful to Edwin and ever watching for the horde of Indian assassins waiting to murder him. When Edwin disappears, Jasper fears the worst, while Edwin himself, who does *not* die, mistakenly believes Jasper to be the guilty party, along with all the other characters and the reader too.

There is a remarkable amount of extrapolation at work here, to put it mildly, rendering Aylmer's frequent insistence on truth and evidence as all the more ludicrous. The grand ending Aylmer envisions rests around Jasper's deathbed. Jasper has stepped forward heroically one last time to save Edwin, who is now returned and weeping over the noble choirmaster's selflessness, along with a severely chastened Rosa who is left to regret her mean and unwarranted suspicions. Nor is she the only one who Aylmer imagines feeling suitably reprimanded:

> *The effect on the reader, when the ultimate disclosure was made, would have been, I fancy, not merely pleasurable surprise at an unexpectedly happy ending but also shock at having been on the verge of condemning an innocent man to death.*[236]

It is very difficult to ascertain Aylmer's intentions on reading this statement. He imagines the reader feeling shocked at almost condemning an innocent man to death. But Jasper is not a real person, innocent or not. It is telling that Aylmer speaks with confidence of the likelihood that 'Dickens originally intended to bring Jasper and Rosa together in the end', citing as evidence that 'Jasper stood in his author's shoes and Rosa in Ellen Ternan's', so that 'to have done otherwise would be to admit the final failure of his own domestic experiment'.[237] If Jasper is Dickens, as Wilson had suggested, then Jasper must have been intended to have a happy ending. Aylmer's passion and intensity has blurred the lines between the author and his creation.

He has also blurred the lines between fact and fiction. He dismisses Forster's statement as 'hearsay evidence' that 'would be excluded in a court of law' as though it were a legal proceeding.[238] Like Duffield before him, he is approaching the plot not as the imagined fiction of an author, but real-life events demanding the full solemnity of matters concerning the law. Then, taking references in the book to the building of the railway, and combining that with information from almanacs, he deduces that Edwin Drood is murdered on 24 December 1842 precisely. The fact that Dickens does not concern himself with setting it in an exact date is not a warning to Aylmer that he has gone too far, but rather encouragement to go further:

> *His refusal to make explicit mention of the fact shows that it has some connection with the concealed story.*[239]

In Aylmer's hands, black becomes white and up becomes down. The book is so blatant in its dismissal of common-sense and absolute acceptance of the wildest ideas that it is hard to imagine how one might go about demolishing such an idea. It is not the work of a moderate Detective, not an idea open to logical debate, but a statement rooted in absolutism and believed in utterly by the author. It is more religious dogma than literary criticism. It is possible, at a stretch, to read a subtext of saving *Drood* from the Academics, or rescuing the book from claims of inferiority as a work such as earlier Detectives had sought to do, but ultimately the sense one is left with while reading this work is that there is no subtext to it, and that it should be read at face value: Aylmer is trying to save Jasper.

The punchline of the work is that Aylmer believes *Drood* was intended to be 'a demonstration of the danger of relying on circumstantial evidence', blithely unaware that he has created an entire book himself that does that very thing.[240] It speaks volumes of the range and intensity of *Drood* solutions, that Aylmer's should be, in my opinion, the *second* most bizarre theory, though it would be another thirty years before its conqueror would emerge to claim the title. Ultimately, Aylmer's solution found little support. Philip Hopsbaum is one of many to note its idea of a foreign assassin as 'a fabric of circumstance, remarkable for its ingenuity, but founded upon not the slightest hint in the book of any such Visitor [sic]'.[241] Rather than inspiring new ideas for *Drood*'s ending, it stands as a warning tale of taking the investigation too far.

Digging in: the Academics' siege

The intensity of Aylmer's extreme interpretation of the ending is counter-balanced by its relative isolation: the high Droodism of the Detectives was reaching its swansong. The development of *Drood* towards more sober and reserved readings played out on a wider battlefield of Dickens studies in general. Contemporary to Wilson's essay, George Orwell had written 'Charles Dickens' in 1940 in which he simultaneously praised Dickens and called for a more critical approach, rather than blind admiration, noting the great divide between what was popular and what, to Orwell's generation, were works of merit:

> *Significantly Dickens's most successful books (not his best books) are The Pickwick Papers, which is not a novel, and Hard Times and A Tale of Two Cities, which are not funny. As a novelist his natural fertility greatly hampers him, because the burlesque which he is never able to resist is constantly breaking into what ought to be serious situations.*[242]

Orwell, like many literary writers of the time, praised Dickens with the heart and criticised him with the mind. For too long critics had struggled with their own embarrassment of writing on an author so overtly popular. Walter Allen summarised the problem in 1954 when he stated 'Dickens was the great novelist who was also the great entertainer'.[243] Early twentieth-century writers had wavered between praise of his vivacity and a cautious distancing from a writer they felt to be enjoyable but not technically accomplished. As the century developed, essays such as Wilson and Orwell's prompted a necessary shift towards taking Dickens seriously, and the subsequent reclaiming of *Drood* as a work foreshadowing Dostoevsky, and most certainly *not* a reader's digest teatime puzzle, was a key conflict in the larger war.

Against the idea of a darker Dickens and psychological *Drood*, a few still persisted in speculative investigations into the end of the book. D. W. Bilham, writing for the *Dickensian*, accepted Forster but was still prone to over-reading the characters as though they were real figures, arguing:

> *Since John Jasper is of criminal type and tendency, it may well be that his sister is streaked with the same family taint. Here we arrive logically at the "Princess Puffer".*[244]

But in the same year, Charles Mitchell's essay on '*The Mystery of Edwin Drood*: The Interior and Exterior of Self' took Wilson's idea of duality and explored that theme throughout the novel, examining the shallowness of Sapsea, or the disconnect between Rosa and Jasper's externalised idea of her.[245] In other words, this was very much a literary exploration, not concerned at all with endings but focusing on the work's style and construction instead.

Mitchell's essay was a promising step for a re-appraisal of *Drood*, and a necessary one to move the dialogue away from endings to other subjects. Unfortunately, the work of Wilson and Collins to end the musings of the Detectives had, in many cases, prompted not a new wave of discussion but an absence of it. In a number of larger works on Dickens that emerged at this time, scholars had little more to say on *Drood*. J. Hillis Miller's *Charles Dickens: The World of his Novels* systematically works through his works from *The Pickwick Papers* up to the penultimate novel *Our Mutual Friend*. Barely a couple of pages are afforded to *Drood*, much of which is comparing it to the previous work. Miller regretfully speaks of it as something that, completed, 'might have marked a new departure for Dickens', but refrains from speculation or discussion.[246] Barbara Hardy wrote comparatively little on *Drood* in her 1968 book *Dickens: The Later Novels* compared to Dickens' other works, and what she does write is not flattering. She sides with Collins over Wilson in terms of the book's quality, suggesting 'it is probably the one Dickens novel from which one could quote passages not immediately recognizable as Dickensian', and argues that 'the novel's chief pleasure must lie in such guesses at riddles'.[247] The centenary of Dickens' death resulted in a number of essay collections being published, many of which contained focused studies on specific novels or short stories, but not *Drood*.[248] John Lucas's influential work *The Melancholy Man* omits *Drood* entirely from his study of the novels save for one quotation from Mr Grewgious used to reflect on *Our Mutual Friend*.[249] Angus Wilson offers a brief account in his 1970 work *The World of Charles Dickens*, refraining from speculation or extensive analysis because 'only the whole gives the key to the whole'.[250] As scholars approached Dickens with greater appreciation for his ability, rather than as the popular entertainer he had been categorised as earlier in the century, more attention was paid to his later social satires than his early comic work, and increasingly it was *Our Mutual Friend* that was hailed as Dickens' final (complete) contribution to literature, with H. M. Daleski referring to it as 'one of the greatest English novels of the nineteenth century' in a book that, predictably, does not afford any discussion towards *Drood*.[251]

The irony of Wilson and Collins' arguments against the Detectives was that it was still being treated within the framework of a detective story. They had argued successful that Forster was right, and therefore the case was closed. Hardy's comment that the chief pleasure of *Drood* lies in its riddles betrays the problem of what was left to say now that the riddle was solved. Without the end to debate, there was felt to be little else to talk about when we talk about *Drood*. This was exacerbated by arguments such as Angus Wilson's that an incomplete novel was best left unprobed as it could not be fully understood. Where once its incompletion prompted discussion, now it was prohibiting it in favour of the great late novels and praise of their craftsmanship. Perhaps

Drood's fragmentary state excused the shorter attention, or perhaps the taint of Droodism could still be felt, and respectable critics felt it best to keep a wary distance. A poisoned chalice, *Drood* was being acknowledged as a work of promise but dropped from conversation on the grounds of incompletion. Geoffrey Thurley began his chapter on *Drood* by stating: 'The vast majority of the critical matter on the novel is really irrelevant to its real interests and purposes.'[252] Yet irrelevant did not necessarily translate as obsolete. Much as this new wave of literary critics sought to ignore the past and see their work as new, Thurley still relented to the idea of Edwin surviving despite noting the very clear evidence to the contrary as presented by Forster: 'The literal resurrection of *Edwin Drood* completes, I think, the pattern of Dickens' work.'[253] This pattern, Thurley felt, 'is more important' than 'proving the thesis from the evidence, or rather the lack of it'.[254] The recognition of Dickens as a literary writer was proving to be a Trojan horse for new suppositions, finding their legitimacy in the idea of a specific and identifiable Dickensian way of writing. It is, of course, Proctor's, and later Wilson's, same approach coming through of arguing for *Drood*'s end through the precedent of his other novels, but argued in such a way that suggests a recognition of literary style is more conclusive than trifling details such as evidence.

To further cement the idea of Dickens as a serious writer, and *Drood* as a serious work, a number of attempts were made during this period to redefine the work within the context of another author, much as Wilson had used Dostoevsky's borrowed plumage. In 1969, James Walton's 'Conrad, Dickens, and the Detective Novel', for instance, had positioned Dickens as a major influence on the later writer, and George Wing argued in 1973 for the similarity between Dickens and Thomas Hardy, comparing *Drood* with Hardy's first work *Desperate Remedies*. Both books were sensation novels after all, and both were seen to sit uneasily within the canon of their authors. In doing so, Wing's essay re-appraises each work within its genre and investigates *Drood* as literature, not a mystery, casually dismissing such an approach when he states, briefly, that 'Speculation on how the second half of *Edwin Drood* would have been written is a waste of time'.[255]

The comparison to Wilkie Collins had been made several times already, with the inherent question being, who did the sensation novel better of Dickens and Collins? Una Pope-Hennesy saw it as Dickens' attempt to out-do the younger author:

> *Dickens, who had published The Moonstone in All the Year Round, found Wilkie Collins's method of telling this story extremely tiresome. He was sure he could do something better in the way of a murder mystery himself.[256]*

Several, like George Ford, saw it as an over-ambitious reach on Dickens' part that was doomed to fail: 'Dickens was competing with his own disciple, Wilkie Collins, in what had becomes the disciple's own speciality.'[257] The key term here is 'disciple', with the undertones of discussion revolving around the degree to which Dickens could be held responsible for Collins' success. Rather than reading it as Dickens aggressively challenging Collins, Sue Lonoff saw it more as a moment of the disciple teaching the teacher, arguing a long trend of Collins influencing Dickens novels before the final culmination where 'The traces of Dickens' indebtedness to Collins are most apparent in *The Mystery of Edwin Drood*'.[258] The comparison of *Drood* to *The Moonstone* was a familiar one, especially on the point of each book's use of opium, but what makes Lonoff's argument particularly interesting is the rejoinder she received two years later from Ross Murfin's article 'The Art of Representation: Collins' *The Moonstone* and Dickens' example', which he envisions as 'offering the first half of a two-part argument that Ms. Lonoff completes'.[259] Murfin's self-styled prequel argues that if Dickens *was* inspired by Collins, Collins in turn had been inspired by Dickens first. In short, *Bleak House* spawned *The Moonstone*, which spawned *Drood*. It is a curious battle of credit and intellectual property. Defining *Drood* as a work that inspired later novels added to Dickens' credibility, but seeing it as an attempt by Dickens to emulate others was emasculating. Murfin's article gave that innovation back to Dickens. It harkened back to Wilson's championing of Dostoevsky as a legitimisation of Dickens and what Albert Guerrard calls the 'century's obsession with influence'.[260] This insecurity over Dickens' status speaks of the infancy, even in the 1980s, of Dickens as a writer to be taken seriously in critical circles, and the need of those writing on him to confirm him not merely as a popular writer, but an innovative one; not a nostalgic sentimentalist, but a forerunner of urbanisation and modernity.

Wilson triumphant

In 1980, two novels emerged to complete *Drood*. The content of each solution is remarkably similar, but their approach is markedly different. The first, *The Mystery of Edwin Drood* concluded by Leon Garfield, a popular author in his own right, reproduces Dickens' text followed by Garfield's solution, while the second, *The Decoding of Edwin Drood* by Charles Forsyte, an author of mystery stories (actually a pseudonym for a husband and wife, both Dickens enthusiasts working together), dedicates the first half of the book to explaining his reasoning, and the second to providing a fully fictionalised end.

Garfield is doing what Crisp did before him by presenting both original and solution together as one volume, the illusion being one of seamless transition from the 1870 text to the 1980 text. A small note on the content page assigns 'Chapters 1-22 by Charles Dickens, Chapters 23-41 by Leon Garfield', but with no clear divide provided in the main text itself a new reader might not be entirely sure of where Dickens ends and Garfield begins, and indeed this is most likely the point. Forsyte's decision not to reproduce the original text, but instead devote that space to careful explanation of how the solution has been reached at, speaks of a different audience in mind. Garfield is writing for the reader who is new to *Drood*; Forsyte is writing for the reader already familiar with the story so far. Thus, the first is drawing in new readers to the mystery, the second is trying to close the book on it.

Both works draw on the statements of those who knew Dickens, vindicating Forster especially: 'Some have totally rejected Forster's account of *Edwin Drood*,' writes Forsyte. 'Such a view ignores the essential integrity of Forster and his solid relationship with Dickens.'[261]

Garfield's story is introduced by Edward Blishen who, likewise, notes the 'strong hints' given to Forster.[262] Interestingly, both the Forsyte and Garfield introductions pay special reference to Aylmer for his unique position of finding 'Jasper innocent'.[263] As Forsyte argues, 'Wilson and Aylmer cannot both be right; and examination shows flaws in both cases' (a rather generous comment in Aylmer's case).[264] Both Garfield and Forsyte take the idea of Jasper's potential, or perceived innocence, without going so far as to call him innocent. Both take the idea of Wilson's innocent and wicked man, without going so far as to subscribe to Duffield's thuggee framework: 'The Thugs did not normally, if ever, attack Europeans,' Forsyte notes. Nor did they operate outside India nor work alone:

> *And there is an even greater objection. How on earth would Edwin Drood, a typical young English public school boy, have acquired as uncle and guardian a Kali-worshipping Hindu Indian?*[265]

How indeed. Both authors thus pared down the more extreme angles of previous solutions, working ever closer to Forster's suggestions. Droodism was growing up, and becoming more conservative as it did so. The plots in both, thus, do not attempt to rewrite Forster's summary, instead focusing on that promised ending in the condemned cell with 'the review of the murderer's career by himself at the close, when its temptations were to be dwelt upon as if, not he the culprit, but some other man, were the tempted'.[266] Garfield and Forsyte took this, along with Wilson's theory of duality, and presented Jasper as a man with a split-personality. Where Wilson had championed Dostoevsky above all, these authors were pulling on his comparison to Stevenson. Blishen recalls a conversation with Garfield in which he said:

> *[...] had Dickens finished the novel, it might have been impossible as well as unnecessary for Robert Louis Stevenson to write, sixteen years after Dickens' death, another great story reflecting the increasingly unbearable nature of Victorian dividedness: Dr Jekyll and Mr Hyde.*[267]

CHAPTER THREE

A sentiment shared – almost word for word – by Forsyte:

> *Robert Louis Stevenson could hardly have written his story fifteen years later had Dickens completed Edwin Drood, which anticipates the central idea of The Strange Case of Dr Jekyll and Mr Hyde.*[268]

In doing so both authors move away from Wilson's attempt to legitimise Dickens as 'Dostoevsky's master' and instead imagine *Drood* as very much belonging to Victorian sensation, or even Gothic. Yet both champion Wilson against the later attacks of Collins in their insistence that there is more to Jasper than just the wicked man. The variation between endings comes in Jasper's own awareness of his wickedness. Forsyte's Jasper lives in ignorance of his other self, rendering his quest to find Edwin's murderer as an honest and earnest one, tragically ending in the realisation that he himself is his beloved nephew's destroyer. As in the solution of Morford over a century earlier, Forsyte's Princess Puffer is instrumental in bringing the confession out of Jasper:

> *'It's not true,' says Jasper, whose hoarseness is suddenly afflicting him again in that tender organ the throat, which is so affected by his mood. 'Neville Landless killed him'*
> *'So you say now. It's not what you said afore your visions.'*
> *[...]*
> *The opium woman falls silent, sensing that no more needs be said. John Jasper stands rigid in the centre of the cell, not speaking, his face a mask. Yet she knows that within him some of her words – she does not know which – have started up some great irresistible movement: as a pebble trickling from the summit of a mountain will gather others and still more until a mighty avalanche of rock is thundering down the mountainside.*[269]

Though Garfield's Jasper cuts an equally tragic figure, he in contrast has been aware all his life of the wicked man within and the dark deeds he would urge him to against his better judgment:

> *He has always been the same, even when we were*
> *children. He used to tell me of the wild and terrible things*
> *he wanted to do. I said nothing, because he was a child,*
> *and I hoped it would pass. But it never did, and the more*
> *I tried to turn away from him, to show him my disgust,*
> *the more frightful became the things he talked about.*[270]

While the explicit use of split personality takes the argument further than Wilson intended, the essential core of the character being innocent as well as wicked remains, and paved the way for Jasper to be seen increasingly as an anti-hero rather than a villain.

One final point to note about these two solutions is their approach to style as well as content. Just as scholars and enthusiasts alike were coming round to the idea that Dickens' plot could be reconstructed after all, a great hesitation still arose over the idea of reconstructing his writing style. Dickens was no longer the popular author, but a recognised literary giant, so that whereas the early Opportunists of the 1870s and 1880s quite happily leapt in, these solutions a century later show more awareness of the task ahead. Forsyte opts for deference:

> *I did not try to imitate the inimitable, but rather to find a*
> *style that would be acceptable to readers today and at the*
> *same time follow on the original narrative as smoothly as*
> *possible.*[271]

Blishen notes too the 'gulf [...] of style', arguing that most attempts 'have tripped at the very start over that huge obstacle which is Dickens' manner', but he does so in order to champion Garfield as someone 'with an original gift for language and storytelling not hopelessly unlike that of Dickens himself'.[272] The book's blurb takes it further, noting the presentation in the book of 'Garfield following on Dickens without interruption' and heralding 'that this can be done with confidence is dazzling proof of Leon Garfield's understanding of Dickens' imagination and style'.[273]

CHAPTER THREE

It's a paradox for the marketing department. Dickens must be triumphed as the inimitable to make the book worth reading, but he cannot be championed as *so* inimitable that the accompanying conclusion is not able to emulate and match the merits of the first half. Getting a recognised author on the case certainly helps to manage these dual claims. As it stands, Garfield's understanding of Dickens' style is most evident in his continuing of the book's references to *Macbeth*. Where Dickens had titled his chapter 14 'When shall these three meet again?', Garfield decided to run this idea into the ground, resulting in: chapter 22, 'Excursions and Alarms'; chapter 26, 'In Thunder, Lightning and in Rain'; chapter 39, 'When the Hurlyburly's Done'; chapter 40, 'When the Battle's Lost and Won!'; and my personal favourite, chapter 33, 'Enter a Porter'. On a roll, Garfield's additional inclusion of *Hamlet* in chapter 32, 'The Play's the Thing!' does perhaps warrant a reminder that he is attempting to imitate Dickens' style, not Shakespeare's. It is one example of a particular strain Dickens has hit upon that others then draw upon to create a mirage of continued authorship (one can also point to the letters PJT outside Grewgious' front door and the way in which completionists have all joined in Dickens' game of guessing what the letters might stand for). It is moments like this, taking a motif from the first half and repeating it incessantly, which both alludes to the illusion of reading it as if Dickens himself wrote it, while also tripping the reader up with such explicit attempts and bringing us out of the narrative and ever more aware of the strings holding the trick together.

Both Garfield and Forsyte attempt to consolidate rather than provoke. They come not to explode and ignite *Drood* studies, but to bring closure. That this should be at a time when scholars were increasingly dismissing *Drood* as just for riddles, or accepting Forster without question, shows how the exploration of *Drood*'s ending was slowing in pace at last. After the frantic back-and-forth between Droodists of the early twentieth century, the middle of the century revealed a winding down of ideas as scholars moved on to consider weightier themes in the novel, or else ignore it as a fragment while turning their attention to the other works in the Dickens canon.

The *Drood* debating had reached a point of redundancy, bordering on irrelevance. That two solutions could come out in the same year and essentially present the same idea showed the limiting of interpretations, and the calming down at last from the hysteria of before. The Senate House Library in London holds the unpublished manuscript of Katharine Longley, *A Whispering Reed: Dickens's Last Novel, its making and purpose*, donated in 1986. Like Aylmer before her, Longley's prominent contribution as a Dickensian was her work on Ellen Ternan, and here she was now using notes gathered in that research to present ideas on *Drood*'s end contradicting Forster's statement, to wit that Edwin was alive (in fact Longley went one further, attacking Forster's credibility and suggesting that 'unable to find the sixth number plan, he took a folded sheet of Dickens's blue writing paper, and wrote on it in pencil', forging the notes for the final part).[274] That her work did not get published feels somewhat ominous, and may perhaps be read as an indication of perceived dwindling interest in another *Drood* theory. Scholars, meanwhile, keen to prove their seriousness and distance themselves from the enthusiasts, would not be drawn into discussions of the mystery, and attacks on Forster were hard to maintain without betraying a subjectivity ill-becoming of an Academic. For discussions of *Drood*'s end to achieve again anything like the intensity of earlier generations, an entirely new approach was needed, and in the mid-80s it arrived – with music.

CHAPTER THREE

John Jasper:
Millions and billions of times

> Well; I have told you. I did it, here, hundreds of thousands
> of times. What do I say? I did it millions and billions of
> times. I did it so often, and through such vast expanses of
> time, that when it was really done, it seemed not worth
> the doing, it was done so soon.

*Imagine your worst moment. Imagine living it over, and over. Such is
my fate. Such is my life, as it is.*

*I killed him. Not once, but hundreds of times. Every new reading,
every new theory. I do it over and over again.*

*Sometimes I strangle him. Other times I strike him. Or push him
from the top of the cathedral. Or drown him. Or drug him. My dear
boy, my Ned. It is not enough that I betrayed him, but I must experience
it a thousand times. My multidrood of sins.*

*Here I am in the dark, always in the dark. Under the watchful eye
of Cloisterham and the world beyond. Everyone reading my secrets,
my diary, observing my actions over and over again. This grinding of
my brain, this pain within, it will not be assuaged.*

*Closure is the only thing that can help me now. I must draw a line.
I must reach the final chapter. There has to be an end, to this, to him,
to me. To all of it. Instead I just sit here, with each turn of the page,
doing it all over again. Millions of times, the never-ending ending
of Ned.*

*Here, alone in the dark, I see myself, both the choirmaster and the
wicked man. Sometimes we are quite distinct, other times we are one
and the same, but we are both guilty. We will never be caught, we will
never be charged, but we will always be punished. I will always be
punished. Every time I have to relive it again.*

*And here I am once more. The billionth time. Over such vast
expanses of time too. The details change, the fashions change, the
readers change, but the event – the key event – stays the same. I did it.
I do it. I will do it. Again and again. Without end. Without rest. Without*

peace. This is my cell. This is my judgment. I am the condemned man, and this is my penance.

I said I would not rest until my boy's killer was destroyed. He will never be destroyed. And so I will never rest. And it will never end.

CHAPTER FOUR

Music and Comedy: A Return to Irreverence 1985-2018

The Academics hold court

As the last chapter showed, Wilson's argument started a slow but certain shift of power away from the Detective Droodists, gleefully hurling theories and insults back and forth, and towards the new generation of Academics seeking to reclaim both Dickens and *Drood* from the enthusiasts. As the concept that Forster's ending might be legitimate became ever more established, the way was set for Academics to explore other aspects of the novel in a tone more expected of higher research. Roy Roussel used the unfinished state of *Drood* as a lens through which to read the novel, arguing that it 'is an incomplete novel which raises the issue of completion on several levels'.[275] Roussel identified several characters with unfulfilled ambitions, doomed to repeat a cycle and desperate to break it, arguing particularly of Jasper and Rosa that 'both their stories are concerned with their attempts to realise their dreams and, in this sense, finish their stories'.[276] Articles such as Roussel's were increasingly to focus on Dickens' text and not the spectre of what might have been written.

One of the most significant works on *Drood* of this period was Eve Sedgwick's chapter 'Up the Postern Stair: *Edwin Drood* and the Homophobia of Empire' in her 1985 book *Between Men: English Literature and Male Homosocial Desire*.[277] As the title suggests, it explored the relationship between Jasper and Edwin, contrasting the choirmaster's destructive care with the more nurturing homosocial bond that Crisparkle forms towards Neville Landless. This in turn

119

linked back to the ideas of orientalism that had been attributed to the book since Duffield and earlier (though the thuggee element that had formed the basis of his argument was becoming ever more side-lined). Sedgwick posits that the difference between Jasper and Crisparkle's care for other men lies in the othering of Jasper:

> *The organisation and the manipulability of male bonds after the secularisation of homophobia depend exactly on a visible arbitrariness in assigning "good" or "bad" names to the array of homosocial bonds. In a narrow, psychologising view, Edwin Drood could well be called a novel about the homosexual panic of a deviant man.*[278]

Jasper's most prominent deviant behaviour, and the one that provides his link to orientalism, is his opium addiction, which offers him a hint of the escape that Edwin plans to achieve in Egypt. But while Edwin, like a good colonialist, seeks to venture out into other countries, Jasper is inviting the culture of other countries in. Sedgwick's article is a fascinating one that has been frequently referenced by subsequent critics of *Drood*, but what it does not do is discuss the end of the story. Like Roussel, Sedgwick focuses on the bit that Dickens did write, and as such it's another nail in the coffin (or body in the Sapsea tomb) for the Droodists of previous generations.

In 1985, Marilyn Thomas's '*Edwin Drood*: A Bone Yard Awaiting Resurrection' explored *Drood* as a critique of the organised church, a theme further explored in 1990 in John Thacker's *Edwin Drood: Antichrist in the Cathedral*. Thacker extended the thematic exploration of *Drood* to an entire book. It makes the direction of analysis clear in the introduction, and it is a statement that holds true for most Academics of this time:

> *To many people Edwin Drood has been only a puzzle; the puzzle is fascinating enough, but study of the fragment brings more satisfying rewards.*[279]

CHAPTER FOUR

Thacker was reaping the rewards of Wilson and Collins' fight, moving towards a point when it is possible to write on *Drood* without first having to address and defend a concept of the ending. That said, the fight was not over, and the question still requires a cursory note in both Thacker's book and Thomas's essay. Thomas's concluding line focuses on how the end might have wrapped up this theme of repressive religion:

> *Although Dickens never got so far, it is safe to deduce from the available evidence that the demons were to be expelled and Cloisterham was to be delivered from the same demonic possession and experience a rebirth.*[280]

Thomas hedges her bets by making a 'safe' deduction, safety in this case equating to vague, but nonetheless contestable. She makes as much reference as she needs to anticipate the reader's question without involving herself too heavily in the argument. It is simply not the focus of her essay. For Thacker's longer work, it is not as easy to pass over the end quite as quickly, he himself noting:

> *It is, however, quite impossible to read an unfinished work of such power as this without forming a few arbitrary opinions which, though implicit in the text, cannot be fully justified either from there or elsewhere.*[281]

Thus, as much as he defers to Forster, he still has to add that he has 'very little doubt that Datchery is Tartar'.[282] Perhaps in a work the full length of a book it is impossible, as Thacker suggests, not to discuss how it might end, as it becomes necessary to anticipate how a theme or motif, be it religion or homosocial desire, might develop. Academic articles, however, with a stricter wordcount, can have that luxury of steering clear of the entire area. Miriam O'Kane Mara's 2002 scholarly reading of colonialism in *Edwin Drood* feels no need to discuss the end of the text beyond a brief footnote stating simply: 'My reading of *The Mystery of Edwin Drood* begins with the assumption that Edwin's disappearance is a result of his death, and John Jasper is the murderer.'[283]

Such an approach is the very opposite to the lengthy literary duels that occurred in print in the early twentieth century over Datchery's identity or Edwin's fate. Thanks to the previous generation of Academics, the backlash against Forster had lost its momentum, and *Drood* finally reached the point that it might have done had Forster simply published his statement at the end of the sixth number in September of 1870. With a generally accepted conclusion from a trusted friend of Dickens now seen as more likely than not, the wind had been taken out of the Detectives' sails. One would think, then, that this would mark the end of *Drood* investigations. Thankfully, this is not so. In 1985, the same year that Sedgwick published her book, another significant work arrived that would provide a new, all-singing all-dancing outlet for extreme and outlandish ideas of how *Drood* might end.

Drood hits Broadway

In 1985, Rupert Holmes' musical *The Mystery of Edwin Drood* premiered at the New York Shakespeare Festival before transferring to Broadway (see fig. 24). All previous attempts to place *Drood* on the stage had centred around the grand reveal of an ending, much as written continuations had done, but Holme's musical was altogether different. Writing retrospectively of the creative process, Holmes expressed an approach distinctly unique among Droodists by asking himself the question 'How could I resolve Dickens's tale *without* implying that I alone knew the ending the great man had envisioned?' (my emphasis).[284] Amongst Detectives and Academics alike, it had previously been a given that all those expressing their ideas would point to 'evidence' in the text to determine that they were presenting precisely the ending that Dickens had envisioned, and now Holmes was keen to do anything but. The idea he hit upon was to go metatheatrical, setting the play up as part of a fake Victorian music hall, with the actors playing Victorian actors performing the part of Dickens' characters (e.g. Sapsea being played by the company's chairman 'William Cartwright'). Thus, the actors switched between Dickensian roles and the Victorian players representing them, constantly reminding the audience of the interplay between the plot and the people in front of them recreating it live. It became a living story once more, rather than a preserved text from over a century ago, and as such one still liable to go in any direction, which is where Holmes' master-stroke came in:

> *I wouldn't create my own mock-Dickensian ending for Drood. I'd let the audience decide who was the murderer, who was the Detective in Disguise, which pair of lovers had a happy ending.*[285]

The mechanics of this lay in presenting the bulk of Dickens' plot in the first half of the play, with the second half more devoted to the actors coming forward as their Victorian music-hall counterparts to discuss the plot and possible endings, before then asking for the murder suspects to line up and the audience to cheer for who they wanted the murderer to be. The same process was also used with the remaining male and female cast members to choose a romantic pairing, and also to find the identity of Datchery. The fate of *Drood* was handed back to audience speculation just as it had been in those first four years after Dickens' death, before Forster's statement arrived in print. It was, and remains, a tremendous exercise in freedom of expression and joyful irreverence, with audience members voting less on what they actually thought Dickens intended, and more on the strength of actors (those selected as murderer, romantic couple or Datchery having the opportunity to sing once more), or a simple wilful streak of mischief. In Holmes' musical, Rosa Bud could be the murderess, while Princess Puffer could marry Deputy. Indeed, the more ridiculous the result, the better. Holmes noted with pleasure 'that during the entire run on Broadway and in Central Park, no audience ever elected Jasper as murderer'.[286]

For all the elements of freedom of choice, there was also some gentle shepherding at work here. As the Victorian players discussed the plot (the musical is supposedly set in 1892, thus allowing a fictional gap of two decades for solutions to emerge), the chairman dares the audience: 'So how stand you? For the obvious answer – or for a more perplexing solution?'[287] It is a provocative stance that discourages the 'obvious' vote and calls for something more unexpected, and indeed the unexpected answers best complement the comic tone of the play. That said, the first half of the play is unafraid to lay heavy emphasis on the more ominous moments and striking clues in Dickens' text. When Jasper exits the opium den and Princess Puffer proclaims 'Who are you then? And what are you?', the actress is invited by the chairman to step forward and repeat again 'that meaningful statement'.[288] The sudden absence of Bazzard is noted as strange and unlike Dickens, in such a way as to clearly hint at the likelihood of him being Datchery. Likewise, most of Jasper's actions are accompanied by unsubtle musical chords to denote without doubt his villainy. Thus, Holmes' play offers an implicit commentary that some aspects of Dickens' book are really rather obvious after all. The genius of Holmes' approach is not to say that the obvious answer is wrong, but rather that it does not matter. The most important judgment, and the final one, is what the audience thinks, and Holmes, through his chairman, encourages them to think of something original. It reclaims the freedom of the early solutions back in the 1870s and 1880s, using Dickens' text as a starting point for any number of solutions, rather than a prescription for one definitive destination.

The musical also makes interesting commentaries upon Dickens' text along the way. The race of the Landless twins, always an ambiguous point, is playfully teased at. They sing of their despair of 'blending in/With this my shade of skin', while the Victorian musical players give them a 'geographically untraceable accent', so that even the cast playing them are unsure what their ethnic origin is supposed to be.[289] Equally the asexual relationship between Edwin and Rosa is emphasised by the casting of a woman – a male impersonator – as Edwin. Admittedly, this could be further interpreted as adding an entirely new homoerotic tone to the relationship, but in practice the playing of the part as a woman in drag tends towards the demasculinity of the character rather than an overt attempt to tease at any lesbian lust. At any rate, it's certainly a far step removed from previous interpretations of the novel.

So does Holmes' musical mock or celebrate *Drood*? A little of both, and the Droodists too. The framework of the Victorian music hall does have the effect of simplifying characters to melodramatic types rather than the three-dimensional psychological explorations and forebears of modernity that Wilson and subsequent Academics have argued for. Durdles is played by the 'clown prince of the Musical Hall', who drops out of character to deliver several one-liners, while Rosa is played very much as the fair and innocent maiden. Holmes himself in his script advises future directors to: 'please try to keep your actors away from Mr Dickens' sombre and poetic novel at all costs, at least during rehearsals – for neither the Music Hall Royale nor the characters they portray are to be found there.'[290] In conversation with Holmes, he revealed to me that his stance on this had now changed, but that his original fear was that reading Dickens 'might inhibit the comedy', something he now sees as less of a concern.[291] Even when arguing for distance from Dickens' text, Holmes' script still advises the director to not descend into 'outright parody', and notes that even with the comedy of the framework, 'the "serious moments" of the story and score […] will work as such, no matter how much comedy surrounds or intrudes upon them.'[292] If Holmes' characters are irreverent, that is not to suggest Dickens' characters are, and much of what the musical achieves is only possible because Holmes went to such lengths to ensure his play would not be confused with Dickens' original. The framework of the music hall setting clearly announces that this is an interpretation, not a direct reading of the original. By stepping away from the reputation of Dickens and his text, Holmes presents a story that can, and should, be manipulated and played with at will, and the result is extraordinarily liberating. Coming in the 1980s, it presented a new model in which outlandish theories could still be presented in the austere age of the Academics, with participants being invited to switch off their concerns of authenticity and simply have fun with the possibilities of an open-ended text.

All approaches at once

The arrival of Holmes' musical marked a new approach, while the Academics continued to establish their own authority over *Drood*, but against these twin threats the Detectives still managed to set forth a few volleys. In the last chapter, I discussed how Aylmer's remarkably far-fetched solution came at a time when moderate Detectives were holding back and only the most extreme continued to pursue their investigations. A similar circumstance was now in play for a Detective to stand forth against the tide once more. I also stated that Aylmer's was the *second* most bizarre theory. First place has to be awarded to the work of Benny Reece. His self-published 1989 book *The Mystery of Edwin Drood Solved* demonstrates the same level of extreme Detective traits that Aylmer showed back in the 1960s. Reece himself was not a Dickens enthusiast, but a professor of classical languages whose work on Drood 'is the result of a recent sabbatical, during which Dr Reece undertook to read the entire writings of Charles Dickens', leaving *Drood* for last.[293] Where others had hastened to spot Dickensian patterns and precedents in the plot of *Drood*, Reece recalled:

> When I began to read the final work of Dickens, I assumed that I would encounter the same types of settings, characters and situations that I had for the past year become accustomed to look forward to. Not so.[294]

Given his background, and being a newcomer to Dickens, meant coming to the book from an entirely original context which in turn resulted in Reece reading the book in a *very* different way:

> Early on, names in and allusions to Greek and Roman mythology and classical associations occur: 'muttered

*thunder' at the end of chapter one; 'classical' Mr.
Crisparkle, in chapter two' the 'Roman name for
Cloisterham' in chapter three, Sapsea's father in a 'toga'
and 'Sapsea's 'Muse,' in chapter four; 'the ideal painting
of woman as Juno, Minerva, Diana and Venus all in one,'
in chapter eight; '(a mythological turn) of sacrificing to
the Graces,' to describe the act of Twinkleton dressing,
and 'Celestial Nine [Muses,]' in chapter nine; 'sound
mind in sound body,' quotation from Horace, in chapter
fourteen; 'pick up your crumbs' from Aeschylus [...] in
chapter sixteen [...]*[295]

Yes, that's right. Reece thought the whole book was rooted in references to the classical world. Noting in particular that the Landless twins were, well, twins, he pondered, 'Could Dickens have based their characters on those of Artemis (Diana) and Apollo?'[296] Instead of answering no, as most would, Reece decided most positively yes. He then determined that the most senior figure in the play must be Honeythunder, in an unintentional echo of those early 1870 poetic tributes, but not because of his comic potential, but rather as 'the name is immediately suggestive of Zeus and his thunder and lightning'.[297] Jasper becomes Pan, Edwin is Orion, Durdles is Pluto, and so on, with a number of less-familiar figures cropping up, such as Pyramus, Cephalus and Paniscus, while more obvious Classical characters like Ares, Heracles, Athena, Aphrodite or Prometheus are absent. So not only is Reece suggesting Dickens is basing his characters on classical mythology, he is also suggesting he is basing them on some of the lesser known figures, implicitly suggesting Dickens to be an expert in the field. The connections are often as tenuous as the Honeythunder/ Zeus link: Crisparkle's Greek identity is identified because 'Cri*sparkle* suggests that "sparkle" of Arcturus'.[298]

Having assigned everyone in Cloisterham to a mythical counterpart, Reece's solution then consists of presuming each character to follow the same plotline as their classical precedent. This results in a number of illegitimate children for Honeythunder, who in his role as Zeus becomes the parent of Neville, Helena, Miss Twinkleton, Mrs Tisher, the Billickin, Jasper *and* Crisparkle. The family ties continue with Honeythunder himself being the child, along with Tartar and Durdles, of Princess Puffer. Moreover, with classical storylines now at play, Edwin/Orion has raped the granddaughter of the Topes (the Topes have no children in *Drood*, but Reece having identified them as Bacchus and Ariadne, his logic dictates they are grandparents of Merope who is raped by Orion, and therefore *must* have grandchildren). Edwin is also supposed to have attempted to rape Helena/Artemis, which in turn leads to the identity of Helena as his murderer. Of course, in the true tradition of Detective Droodists, Reece insists he is 'convinced' that he has found 'the correct trail of clues and the proper interpretation of them'.[299] Reading Reece's solution is baffling and bewildering. It is an utter curve-ball in the history of *Drood* solutions, and a defiant statement that *Drood* was still open to any number of interpretations.

In comparison, Peter Rowland's completion two years later, *The Disappearance of Edwin Drood*, feels positively nostalgic for the earlier works of the Detectives, not least in his employment once more of the greatest of them all, Sherlock Holmes. Where Andrew Lang had set Holmes to work on the fictional puzzle of Dickens' last book, Rowland imagines Holmes living in the same world as Dickens' characters and walking the streets of Cloisterham. The twist of the novel is that it is Jasper himself who comes to Holmes to seek his nephew's murderer, leading towards the trope seen in Forsyte of the man with multiple personalities living in ignorance of what his other self has done – Rowland's book is a blending of the Detectives' and the Academics' two schools of thought, an attempt perhaps to reconcile the two warring factions to find a mutually agreeable way forward. However, the blending of Doyle's world with Dickens' is not perfect, with Rowland presuming the events of *Drood* occur in the year it was published, rather than the 1840s where it is commonly recognised to be set. Even so, this still calls for some delay between the disappearance of Edwin and Jasper meeting Holmes in 1894, and really the work is more in the style of Doyle than it is of Dickens, though the latter does get to have a starring role, being none other than the true identity of Datchery, or, as Rowland's Holmes argues it was originally intended to be, 'Dalchery, an anagram of Charley D'.[300] In this playfulness, Rowland's work also falls into that same vein of irreverence begun with Holmes' musical (Rupert, not Sherlock). It is thus a work that encompasses many approaches to *Drood*, satisfying the desire of the Detectives for a twist and mystery, the Academics for the psychological troubles of Jasper, and maintaining the necessary distance of the later Irreverent works. This is not a book that proposes to present what Dickens intended, but rather one that has fun in the confines of its mystery. It is contrasted by Ray Dubberke's *Dickens, Drood and the Detectives* which, as the title suggests, plunges *Drood* back into the genre of detective fiction. Like Duffield before him, Dubberke draws 'on material from Dickens's other works and from other contemporary writings [...] from the cornucopia of Victorian mystery fiction to the history of the Metropolitan police', though he refers just as equally to the wealth of Droodists before him.[301] It is a work seeped in the heritage of *Drood* studies and theories, recognising the work of the early twentieth-century Detectives and continuing their style of investigation. Dubberke concludes Datchery to be a new character, Edwin to be dead and Jasper to confess in the condemned cell to Helena disguised as Neville.

There is another significant work on *Drood* that appeared at this time that remains to be explored, which most successfully picked up the playfulness of Holmes' musical and turned Droodism in on itself: *The D Case* (fig. 25). First written in 1989 by Carlo Fruttero and Franco Lucentini as *La verita sul caso D*, but not translated into English from the original Italian until 1992, *The D Case* is a book that both reports on the phenomena of *Drood* solutions and utterly confounds them. The book alternates between the original chapters of Dickens' work and a fictional framework created by Fruttero and Lucentini in which 'An International Forum on the Completion of Unfinished or Fragmentary Works in Music and Literature' is underway.[302] While other rooms in the forum focus on Schubert's Symphony, or Poe's *The Narrative of Arthur Gordon Pym*, the reader is ushered into the room exploring *Drood*, where the participants are all famous fictional sleuths. As if Sherlock Holmes had not already solved it enough times, he is now joined by Hercule Poirot, Father Brown, Philip Marlowe and several others who are led through the book by Dr Wilmot, a fictional editor of *The Dickensian*, and the seminar's hostess Loredana. After Loredana reads each chapter of *Drood*¸ Dr Wilmot opens discussion, with the Detectives squabbling among themselves and nit-picking over small details. Thus, Holmes pedantically asks a question after the first chapter:

> *'There is one small point I would like to clear up,' says the expert in fluorescent hounds. 'The man who comes hurrying into the cathedral of X and who joins the choir in intoning "When the Wicked man": is this the same man we saw leaving the opium-den at dawn? I would have you note that the author does not say so explicitly.'*
>
> *The director of The Dickensian sighs. The proceedings are likely to be lengthy, with a quibbler of this calibre.*[303]

For the most part, the Detectives are as intent on proving their own sagacity in front of their peers as they are on solving the case – and in Fruttero and Lucentini's hands the story quickly becomes the most perplexing and confusing of mysteries. The subtext is whether the reading of *Drood* as such is due to the text itself or the nature of the people reading it. Strange and new theories erupt throughout the reading. Sergeant Cuff of *The Moonstone*, in conversation with Dickens' own Inspector Bucket, deduces that Dickens' trouble with the plot must mean Jasper is not the culprit, 'unless Jasper is in some way *working with the twins*.'[304] As much as Fruttero and Lucentini take time to point out previous theories – especially that of 'Jasper's eminent defender', Aylmer – they have just as much fun including several new and utterly groundless theories too.[305] This is all part of the book's mischievous ethos. It places the ultimate detectives in a room with *Drood* and invites us to watch as their skills derail the book. It gently mocks the Detectives' tunnel vision that prejudices them into spotting mystery and conspiracy at every turn. The more the sleuths search for the unexpected in the book, and congratulate themselves on their high levels of perception, the more the reader laughs at their convoluted extrapolation of extraordinary conclusions from commonplace events. It is a mockery of everything the Detectives had done in the early twentieth century, except...*except*...the resulting work is so joyfully exuberant that the reader ultimately cheers the Detectives on. Consequently, as much as it is parodying the Detectives, the sheer fun of the book shows how amusing it can be to treat *Drood* as such a puzzle, rather than a work for serious literary study. While the real-life *Drood* Detectives may be the obvious target, ultimately it is the more reserved approach of the Academics that comes off the worst from this book for not carrying that same *joie de vivre* into their own analyses.

These four solutions, emerging in short succession of one another, demonstrate a very splintered reaction to *Drood*. Fruterro and Lucentini's glorious sending up of the Detectives, Rowland's playful Holmes homage, Dubberke's dogged detection in the grand tradition of early-twentieth century solutions, and Reece's...unique take on the story all seem a world removed from the contrasting unity of Academic voices, such as Sedgwick and Thacker who were writing at this time on the themes of the novel while presuming the plot to be beyond question. As much as Dickens scholars were closing rank, and closing the case, elsewhere the question of *Drood*'s ending was being prised open and some enjoyably diverse works were being produced as a result.

Academic consolidation and cataloguing

The gleeful irreverence of Holmes' musical and *The D Case* was still standing against a larger tide of academic study. Even in film, the influence of the Academics was evident. In 1993, *Drood* returned to the screen with Timothy Forder's film starring Robert Powell as Jasper (see fig. 25).[306] The plot is distinctly in line with the completions of Forsyte and Garfield, and does not stray very far from Forster's statement aside from the usual level of cuts and abridgments expected of a screen adaptation of a novel. It does, however, shy away from the innocent and wicked man proposed by Wilson and veers towards Philip Collins' more straightforward wicked man. It is gritty and sombre, with a number of scenes shot in the mist or the dark, while the decision to show the decomposed body of Edwin confirms the film's debt to Gothic horror. Where Claude Rains' Jasper fled up the stairs of the cathedral to his doom, Powell's Jasper confronts Rosa in her London home, his arms outstretched either to embrace or strangle her, before he is stopped by Crisparkle, who here fulfils the role of Tartar, who has been cut once again from the script. Jasper thus ends the story not hanged, or falling from the spires, but eerily unrepentant in his cell, staring directly at the camera. His is not a tormented mind so much as an utterly depraved one. With Tartar omitted, Edwin dead, Jasper without redemption and Crisparkle playing the hero, it is left for Neville to be a sort of romantic interest for Rosa, though this is only hinted at in mutual smiles between them at the end. Forder's film is one that revels in the dark deed of murder rather than a happy Dickensian finale of wedded bliss. It is a good film, but a glum one. It is true to Collins' vision of Jasper, yet somehow in being so, it does not feel true to Dickens, insisting on the darkness not only of the man, but of the entire story, above all else.

Meanwhile in print, Gerhard Joseph was making an interesting stand in arguing that *Drood* 'comes to a satisfactory close with what we now have in chapter 22: there is not, nor need there be, any more'.[307] The provocative title of his article, 'Who Cares Who Killed Edwin Drood?', is a slap in the face for the Detectives, though Joseph is equally critical of Wilson and Collins, arguing that their Jasper, be he Dostoyevskian anti-hero or plain villain, is merely repetitive, whereas the abrupt unplanned ending brings real originality to the whole work. He thus turns to the final chapter to seek what closure and reflection it offers on the plot before it. Joseph's approach is intriguing, and while unique in one sense it is also representative of a larger push to taking *Drood* as we have it.

The following years produced a number of Academic studies looking at the back catalogue of solutions. Steven Connor edited *Drood* for Everyman in 1996, and David Paroissien for Penguin in 2002.

Connor devotes an appendix to 'Unfinished Business: The History of Continuations, Conclusions and Solutions', recognising the inspiration Dickens' text had provided to several decades of conversation. He proposes 'four broad forms of explanation' over the years – 'melodramatic-sensational', 'forensic-investigative', 'exotic-psychological' and 'textual-ironic', which roughly correspond to my own four distinctions in this work.[308] Where Connor looked at works after *Drood,* Paroissien focused more on what came before. His introduction chooses to treat *Drood* in context, examining the statements of Dickens' friends and family (much more objectively than Brend's attack in 1956), and looking for possible inspirations in other literary works and real-life events prior to 1870, identifying the work of both Jolly and Bulwer-Lytton as possible precedents. Both Connor and Paroissien demonstrate a more detached approach to discussing previous solutions and the likely end respectively. They are both content to lay out the evidence and leave the readers to make their own assumption based upon that, rather than argue for their own theory of the book's end, a far cry from the fevered debates at the beginning of the twentieth century. Where they differ from each other is in their final summary of the text and its potency. For Paroissien, *Drood* was reduced but nonetheless impressive:

> *Smaller in scope than any of the five he published in weekly instalments, diminutive in comparison with the panoramic novels of his maturity, Dickens's last fragment nevertheless carries the signature of his greatest fiction. What an accomplishment, one might exclaim, what wholeness when so much is missing, what totality hinted at and yet unfulfilled. Like the lovers on Keats' Grecian Urn (1819), readers of The Mystery of Edwin Drood are for ever panting, for ever drawn to a song whose melodies, though sweet, are never heard in full.[309]*

For Connor, in contrast, the novel's incompletion did not render it a great work made less, but a normal work made more.

The paradox of the novel is that Dickens's death at once lifts it out of time, indefinitely suspending its workings, and surrenders it to time, opening up the question of its end to endless speculation, and refusing that refusal of time which an ending of a novel is designed to embody. Had Dickens completed the novel, it might well have achieved routine immortality. As it is, it possesses another quality [...] Let it perhaps be called undyingness.[310]

Between the publication of these two editions came Don Richard Cox's annotated bibliography of *Drood*. It is an impressive work and a great boon to all subsequent *Drood* scholars. This catalogue was, due to the nature and volume of *Drood* criticism, dominated by the many solutions, but like Connor and Paroissien, Cox's tone is objective. Previous catalogues had often been done by those looking to propose their own theory, or who already had, such as J. C. Walter's *Complete Mystery of Edwin Drood* in 1912 or Duffield's unpublished manuscript. Cox had no such axe to grind, allowing him to present the solutions alongside criticism of the novel as part of a history of *Drood* discussion. That said, he defends the inclusion in his bibliography of 'sometimes trivial arguments [...] quarrels that rage back and forth for weeks or even months with neither side retreating on a single point', if only because it might 'prevent future scholars from wasting their time tracking down these articles and letters only to discover there is little of substance contained within'.[311] Nonetheless, Cox's individual reports on each work are without judgment, leaving the reader to determine their merit from his notes.

Ray Dubberke's 2004 article '*Edwin Drood* by the Numbers' for *The Dickensian* used the catalogues of past Dickensians (though not Cox, interestingly) for interrogation of statistics.[312] Drawing on his previous research, Dubberke looks at previous solutions from an analytical perspective, presenting the solutions as numbers to show where popular opinion fell among the various published solutionists, noting that of 252 writers, sixty-three percent thought Edwin dead.[313] Dubberke is not treating the solutions of the past as theories to challenge but data to mine. In his, Cox's bibliography and the scholarly editions of Connor and Paroissien, the mania of the twentieth century was being catalogued and preserved instead of ignored, with that very calmness of approach being in many ways more fatal to the way of the Detectives than an outright attack. So long as Wilson and Collins had berated the Detectives as 'old duffers' or unintelligent, they had something to react against, but increasingly, *Drood* solutions were being treated as an object of the past, a discussion that was popular when we did not know better. This is, of course, a note that had been struck before by several bemused critics in the height of *Drood* discussions, such as B. W. Matz and his failed attempts to ban further *Drood* articles in *The Dickensian* on the grounds that it had all been said. But where Matz was fighting against the tide, now it had turned and was on the side of those calling for a more level-headed, less argumentative approach.

Seeing Dickens through *Drood*

The return of *Dr Who* to television screens in 2005 also marked the timelord's first meeting with Charles Dickens. Simon Callow, a seasoned performer of Dickens on the stage, returned to the role in an adventure involving ghosts (actually aliens) terrorising Victorian London. At the end of the adventure, Dickens finds a new burst of life from his near-death, extra-terrestrial experiences, and announces his plans to incorporate these events into his latest book:

> *The Mystery of Edwin Drood still lacks an ending. Perhaps the killer was not the boy's uncle. Perhaps he was not of this earth! 'The Mystery of Edwin Drood and the Blue Elementals!' I can spread the word, tell the truth!*[314]

It's a passing joke, albeit one the doctor has to explain to his companion (and presumably a fair portion of the audience as well), given that Dickens will never finish the book, and the world will never read

Dickens' first science-fiction work. *Drood* was reduced to a gag in a larger narrative about the author. In print, however, this idea of framing *Drood* within a narrative focusing on Dickens would take flight. As Academics catalogued and constrained the wilder theories of the past, and critical, as well as general, consensus moved further towards the idea that Forster's statement had been true after all, an alternative branch of *Drood* mysteries emerged which aimed to reinstate the mystery by rewriting history. Drawing on the idea noted by many Detectives that the lack of an end made *Drood* the greatest literary mystery of all, recent authors have been tempted to focus on stories *about* the unfinished novel rather than the novel itself. Dan Simmons' *Drood* (2009), Mathew Pearl's *The Last Dickens* (2010), John Paulits' *The Mystery of Charles Dickens* (2012) and Lyn Squire's *The Last Chapter* (2014) all focus their efforts on the last days of Dickens, or immediately afterwards, taking the air of mystery and murder that had previously been seen in *Drood* and applying it instead to the life of its author. In this way, Simmons, Pearl, Paulits and Squire all attempted to imply a mystery behind the mystery, a true-life crime for which the solution was hidden within the pages of this half-finished book. It effectively out-detectives the Detectives who had all been so keen to present themselves as the first to truly understand Dickens' intentions, by suggesting a whole other layer through which to read the book that is entirely more personal to the author.

Ironically, the idea had already been considered – and parodied – in *The D Case*. There the assembled fictional detectives not only find increasing significance in minor elements of the plot to utterly exonerate Jasper, but had also found what they considered irrefutable proof of Dickens' own murder and the culprit. Fruttero and Lucentini's plot is perhaps the logical extension of the Detective approach to *Drood*. Once you start looking for conspiracies and hidden meanings, where will it stop? Of course, Simmons, Pearl, Paulits and Squire are not suggesting that their theories are true, but instead they are cleverly playing on the general reader's anticipation that there *could* be such a significance to Dickens' final book, that art could reflect life, or life reflect art. It satisfies that yearning for a twist that had fuelled the barrage of solutions a century earlier, while also maintaining an objective distance by presenting the entire theory as fiction. The reader is not being told that there is a mystery, but being invited to imagine that there is. This, of course, gives licence then to the wildest of solutions without impacting on the credibility of the author. They can have their Edwin and bury him, to coin a phrase.

Without wishing to spoil the stories, suffice to say that Pearl and Squire both begin after the death of Dickens, with Pearl's focus upon finding the missing manuscript that offers the second half of the text, and Squire's shared between this and the detective's early suspicions of foul play concerning Dickens' death. Both works literalise the quest to complete *Drood* by imagining a physical conclusion for the budding detective to find. Squire's work is interesting for its central character Dunston Burnett, a fictional nephew of Dickens and a source of embarrassment for the family who think of him as 'Mr Plod'. Consequently, when Georgina Hogarth shares her suspicions that Dickens was murdered, Dunston's announcement that he will solve the case is not met with gratitude, but mortification at the idea of this bumbling detective throwing accusations around:

> *Georgina remains motionless and, fortunately for Dunston, speechless, her mind racing in a dozen different directions but, whatever the direction, the final destination inevitable has disaster written all over it. The Guardian of The Beloved Memory is horrified at the thought of Mr Plod intruding on the grief of Charles' family and friends and grilling England's literati, a sleuthing plan to be avoided at all costs. Time for her own plan, time for the wild goose.*[315]

The wild goose, it turns out, involves convincing Dunston that there must be some significance in *Drood*'s end to explain Dickens' death, which thus sends the budding sleuth off out of harm's way while the professionals investigate the real crime. The reception of Dunston by other Dickensians (literally Dickensians in this case, being members of the family) offers a parallel for the treatment of later Droodists among the growing Dickensian fraternity. That the detective himself is over-zealous and quick to leap to various conclusions only strengthens the parallel.

Meanwhile, Simmons and Paulits both centre their attention on the last days of Dickens, each imagining a real-life mystery consuming him and inspiring the final novel. Paulits imagines Dickens himself as the hero, and *Drood* his coded attempt to unmask a crime by Emile de la Rue, wife of Augusta de la Rue, who had been treated by Dickens during his stay in Genoa in the 1840s. Simmons, however, places his first-person narrative in the hands of Wilkie Collins, writing of Dickens' strange behaviour from the outside and becoming increasingly worried about his friend as he begins to suspect a real-life inspiration for *Drood*. What is interesting in all of these books is how they simultaneously celebrate and sideline *Drood*. Each book is freeing *Drood* from the restrictions of truth and Forster's statement in order to allow the imagination to run wild and have great fun along the way, but each book is further confirming that same backhanded compliment of the Detectives that the original story in itself is not nearly so mysterious as its subsequent tale of incompletion. Furthermore, in the case of Simmons, Paulits and Squire, it robs Dickens of his own imagination in suggesting that he is copying real-life events. I do not believe this is the intention at all, but an unfortunate side-effect of that very human desire to see fiction come to life (to this day, visitors to Rochester can see a sign above the building next to the gatehouse proudly proclaiming that 'This was the home of Mr Tope, the chief verger of the cathedral in "The Mystery of Edwin Drood"', the directness of 'this was the home' confusing fiction and reality). Bringing the characters or circumstances of *Drood* to life is not an attempt to minimise the plot but to enlarge it beyond the limitations of the book. But it has, in turn, the implication of suggesting that, if left alone in those limitations, it is somewhat lacking. It is only left to add that Pearl and Simmons' books both received rave reviews and good sales. Jed Rubenfeld's back page blurb on *The Last Dickens* proclaiming it 'an engrossing mystery, which grips the reader from harrowing start to tantalising finish' is really offering the kind of summary that the Detectives had long yearned to hear about *Drood*.[316] It is the *Guardian*'s review of Simmons' *Drood* as 'a labyrinthine piece of hokum' that perhaps best sums up these stories.[317] They are utter nonsense, but enjoyable nonsense, and a welcome treat for those faced with the sober conclusion that Forster was right after all.

Alternatively, repositioning the book within a larger mystery can serve for further doubts on Forster's credibility. Christopher Lord's murder mystery *The Edwin Drood Murders* stands slightly askew to the other books here.[318] It does not concern itself directly with Dickens himself, or even the nineteenth century. The second of Lord's *Dickens Junction* series (following *The Christmas Carol Murders*), *The Edwin Drood Murders* instead showcases a host of characters sharing names with Dickens' creations who play out their lives in modern day Oregon. The hero Simon Alastair, bookseller and amateur detective, has organised an academic conference on *Drood*, at which the big event is the arrival of pugnacious Professor Drab's announcement that he has found the missing plans for the last six numbers of *Drood*. Such is the frenzy around this that murder is not far off, and in his pursuit of the killer Simon encounters, among others, blogger Daniel Quill (commonly referred to as Quilpy), actress Jennifer Wren, mesmerist Morgan Grewgious, enthusiast Silas Cheeryble, and student Lionel Tartar. Even Wilkie Collins' Sergeant Cuff gets a name-check as the hotel's head of security. Lord's book is clearly written by a fan and happy to immerse the reader in minutiae of a Dickens world. His take on *Drood* is simultaneously one that stands on the outside, somewhat dumbfounded at the intensity of academic argument, whilst also being firmly in the group and sharing an enthusiasm for the subject. It feeds the idea of Forster's deliberate suppression of the final parts, and the concept that a tangible external objective source for Dickens' intention exists to be found. As much as Lord rewrites and relocates his Dickensian characters and plots, the subtext is a longing for the certainty of an undeniable ending.

Drood in the bicentenary

The 200th anniversary of Dickens' birth in 2012 understandably resulted in a flurry of books, exhibitions, conferences, plays and television shows.

The BBC announced a Dickens season, including yet another adaptation of *Great Expectations*…and *The Mystery of Edwin Drood* (only the second time the BBC had adapted it), with a new ending written by Gwyneth Hughes. Just the previous year a new completion had appeared in print, written by David Madden. The last time two completions had appeared in such close proximity, back in 1980 with Garfield and Forsyte, both went down a remarkably similar track, showing the dominance of the Academics' acceptance of Forster and Wilson's view of the book. Now, however, the two completions of Hughes and Madden were poles apart both in content and their approach to the mystery, and that contrast in response demonstrates the breadth of *Drood* solutions in recent times.

Madden's book stays close to Forster's summary, with some slight variations and his own interpretation of who Datchery might be. In his introduction, Madden declares that the characters are not only 'clues', but 'the chief ones, for it is their personalities, and the interaction between them, which will continue to carry the story forward, and tell us how it is likely to end, if we read them aright'.[319] Madden's approach of following the characters allows for more inclusion of the Billickin's disputes with Miss Twinkleton, rather than the more direct focus on the mystery that many solutions often presented. But it also means that the uncovering of the mystery focuses more on those doing the detecting than on the one who first did the crime. Jasper becomes less of the protagonist in Madden's second half, in what becomes a book of two parts – crime and detection – where Jasper as the perpetrator holds our attention for the first (by Dickens), and Datchery as the detective holds sway in the second (by Madden).

Meanwhile, Hughes' screenplay takes an entirely different approach. Speaking at a conference in 2014, Hughes disclosed that it was never her intention to worry about how Dickens would end it, but instead to think how she would like to end it.[320] Like earlier screenplays, her adaptation also had the advantage that it could change Dickens' first half to suit the second. Pressure of time results in several characters being cut again – Honeythunder, Tartar and the Billickin have all disappeared long before Edwin – and Datchery is immediately identified as Bazzard, who does not concern himself in

Hughes' adaptation with wearing a white wig but appears precisely the same as when we saw him in Grewgious' office. With that mystery neutralised, Hughes focuses on rewriting the ending. Jasper becomes step-brother to Edwin once more, and Edwin is alive after all. Jasper has in fact murdered their father the year before, which provoked him to begin taking opium. By the time of the fateful Christmas Eve when Edwin disappears, Jasper is so emotionally distraught by his love for Rosa, and his mind so addled by his drug addiction, that his mind confuses the events of the past with the present and he *thinks* he has killed Edwin. Though the truth comes out, in the end Jasper is so distraught that he takes his returned nephew to be a ghost, and jumps from the heights of the cathedral to his death (but inside the cathedral this time, rather than outside like Rains in 1934). Hughes thus tried to deliver an ending that she felt a modern audience watching a television crime drama would expect, rather than worry about what a nineteenth-century reader of Dickens could anticipate. In her hands, Jasper becomes a tortured anti-hero, genuinely in love with Rosa and equally tormented by the idea that he has killed his beloved nephew. Rosa, more interestingly, does not marry Neville, nor Edwin, nor anyone else, Hughes proudly claiming that it was her 'great pleasure to rescue 17-year-old Rosa from the Dickensian fate of an early disastrous marriage'.[321] Rosa was given a twenty-first-century conclusion to satisfy a twenty-first-century writer (and audience), rather than be confined by Victorian values. Like Holmes, Fruttero and Lucentini before her, it is an utter disregard for an authentic conclusion, and that freedom is much to the benefit of the production.

Madden and Hughes' conclusions are both enjoyable in their own ways. The intention of Madden, like Forsyte and Garfield before him, is to try to offer what might have been the full work, and therefore it is not his aim to introduce a wildly controversial theory nor to slam down any previous solutions. Instead, the book provides a pleasant illusion of what might have been, and attempts to flesh out the bare bones of Forster's one-paragraph account. It is a solution for the first-time reader of *Drood*, or the many for whom one solution is enough. Hughes' adaptation is more provocative, refusing to offer what

Dickens would have done and using his book as a launchpad instead for her own ideas. It not only follows the footsteps of the musical and *The D Case*, but moreover harks back to the early solutions of the 1870s. For someone who has read a number of *Drood* solutions, it is refreshing to see a different idea put forward, but that can lead to frustration for those who like their *Drood* to be authentic. When I ran a session with Madden and Hughes in 2014, there was a distinctly pleasant lack of antagonism – neither was trying to debunk the other's approach. Madden was not attempting to close the book on *Drood*, while Hughes' adaptation threw it wide open. 'There will never be a definitive answer to the Mystery of Edwin Drood,' she suggests in the accompanying edition of the text, 'But I hope you have enjoyed mine.'[322] Both writers were trying to tell a good story rather than present a manifesto as the Droodists of the early twentieth century had done. As distinct as these two conclusions to *Drood* were, they were capable of existing in harmony, because in having two distinct aims, neither one threatened the validity of the other.

Drood now and beyond (1): the Academics

Thus, while a number of responses acted deliberately in defiance of Dickens' end, not as an attack on Forster, but a celebration of imaginative diversity, simultaneously the Academics persevered in their focus on *Drood* as we have it, with less concern for the ending. In 2009, Holly Furneaux's *Queer Dickens* continued the work of Sedgwick in exploring homoerotic and unconventional relationships across Dickens' work. Of *Drood* she notes the theme of 'homoerotic orientalism', and the perceived deviance of the East infiltrating Victorian society through opium, Edwin's Egyptian plans, and the Landless twins.[323] Of the twins in particular she finds root for a confusion of Edwin's sexual orientation in his attraction to Helena, as her similarity in looks to Neville 'creates an explicit physical and psychical parity of male and female bodies', which 'does little to bolster [Edwin's] insufficient performance of heterosexual lust'.[324]

However, the confusion caused by the twins' similarities also has an impact on Furneaux's reading of Rosa:

> *In this final novel's bold statements of the parity of Neville and Helena Landless's romantic feeling for the highly appealing Rosa Bud, Dickens's exploration of the homoerotic possibilities of opposite-sex sibling love plots reaches its culmination.*[325]

In this she thus furthers Sedgwick's consideration of Edwin and Jasper's relationship by mirroring it with the female counterpart of Rosa and Helena:

> *The foreignness that renders Jasper's intense feeling for his nephew visible as homoeros, has continuities in the relationship that the repatriated Helena Landless enjoys with the English Rosa.*[326]

Furneaux's analysis of *Drood* is one of deep reading of the existing text, peeling new layers within the story rather than pasting new pages at the end.

As Furneaux continues the path set out by Sedgwick, so Lillian Nayder's 2010 work on Dickens and Collins expands the previous discussion of potential influences in *Drood*. In her balanced consideration of the two authors, Nayder notes in contrast how:

> *For generations of Dickens critics, the "unclean spirit of imitation" that pollutes John Jasper became a symbol of Dickens's own, as the "master" of English fiction unwisely modelled himself on his artistic inferior, Wilkie Collins.*[327]

Nayder is able to approach the subject more objectively. The exploration of orientalism in *Drood* continues, with Nayder's summary of Dickens' book as 'the disappearance of an imperialist-in the-making' that 'addresses the theme of empire and crime in several ways'.[328]

With this vision of the text, Nayder argues that all the solutions share a common bond, that:

> *Despite the variations among these solutions, and regardless of their plausibility, each one reflects and extends a single strategy on Dickens' part: the displacement of crime and criminality from West to East.*[329]

The significance of Nayder's approach is a) in her objective consideration of the two authors, rather than the search for superiority or mastery, and b) her use of solutions not as a springboard for a new solution, but as a veiled form of commentary on Dickens' text. No longer was Academic exploration of *Drood* working in defiance or denial of the solutions, but actively utilising them as part of the critical heritage.

To further explore this meeting of Droodists and scholars, I myself organised a conference held in Senate House, London, on 20 September 2014, *The Mystery of Edwin Drood: Solutions and Resolutions* (see fig. 27). It was here where the aforementioned meeting of Madden and Hughes occurred, rather symbolically, as my intention for the conference was to celebrate equally the solutions to the text alongside the surviving half of Dickens' novel. Accordingly, the speakers covered a mixture of topics looking both within *Drood* and after it. Throughout the day papers considered specific solutions and completions, general trends in those solutions, as well as re-evaluations of themes in Dickens' novel. In other words, it tried to do everything seen in the various approaches tried since Dickens' death, without any one strand trying to maintain dominance over the others. Quite the contrary, the atmosphere of the conference was warm and collegial as each paper was informed in some way by those surrounding it. This was not an attempt to promote one way of approaching *Drood*, but to enjoy and appreciate all approaches. The conference attracted the attention of critics of other writers (e.g. George Gissing or M. R. James) to share their author's insights and interpretations of *Drood*, alongside a number of Dickensians who were encouraged to investigate the novel for the first time. It also involved a number of pre-existing *Drood* scholars. In addition to Madden and Hughes, Don Richard Cox and David Paroissien were both present to share their expertise. But most of all, it was promising to see new *Drood* scholars sharing their research, and to see the shape of *Drood* scholarship to come.

Camilla Ulleland Hoel's talk came on the back of her doctoral thesis on *Drood*. As the title suggests, *The Completion of Edwin Drood: Endings and Authority in Finished and Unfinished Narratives* uses *Drood* as a keynote to explore the idea of endings in unfinished works, and its implications for our idea of authorship:

> *This inability to furnish readers with an ending sanctioned by the authority of the author is the central problem of the volume of textual production referred to as 'Droodiana': the author's death and subsequent inability to finish his narrative means that the very foundation for interpretation is incomplete; the lack of any authorial plan for the later chapters means that the confidence in the end, which as I have shown is part of our desire for anagnorisis, the consonance of the end, is disturbed.[330]*

Hoel notes the anxiety of a work without an authorised end and the way *Drood* exposes our need for a conclusion to make sense of what has come before. It is not only an exploration of *Drood* but a utilisation of *Drood* to make sense of the practice of reading in general. Her thesis draws reference to Foucalt, so is decidedly scholarly, but she is markedly different from Wilson and Collins' ilk by being unafraid to explore the completions and solutions presented on *Drood*. Rather than dismiss them out of hand as silly nonsense, Hoel looks to them as a commentary on *Drood* and Dickens, and takes time to analyse why we have reacted to them as we have, raising the question of what ideas we as readers have of a Dickensian style that prompts us to accept or reject these completions as authentic endings to the original text: 'because Droodian speculation has continued over almost a century-and-a-half, it also makes it apparent how our assumptions change over time'.[331] What is encouraging in Hoel's work is to see an objective approach to the various solutions that seeks neither to champion nor demonise them, but rather to use them as source material for her own theories. The wave of irreverence that has emerged in the twenty-first century has allowed us to get past our shuffling embarrassment of *Drood* and approach them anew with an aura of calm.

Shortly after, another analysis of *Drood* solutions has been conducted for a doctoral thesis: *Not Just the Facts: Victorian Detective Fiction's Critique of Information*, by Beth Seltzer. Where Hoel is interested in theories of the question of novel, the author and conclusion, Seltzer utilises computational models to analyse the solutions and our responses to them, drawing up a running commentary in the process. She notes, as I have in chapter two, how 'Over time, critical interest in the novel starts to shift from the text itself and Dickens the supposed authority on the text, to a wider range of readerly interpretations'.[332] As part of a larger study of Victorian detective fiction and the act of readers trying to work out the endings, she suggests that *Drood* 'offers an almost unique case-study in how reader response to the same text changes over time'.[333] What is key to Seltzer's work is her employment of computers in her analysis, resulting in several interesting graphs and statistics – using Cox's bibliography to establish a canon of solutions, she notes for example that thirty percent of them appear in *The Dickensian*. But importantly – and rather ground-breakingly for *Drood* studies – she assesses and compensates for her own subjectivity, not only conducting searches for key terms of her choice but also using 'the digital humanities to open a space for including aspects of these texts which I might not myself notice'.[334] Computers allowed for absolute objectivity, a dispassionate interest that searched for terms a human would not think of when analysing the various solutions. Both Hoel and Seltzer's work are to be congratulated for approaching the work level-headedly, not disregarding the solutions out of hand, but accepting them as a body of work and reading them objectively for the implicit commentary within. It is my contention that this new wave of objectivity has been made possible by the irreverence that has arisen outside the academy. In effect, the attitudes displayed in Holmes' musical or *The D*

Case allows for an exorcism of all the wildest theories, so that scholars are able at last to approach the solutions without revulsion but as archival sources free of controversy.

I am acutely aware of all those who have preceded, and the confidence in which Detectives, then Academics, have looked back on the movement before them and berated their predecessors for mistakes made whilst championing their own superiority. As a Droodist who is keenly among the Irreverent, I do not wish to fall into that trap. The irony is that the mistake I would note in the previous two movements is precisely their identification of mistakes in those before them, dooming me to repeat that error whatever I do. But nonetheless, I do take pride in the attitude of my contemporaries in not attacking the ideas of predecessors with the same vehemence that they in turn criticised those before them. Granted, the works of Aylmer, Reece or T. P. James warrant at least a raised eyebrow, if not a little teasing, but in all this their folly is balanced by their value as commentary on *Drood* and its reception. The Irreverent movement has allowed for the removal of all the baggage Droodists previously had to carry. Rather than feeling the shame of discussing *Drood*'s end, or indignation at those who dared to do so, it has become increasingly possible to discuss it rationally, but not the less enthusiastically for that. *Drood* still has a place in the academy and is likely to continue to do so.

Drood now and beyond (2): *Drood* online and in public

In his 1996 review of *Drood* solutions, Steven Connor closes by looking at what might come next, and suggests the novel 'might in the future best be read in the form of an electronic hypertext', and this forecast has proved correct.[335] While *The Dickensian* afforded space for Droodists to share their thoughts in the early twentieth century, the twenty-first century has seen a larger arena made available through the internet. Through blogs, website and social media, discussion of *Drood* has been made open and available to anybody with a computer. This has meant that moderate voices who previously may not have pushed themselves to write for a journal now had a much easier way to share their thoughts. It also meant that those with more extreme ideas need not worry about finding a willing publisher. The full impact of the internet, not just on *Drood*, but all literary discussion, has yet to be fully appreciated and understood, and this will certainly prove an area for future Droodists to reflect upon more fully. For now, however, let us consider what forays *Drood* has made online so far.

Sven Karston has created an excellent site *Droodiana,* which continues the work done by earlier cataloguers of *Drood*, compiling notes on the main solutions and sharing them with a wider audience.[336] In addition, Karston has included his own research, which predominately focuses on looking for real-life inspiration for several of the characters (he presented his theory of Thomas Edmett, Mayor of Maidstone in 1842 as source for Sapsea at the 2014 conference). In doing this he steps away from the fictional forensics of Duffield, not considering the crime as a real situation but instead viewing it all as the imagination of Dickens and looking for sources in the life of the author, not the world of the novels.

My own website *The Drood Inquiry* launched in 2014.[337] The name drew inspiration from the Leveson Inquiry that had dominated the UK media's attention the previous year. Given the number of investigations and trials that already been held on *Drood*, I felt an inquiry was a more appropriate response, allowing me to investigate the solutions themselves rather than start a fresh one. The purpose of the site is to summarise the tale and introduce new readers to the mystery. Alongside a full version of Dickens' text can be found a synopsis of the main theories, but arranged thematically, rather than chronologically as here. To further aid the introduction of new readers to the text, a real-time reading project ran from April to September 2014, where the monthly instalments were released online in synchronisation with their original publication in 1870, with discussion among readers being shared on the sister-site, *Cloisterham Tales.*[338] I invited Alys Jones not only to create new illustrations of the characters (some of whom, such as the Billickin, or the Topes, were never illustrated by Fildes), but also the graphic novel pages reprinted for the introduction of this book. The aim was to make the story as vivid and multimedia as possible, though my intention to also include sound effects and quotations have not materialised (yet).

In all of this the motivation was to encourage visitors to judge and decide on their own solution, and the joy of the internet is the potential it allows for such interaction. The site thus includes a verdict page where visitors register their own beliefs and the results are immediately updated to show the most popular ideas. At time of writing, this shows that over sixty-five percent believe Edwin is dead, eighty percent think Jasper killed him (or tried to), and sixty-five percent think the method of murder was strangulation. In short, the most popular theories are those that adhere to Forster's original statement. This is a remarkable result. Where Holmes' musical deliberately encouraged unusual responses, *The Drood Inquiry* was asking how visitors thought Dickens intended the story to end, and thus generated less outlandish results. Prior to this, with only the solutions as our guide, the overview of *Drood* theories was one of extreme ideas working against one another. By allowing everyone a voice, it meant that more moderate voices could be heard, and rather than the diverse views of the minority being the only ones seen, it was possible at last to see what the silent majority thought. In agreeing with Forster, it suggested that Wilson and Collins were triumphant at last, and that the arguments over Dickens' intentions were at an end.

This general agreement by no means signals the end of Droodism, of course. The aspects not discussed by Forster predictably split results: the question of Datchery's identity is spread widely, with thirty percent thinking him to be a detective, twenty-seven believing him to be Bazzard, and the remaining forty-three percent spread between him being an actor, Tartar, Helena (relatively popular at ten percent), Edwin, Neville or a new character with a personal motive. Even when we accept the statements of Dickens' friends and family, there still remains much to be discussed over the end of *Drood*. On the back of the website's success, I co-curated a special exhibition at the Charles Dickens Museum in London in 2015, *A Dickensian Whodunnit: Solving the Mystery of Edwin Drood*, to further encourage wider participation with the novel and theories of its end (see fig. 28). This then attracted coverage in the national press regarding the website and subsequent exhibition. *The Times* announced in a full-page article that 'academics have now turned to crowd-sourcing to find a convincing conclusion to Dickens' last, unfinished novel'.[339] This was not my intention, the site instead being there simply to encourage participation. But the media angle that garnered most interest was to rest on this idea of authority through the people: a democratic decision on the correct solution. Over a century on from the attempts to feign authority through Dickens' friends, ghost or the employment of Sherlock Holmes, a new master was being proposed for the final verdict: we the people. For all my efforts to step away from the idea of solving *Drood* definitively, I was powerless against a larger narrative that hungered for the simplicity of a straight answer. The story was picked up by the *Daily Mail*, which in turn meant that, through the joys of the internet, *Drood* became a subject for online *Daily Mail* readers to share their views. Ignoring the first basic rule of internet use, I read the comments.

They could generally be grouped into three types of response to the idea of solving *Drood*. The first was passive-aggressive bewilderment that people were even talking about this. One anonymous commenter from London said:

> *Scientists are saying that computers are already intelligent enough to produce creative work better than humans, so why don't they get a computer to read all Charles Dickens' works and then provide an ending for this story?[340]*

Literature was reduced to a simple formula easily interpreted by the magic of computers. Peter the Painter had a similar view of the needlessness of all this:

> *The BBC did a play on this and somebody has written the end which fitted in quite nicely as to the way Dickens might have finished it off. So what's this all about?[341]*

Thankfully, a second group of commenters were more keen to impress the genius of Dickens and the allure of his final novel. Henry Noel, injecting an air of mystique into proceedings, said:

CHAPTER FOUR

It's spooky reading that last chapter, knowing that with the final sentence, the great author set aside his pen, went to dinner, and was stricken that very afternoon with the stroke that killed him the next day.[342]

The 'spooky reading' harkens back to that same trend noted before of reading *Drood* as a foreteller of Dickens' own death. It is the romanticising of the author-figure: had Dickens been a taxman no one would be saying it was spooky that he was doing tax returns when he had a stroke. But Dickens writing shortly before his death adds a pleasing aura of 'spookiness' to the novel. Colonel Steve Zodiac, from Space City, Micronesia, extended the sentiment:

Although Dickens died too soon (just 58 years old), he did have perfect timing. The true mystery of Edwin Drood is that we shall never know how it ends.[343]

Passionate as Dickens may have been about his books, we can confidently assume that he would have been more passionate about continuing to live, and that as he lay there after his stroke he was not congratulating himself on the perfection of his timing. Still, this second group of commenters betray that idea of Dickens' own death and the very incompletion of *Drood* as his final, *intentional*, stroke of genius.

And then the final strand of comments, and far more angry. Earwig-O said: 'The only ending of any real significance is the one CD intended. A pity it was never revealed, but best that it be left a mystery. Otherwise, readers of Dickens can imagine their own ending if that gives satisfaction. Anything else is not Dickens and therefore inconsequential' – dismissed with a Podsnappian wave of the hand.[344] Likewise the grandly named catdog71 said:

I don't see how an ending done in any way can be the same thing as the original would have been. None of us can know what was in Dickens' head so the story can never be truly real. I was always a bit dubious about reading this, knowing it was unfinished, but did so in the end. I was really enjoying it too when it came to its abrupt finish. Shame, as I thought it one one of his better stories. I almost regretted starting it in a way as I was disappointed at never knowing what would have happened – and still won't as any other ending is STILL not Dickens.[345]

Aside from the unnecessary capitalisation of 'still', what is worrying here is catdog71's idea of a Dickensian ending makes no mention of technique or characterisation but focuses purely on what happens, as though the plot alone would be imbued with Dickensian DNA. In short, for all the previous congratulation echoed in this chapter at a new wave of Droodists cheerfully engaging in irreverent solutions while maintaining a healthy respect for the original, there remains still among the wider public (or *Daily Mail* readers at least) a broad range of former prejudices against the book and the best approach to solving the mystery.

From one extreme to another, and while *Daily Mail* readers were making their views known on *Drood*, a new generation was being introduced to Dickens' last novel via a video game. Ubisoft's *Assassin's Creed: Syndicate* continued the popular series of historical-based games with a nineteenth-century location in which players could meet and interact with various famous historical figures of Victorian London, including, of course, Dickens. The author offers the players several missions to engage in, should they be willing. The third of these missions, 'Haunted House', sends the player with Dickens to explore the said residence of ghostly visitations. *En route* in the coach, Dickens recounts the popular myth surrounding the house:

> *This residence was briefly owned by a Mr James Jasper. A choirmaster and an opium addict. His nephew, Edward, was betrothed to one of Mr Jasper's pupils, the fair and delicate Rose. However, Edward disappeared under mysterious circumstances, followed by Jasper himself. Perhaps grief sent him back to the soothing arms of his narcotic mistress.*[346]

Irreverent in one sense for its repackaging of the text into a violent adventure, its brief summary of the text is nonetheless very conventional. We soon learn that Jasper killed 'Edward'. The slight changing of names is explained in the mission's conclusion, after the 'ghost' turns out to be Jasper himself, alive but driven mad by his guilt and put out of his misery by the player. When the action is done and all is safe again, Dickens emerges once more for some final thoughts on the mission, proclaiming that 'I think this has the makings of a rather fine novel. I wonder if I have one left in me...'.[347] Like the fictionalised biographies discussed earlier, the claim is that Dickens is inspired by real-life events. The whole thing is an in-joke in a game that prides itself on its immersion in the world of the nineteenth century (besides Dickens, players can also interact with Charles Darwin, Queen Victoria, Florence Nightingale and Karl Marx, among others). It can be argued that it is catering in part, then, for an audience with an appreciation for the Victorian that may well know and appreciate the appropriation of *Drood* in this mission. But equally there will be a number of players who do not know *Drood*, and who will either remain ignorant of the joke or else are introduced to Dickens' text through the videogame. If reducing Dickens' last novel to a minor plot of an optional mission in a computer game seems glib, the sheer sales figures for the game and the consequent exposure of *Drood* to a new and varied audience should not be dismissed. Video games are growing exponentially both in the scale and depth of gameplay, and the audience reach and investment of developers. We have no more idea how this new medium will develop, and to what extent its influence will reach, than the early viewers of silent movies could appreciate the vast cinematic industry that would follow.

Growing technology and the internet has not only allowed for a new outreach, such as *Assassin's Creed*, but also a new level of interaction from the wider public. People wanting to have their ideas heard are no longer reliant on journals, newspaper correspondence or a willing publisher. The internet offers space like never before for free and easy publication of ideas, essays...and fiction. In truth, all of the completions can be regarded in a certain sense as fanfiction, just as

153

the solutions (even the Academics') can be regarded as fan theory. All arise from an interest in the novel and a desire to talk further on it. But online fanfiction can be distinguished in one sense that it clearly identifies itself as fanfiction, a community of writers glad to admit themselves as fans, where Droodists are just one branch of a much larger group. Fanfiction sites include a number of new works inspired by all of Dickens' novels, and the *Drood* ones are delightfully bold in their takes. *Edwin Drood Zombie*, for example, is certainly a fresh angle on how he might survive Jasper's attack:

> *'Jasper,' Edwin began, 'I am a zombie. This is why you could not kill me. This is why you could not tell if my body was alive or dead.'*[348]

One might fear we have dived fully into the imaginative world of Kavanagh, Aylmer and Reece, but in line with the wider context of Droodian irreverence, online fanfiction proudly wears on its sleeve any deviation from the original. Many identify themselves as alternate universe (AU) and not one prefaces his or her story with allusions to uncovering Dickens' intentions. As the title suggests, fanfiction is by the fans, for the fans, and can be categorised as a combination of wilful abandonment and wish fulfilment, taking a 'what if' premise and having fun with the characters. Accordingly, a number of the solutions are very much focused on a handful of characters that the authors are particularly fond of. Many stories are either first-person narrative, or third-person but focusing particularly on the viewpoint of one character. For example, Foosemittee's short work *Drood* consists of three brief monologues from minor characters disgruntled at being side-lined: 'Ever had that feeling?' ponders his Durdles, 'Where maybe you're just vanishing away because you're not important enough to *exist*?'[349]

A number of these works cite Hughes' 2012 television series as a direct influence, imagining their works to follow specifically that interpretation of the story, which in itself explains, or evidences, the freedom from reverence and adherence to Dickens' text. Like other works of fanfiction, the appeal of writing on *Drood* lies as much on entering the existing world of the novel as it does in extending towards the unwritten end. So there are several short pieces that detail plot moments left out of Dickens' first half, such as *Before the Shadow Falls*, which imagines Jasper preparing for his fateful meeting with Rosa by the sundial, or *Absolutely No Shame* that recounts a conversation between Helena and Crisparkle intended to flesh out their growing romance.[350]

The fleshing out of romance brings us to the other recurring element in a number of fanfiction, where writing turns to more adult themes. Building on the aforementioned sense of affection for particular characters, a number of writers have allowed their imagination to run riot, especially with regards to Jasper who now becomes a brooding bad boy for readers to love to hate. In particular, authors have imagined what few before would consider, that Rosa might change her feelings to accept Jasper as her true love after all. *The Blossoming of the Bud* by the evocatively named Roman De la Rose, removes the shadow over Jasper by revealing early on that Edwin is alive and in Egypt. Jasper, who had harboured plans of murder induced by his opium addiction, now overcomes his drug habit and wins the heart of Rosa, much to the initial horror of her friends:

> *'Neville has told me about Mr Jasper,'* [Helena] *said quietly. 'How has this come about? Did he force you?'*
>   *'No. Only by dint of his persistence and his unbending will. There was no force involved.'*[351]

The book, like many other examples of fanfiction, is happy to attempt a Victorian style of dialogue, but incorporate modern day ideology and franker discussions about relationships. Accordingly, Jasper and Rosa's love is expressed not through the eyes of Dickens' young schoolgirl but through those of a mature woman experiencing a more layered form of love (not to mention an innovative use of Jasper's piano during the throes of passion). While the inclusion of sex scenes may baffle those seeking the authentic Dickens experience, *The Blossoming of Rosa Bud* is a positively cautious portrayal of the relationship when compared with *Mr Jasper's Cadenza* by Laurie Love. The author's preface for the second chapter is admirably frank in what it is, and is not, trying to do:

> *Just bear in mind that this is an erotic story; it is not an attempt at finishing Dickens' mystery (although things will tie up eventually). And it is about to contain a lot of sex.*[352]

So. Much. Sex. It might be assumed Jasper had swapped his opium for a performance-enhancing drug given the amount of athletic bouts he engages in with Rosa. Love states her debt to Hughes' series and the portrayal of Jasper by Matthew Rhys: 'clad in black, tightly buttoned, dark features, dark hair, repressed lust, it's all there. And I want it.' (see fig. 29).[353] What unfolds, therefore, is a tale of the mysterious choirmaster wooing and educating the young Rosa in the physical nature of love:

> *'Rosa…' he hummed against her humid skin, 'My Rosa Bud…now you shall bloom.'*[354]

The reader is consequently shown fifty shades of Jasper in a novel that makes Dickens live up to the sexual innuendo of his name. Sadly, despite Love's promise that she will tie things up eventually (the plot, rather than the characters, one hopes), the work currently stands unfinished at the end of its fifth chapter, with no indication of, or concern for, the whereabouts of Edwin, so frustratingly we have yet to reach a climax. Though Love and Rose classify their work as fanfiction, reinventing *Drood* as erotic fiction identifies with the Irreverent for their willingness to liberate Dickens' character from expectations of nineteenth-century fiction. Both authors are able to imagine entirely new takes on the novel beyond the parameters and limitations felt by earlier Droodists.

Considering his attitude to the early completions, it is a deep regret that J. C. Walters did not live to read Love's story. His reaction would have been something to truly savour. The development of erotic *Drood* completions is certainly not one he could have predicted, but is a testament to the potential for variety in responses to *Drood*. There is no limit to where a completion can go. And yet for all this talk of deviating from Dickens' novel, the increased focus on sexual activities in Rose and Love's stories need not be so very far removed from the intentions of the original. Natalie McKnight's article "'A Little Humouring of Pussy's Points!" or Sex – the *Real* Unsolved Mystery of *Edwin Drood*' conducts a glorious investigation of Rosa's nickname 'Pussy' which, she convincingly contends, was a known euphemism at the time that Dickens was writing and therefore absolutely to be read as *double entendre*. This is further compounded by the sexual connotations of a rosebud and the gloves (i.e. condoms) that Edwin buys as the perfect present for her. The most intriguing part is McKnight's own admittance that on first reading she automatically dismissed such obvious hints:

> *I should admit that I had read the incomplete novel a good number of times over the past 25 years before I noticed what now seem to me to be very obvious sexual references. Naturally, the nickname 'Pussy' probably caused me to raise an eyebrow the first time I read the novel, but I must have dismissed my reaction fairly quickly as anachronistic.*[355]

McKnight notes how this 'reflects the persistence of the stereotype about Victorian prudery', one which too is being demolished by a number of contemporary historians. Instead, the outrageous innuendo of Edwin and Jasper's conversation about Pussy in Dickens' second chapter has been automatically overlooked precisely because we take Dickens seriously and as a model of Victorian family values. The erotic fanfiction of Laurie Love and Roman de la Rose, might be vindicated after all. While a reader could all too easily fall into the trap of automatically dismissing erotic *Drood* completions as beyond what Dickens intended, they offer a lesson in re-evaluation of Dickens. Irreverence, be it through fanfiction or rereading of the text, opens our eyes either to new interpretations, or even obvious ones that were always there.

The forays of fanfiction are a world removed from the intense discussion of the Detectives and bear far more in common with those early solutions of the 1870s. What saves them, like the *Drood* musical, or *The D Case*, is the lack of pretension. Irreverence has proved to be the necessary ingredient for *Drood* solutions to continue in their variety without the division of previous approaches. It allows and encourages readers to return to that pre-Forster age of wild speculation, without the baggage of trying to prove those theories were what Dickens intended. The openness of Hughes, Holmes and Fruttero and Lucentini in their disregard for Dickens has not resulted in angering Dickensians, but allowing for their ideas to be taken with a pinch of salt and enjoyed as ideas without the need to debunk or challenge them. After nearly a century-and-a-half of heated debate, be it between undertakers and resurrectionists, or Porfirians and Agathists, irreverence allowed for the existence of two schools – one staying faithful to Dickens, the other open to all possibilities – without the conflict and tension between them.

Rosa Bud:
The unfinished picture

> …the unfinished picture of a blooming schoolgirl
> hanging over the chimneypiece; her flowing brown hair
> tied with a blue riband, and her beauty remarkable for a
> quite childish, almost babyish, touch of saucy discontent,
> comically conscious of itself.

She sits. And waits. Miss Twinkleton reads on from her book of nautical tales, but she barely listens. She is thinking of all that she could be. All that she will be.

Sometimes she thinks of what she might do if Edwin ever returns. Would she embrace him as a brother, or accept him once more as a husband? Or is it her path to mourn – or avenge – the boy who will never return?

Other times she thinks of Tartar. Those thoughts are usually…a little more explicit than the thoughts of Edwin. Older, more mature, a Rosa in bloom rather than the Bud she has been in Cloisterham. Climbing his beanstalk, if you might pardon the expression.

Once she thought of Neville. Safe, dependable, poor, lovely Neville…but then she went straight back to thinking of Tartar.

Of course, there was Neville's sister. Sometimes Rosa had… confusing thoughts about Helena. Distinctly unDickensian thoughts that thrilled for their deviation alone.

And then there was Jasper. Dark thoughts clad in black. Very tightly clad. His inner demons just bulged out…

She sits up and fans herself vigorously, prompting a momentary pause by Miss Twinkleton in her reading. Rosa settles back in her seat, and tries to settle her mind accordingly.

In all these thoughts she focuses on other people. If she stops looking outwards, and looks at herself, the fear she has is that there is nothing there to see. For who is Rosa Bud? A schoolgirl – no, a shadow of a schoolgirl. An unfinished picture defined by those who paint her, and watch her. Nobody knows what she is on the inside, her least of all.

She did break it off with Eddy of course. And she ran away from Jasper. That showed a spirit of independence, didn't it? What might she have been? What might she yet be? Could she set out for a life alone, without being reliant on someone else to define her? Could she take the trek to Egypt in Eddy's stead? Or see the New World? Why should she remain for ever the demure young darling of Cloisterham? Why can't this Rose prove to be a Thorn of Anxiety? She could do something improper, find someone entirely new, perhaps an older, famous novelist for example.

She could marry anyone, or no one. She could go anywhere, or nowhere. The more she sits and waits, the more new thoughts occur to her, more varied and daring with each passing age. She could be the hero. She could be the murderer. Could, could, could – always what might happen, but never what does happen. She never is *anything, only* could *be something. Not fully formed. Instead, she is simply becoming. What the result might be she does not know, only that it has not yet been reached. First Eddy must be found, then she will know her own purpose. So she sits. And she waits.*

Conclusion

The question

How do you conclude a book that is all about a book with no conclusion? The temptation simply to finish off midsentence is –

Nonetheless, noting the implicit irony in concluding the inconclusive, allow me to summarise what *Drood* teaches us, and asks of us. What has been shown in this history of solutions and completions is a narrative divided into four movements: the Opportunists, the Detectives, the Academics and the Irreverent. Each wave of solutions has had to position itself against the one that preceded it, and one recurring element that generates so much theorising on *Drood* is a healthy dose of disagreement. Discussing the end of a novel is not like other literary theories that can exist side-by-side by agreeing to explore different themes in the same text. Where most scholars can present their own theories without the need to challenge others, any discussion of an ending to *Drood* implicitly identifies those that differ to it as wrong. There can be many readings of a text, but when it comes to the end, there can be only one. At least, that is the idea many of my predecessors have clung to, and one I would like to challenge over the next few pages.

If there is an overall trend, it is one that plays against the backdrop of Dickens studies as a whole. We have seen an early tendency to capitalise on Dickens' success that simultaneously recognises the popularity of the author while not feeling overwhelmed or restricted by awe and reverence. The struggle of the Detectives was the fight to take Dickens seriously by whatever means necessary. They wavered between an abundance of praise for the writer without fault, and their own nagging doubts that perhaps his last work was not all that they might hope. They tried to redeem Dickens as a great writer and not simply a popular one. That their efforts should subsequently be seen as unscholarly and ridiculous – the very opposite of what they were aiming for – is one of the great tragedies at the heart of this narrative. Nonetheless, the maturing of Dickensian scholarship with Edmund Wilson and his successors allowed the hopes of the Detectives to come true, or alternatively for their folly to continue. While the Detectives focused their efforts on reinventing *Drood* as a great mystery, the Academics rewrote Dickens as a tortured genius. Finally, the Irreverent arrived to defenestrate Dickens and just revise his stories. It is another rewrite, or rather a dismissal of any writing at all. As ever, the answer lies in balance. We can recognise the darker moments in Dickens without ignoring the comic. We can have fun with Dickens' writing while maintaining a respect for the author. We can explore the intricacies of what might occur while enjoying the fragment we have. *Drood* need not be divisive.

Nor need *Drood* be diminishing. In presenting this history of solutions I do not intend for it to be the last word, but a recap of the story so far. I announced at the start of this book that I did not want to solve *Drood*, and I stick by that. I have been studying *Drood* and its solutions for five years now (I suspect, tracing the path of my forebears, that this is only the beginning of my involvement). In that time, I have spoken at various conferences and discussed my work with several people, and one question frequently hovers in the air: how do *you* think *Drood* should end? In reaching the end of this book I am conscious, therefore, that some readers may now be asking the same question once more of the author. I need only look at those works before me to see the glaring dangers in closing a narrative on solutions by offering my own as the crowning glory. Instead then I shall simply offer the same reply I have given to all those who have asked it of me before: I have less interest in the answer than I do in the question. Any solution to *Drood*, even Dickens', is going to be an anti-climax to some degree. Who on earth wants the depressing job of having 'The Last Word on *Edwin Drood*'? Far from it, I have complete faith that should Dickens' notes for the final six numbers be found, that it would only take a few months before arguments were made on why those notes are wrong. The reason why is because as much as we want to know how *Drood* ends, I believe we have now reached a point where having that end is the last thing we want. It is the question itself that fascinates most of all, rather than any one answer. It is the process of finding the end, rather than the actual discovery, which continues to create so much discussion. So far as the ending of *Drood* is concerned, it is the quest, not the treasure, which offers enjoyment here. Perhaps this is the beauty of Forster's statement, that it offers enough information for closure, while leaving sufficient details tantalisingly open for debate.

Why should we ask this question? Why should we care how *Drood* ends? Dickens is not the only author to die in the middle of writing.

Most authors at any one time are in the process of writing or planning works. So, on reflection it would actually be a rarer thing for an author *not* to leave behind any unfinished work. Most editions of Elizabeth's Gaskell's *Wives and Daughters*, for instance, are content to simply have a short summary after the last surviving chapter detailing the author's plans, and most readers content to accept that. So why should it be different for *Drood*? The ambiguity caused by the lack of written plans is certainly a factor, as is the delay between the publication of the sixth instalment and public awareness of Dickens' conversations with friends and family, allowing the roots of speculation to take hold. The method of publication is equally important. Had Dickens simply been halfway through writing a manuscript at his death, and the fragment been first published in one volume posthumously, I believe it would have had a far different reception. But because it was serialised, readers began the story in good faith of reaching the end, so that they did not approach this knowingly as the last fragment, but were instead denied a promised end. But both this and the four-year wait for Forster's statement speaks more to contemporary reader's reactions, and cannot be held to account for the succeeding 150 years. Another consideration we cannot dismiss is the prominence of the word 'mystery' in the book's title. Certainly, the Detectives were eager to pick that particular gauntlet up. One could argue of the different interpretations of 'mystery', or the anachronism of reading an 1870 text in the mode of twentieth-century murder mysteries, or argue the question of whether the events are meant to be mysterious to the reader, or the other characters. But all these struggle to overcome that initial reaction and expectation of most readers when they first see the title. For better or worse, it *is* a mystery. Would we be questioning the identity of Datchery so fiercely if the story was a romantic comedy? Would Princess Puffer's history matter so much if the novel was a satire? Mystery prompts investigation of all loose ends and unexplained factors.

And then there is the author. Charles Dickens is the most successful and famous British novelist of all time. That in itself guarantees a greater readership and interest in his final book than would be afforded to unfinished works by other authors. The price of fame is great scrutiny. Dickens suffered from this in life, and his last work suffers from it after his death. As I have shown, often the prominence of Dickens has affected the approach to *Drood* as writers have tried to champion the book and make it worthy of its author. The efforts of Proctor and Walters only further identify their insecurity that *Drood* might not be a good book, and even though Wilson and Collins are prepared to accept and praise *Drood* on its own terms, rather than relying on a fiendishly convoluted end to raise it, there still lies behind their arguments that note of triumph in saving Dickens from the ignominy of an ill-regarded final work. To take that fear head-on, perhaps the question we should ask is: What if *Drood* had been a bad book? I do not think it myself, but would it really have such a monumental impact on our appreciation of Dickens had his swansong been a dud? It is this, above all, I think, which provides the continuing momentum for many to step forward and identify themselves as the true interpreter of *Drood* and saviour of Dickens' reputation. The question that haunts us – how does *Drood* end? – is haunted in turn by our admiration for Dickens, and our inability to let the matter go. We will never find an answer that can be completely certain, and so we will always keep asking the question. We are stuck in a loop, at the heart of which is the ghost of Dickens: intangible, multi-formed and open to different interpretation by each reader. But as we continue to generate new endings, and further discussion of those endings, are we still celebrating the real Dickens or have we left him behind for our own version of the writer?

Diamond soup

The anxiety of where *Drood* itself belongs in the tangled web of completions and solutions brings to mind the old folk tale about stone soup. It tells of a poor man who knocks on a rich man's door asking for food. The rich man refuses, so the poor man shows him a magic stone that can make stone soup, the finest soup there is. The rich man,

165

intrigued, lets him in, and the poor man promptly places the stone in a pot of boiling water. The poor man tastes it, then suggests a little salt will make it perfect, which the rich man provides. Then the poor man mentions how a few carrots will top it off nicely, and again the rich man puts some carrots in. The charade goes on with the rich man naively adding all manner of extra ingredients until finally the poor man says, 'Now it's perfect – have a taste.' The rich man tries the soup for the first time, which is by now delicious, and promptly buys the stone off the poor man for a great sum of money.

Working in academia, I am constantly reminded of this tale. How much of the praise and credit we owe to a text or author is due to the source itself, and how much to the extra ingredients we lavish upon it in the subsequent years? In this specific case of *Drood*, what has become more important: the original text or the quest to solve it? I stated above that an ending is the last thing we want, but where does that leave our judgment on the beginning? Is *Edwin Drood* merely a stone? Certainly, Proctor and Walters were arguing for this, unintentionally perhaps, when they claimed the torso to be a poor fragment and trumpeted their own solutions as rescuing Dickens' text – the necessary extra ingredients to make the soup taste perfect. Since Wilson's essay, a new narrative emerged of *Drood* as a diamond in the rough, a good text buried under years of unnecessary speculation and solutions. Many, like Sylvere Monod, have lamented the wealth of 'literature devoted to the mystery of Edwin Drood, not to *The Mystery of Edwin Drood*'.[356] The Detectives saw their solution as reinstating Dickens' genius. The Academics considered them to be both a distraction and obstruction to appreciation of the original. Is *Drood* stone soup or a diamond in the rough? The one analogy berates Dickens, the other berates the subsequent solutions. The model I would like to move towards is a compromise of the two: diamond soup.

The Mystery of Edwin Drood is a great piece of fiction, and does indeed include some of Dickens' best writing. Had it been completed, I am sure we would have a work that would comfortably sit in the top half of his works. But the undeniable truth is that it is not finished, and speculation of *Drood*'s value as a finished work will always amount to just that: speculation. Rather than mourning the loss of a second half, it is better to recognise the opportunities that *Drood*'s incompletion has afforded us. Rather than blocking our view of the original text, the solutions and completions allow us to re-interrogate the original, either to consider a fresh perspective or further cement and defend our original premise of the book. The extra ingredients we have added in the past century-and-a-half need not automatically dictate an absence of value in the original stone at the heart of the soup, but it does allow for many more to enjoy it who might otherwise not do so. This is not to say that the hordes of completions and solutions are doing *Drood* a necessary favour. The book can prosper as a fragment, a notebook of sketches and memorable characters. We can enjoy *Drood* perfectly well with what we have. But nor do I want to side with Wilson and Collins in dismissing these completions out of hand. Philip Hopsbaum considered the Academics and Detectives to have reached an *impasse*:

> *Clearly, this is stalemate. The critics should confess themselves baffled. Dickens, after all, was quite capable of laying an entirely false trail of clues [...] It is all too easy for critics and writers to read their own fictions into Dickens's fragment [...] And so, all we can do with the vast body of Droodiana is to make use of it, as we do other criticism, not to judge intention, but to gauge effect.*[357]

Solutions and completions to *Drood* are subjective and always will be, no matter how vehemently the writer refers to evidence and sources. Interpretation is in the eye of the beholder. If we can come to terms with this subjectivity, and approach the solutions not as final words, but opening dialogues, we can read them first for their implicit commentary on the writer's interpretation of Dickens, and secondly as a counter-factual narrative, an experiment in the diversity of a plot without conclusion. I myself identify as one of the Irreverent, and so am keen to stress the benefit of a healthy dose of self-mocking when delving into Drood, maintaining a necessary distance between asking the question and caring too deeply about the answer. But it is important to note that this is not an anti-scholarly approach. Irreverent does not equal irrelevant. As both Seltzer and Hoel have shown, the wealth of writing on *Drood*'s end offers analysis on *Drood* itself, as much as a commentary on the changing perceptions of Dickens and his work. To read what different generations have considered to be an authentic ending speaks volumes about that generation's concept of who and what Dickens was. We cannot and should not disregard the completions and solutions, but recognise within them a mine of treasures to be dug out and utilised as part of a narrative on the reception of Dickens as a writer.

Drood and the F word

Solving *Drood* is a wonderful exercise in imagination and engagement with a text. Rather than being off-putting, it can be a great introduction into Dickens' writing. In 2015, I received an email from Olivia Griffiths, a school teacher in Vermont, who had been inspired by *The Drood Inquiry* to teach *Drood* to her own class:

> *For their final assignment, each student had to come up with their own theory as to what happened, whether Edwin was dead or alive, who killed him, where was he, who was involved, etc. The classroom was covered in CSI-style crime boards, coloured charts with arrows and crude drawings of dead bodies. Heated arguments broke out as to HOW exactly you could dispose of a body and where given the time period. For those who believed Edwin had fled, there were many ideas of his coming back in disguise, secretly being everywhere from Munich to Cairo, and one theory that had Edwin and Neville running away together.*[358]

It offered a way in to Dickens for new readers precisely because the openness of the ending invited them to stand side-by-side in discussion with Dickens, one author to another. The gift of a project like this is that there are no wrong answers. As much as we have come to trust Forster – and I would argue that trust is justified – there is always the slim possibility that he could be wrong after all. It does not matter if you have been studying Dickens all your life, or have just picked up the book for the first time – any opinion has the same validity as the other, and that democracy of opinion is a rare thing to be cherished.

As seen in the last chapter, the advent of the internet has seen great steps taken in demolishing the ivory tower, not as a defeat of the academy, but the release of it, allowing for scholars and enthusiasts to work together again as they should, rather than encouraging the 'us and them' mentality harboured by the earlier Academics trying to distance themselves from the Detectives. Solving *Drood* need not be solely the work of the academy. What it began as, and should continue to be, is an exercise in imagination. It offers a light-hearted investigation and discussion for people to enjoy debating with the right amount of perspective. The word to describe it, which I have been tentatively circling around, is 'fun'. I hesitate to use the word because 'fun' has come to be something of a dirty word in academia. It lacks a qualitative value, it has twee connotations, and it is only one syllable long. Serious scholars accordingly give the word a wide berth. But solving *Drood* is, and should be, fun.

The mistake of the Detectives was in assuming the best way to get their ideas heard was to ground their theories in as scholarly and serious a tone as possible. The more they tried to convince the wider world of the gravity of their ideas, the more ridiculous they seemed. The early solutions, and this last wave of the Irreverent, have a more healthy approach by not taking it all so seriously. For the early completionists, it was an opportunity, a springboard for new plotlines, and while their occasional audacity in counterfeiting authority for their solutions has left them in the doghouse, the work produced is still entertaining enough to read. Thus, the Irreverent have seized on this same idea, without the blasphemy of pretending to be Dickens' son, friend or ghost. They don't seek to challenge Forster, or attack any of Dickens' friends or family for being fools or liars. They simply take an unfinished text and have fun imagining where it *could* go, without the responsibility of having to prove that it is where the plot *must* go. They have fun. Again, the connotations of that word can dangerously imply a superiority on the part of the Academics. Wilson and Collins took Dickens seriously, and in discussing the works in chapter three it has been tempting to describe the various approaches as 'level-headed', 'objective' or 'rational' compared to those that preceded them. I have often opted for cautious as a better description, as they avoid controversy by avoiding risk. The solutions proposed by the Academics garnered less rebuke because they offered less to challenge the status quo, whereas the Opportunists, Detectives and Irreverent have jumped cheerfully into the fray, vulnerable to ridicule but opening up so much more potential on the way. How wonderful it is that we as a species can look at a character like John Jasper and see in him a madman, a monster, a villain, a guardian angel, a Gothic anti-hero and, yes, a sex-symbol. What fun it is to see Dickens' last roster of characters refuse to behave, but to titillate our imaginations and explode beyond their original confinements into any manner of possibilities.

That Dickens left his final book unfinished need not be a source of frustration, but the ultimate parting word from an author who built his career on his relationship with his reading public. Given the serial nature of his novels, *Drood*'s paused status preserves that moment of anticipation, waiting for the next number to be published and wondering with your friends what is going to be coming up. It passes responsibility on to the reader to continue the story in Dickens' absence. Rather than a full stop, we are left with an ellipsis. In not being given a conclusion to *Drood*, both the book and Dickens are rendered endless, ongoing, forever in the height of the action. David Copperfield grows up and settles down. Oliver Twist similarly swaps his exciting escapades for a life of middle-class mundanity. But Jasper, Rosa, Helena, Datchery, Princess Puffer… even Edwin…all still have their stories and adventures left ahead of them. In stasis, they endure.

CONCLUSION

Edwin Drood:
Schrodinger's Corpse

> 'The proverb says that threatened men live long,' he tells her, lightly.
>
> 'Then Ned – so threatened is he, wherever he may be while I am a talking to you, deary – should live to all eternity!' replies the woman.

Everything is dark. I am here, entombed in lime, preserved and decayed all at once. Everyone is looking for me but I never went anywhere. I am –

– here. Everything is light. Breath rushes into my lungs and I am blinded by the rays of the sun. I am in Egypt, beginning my career and a life alone. Free of my obligation to Rosa, but I may yet return for –

– Helena. Dark again. I am in the weir. He pushed me in. I cannot believe he actually pushed me in. All I can see is the fish and the weeds. Above me, all is light as people carry on their daily lives. I am here. I am right –

– here. I am sat in a room. I am wearing a white wig, and making chalk marks on the wall. I am here, but no-one knows it. Edwinconspicuous. Breakfast is before me and I realise I have not eaten for over a century. I fall to with an –

– appetite. The dark comes back. I am lying in a tomb. Dark, close, musty. All is done. All is –

– finished. I am in London. I was attacked, but not killed. I am recovering thanks to my friend. It may be Grewgious. It may be Durdles. It's hard to concentrate when I keep changing –

– places. Dark again. The tomb again? The same tomb, or the one next to it? How will they ever find me when I keep –

– moving? Egypt again. Broken-hearted and dreaming of Rosa. Breaking off the engagement was a mistake. I should go back to –

– Cloisterham. The cathedral. The crypt. The tomb. Back again in the dark. Sometimes the lime preserves me, sometimes it leaves nothing but the ring. But I am here. I am –

– dead. No, alive. Datchery again. Watching out for Jasper. He does not suspect I am –

– here. In the tomb. Is it over? Can it ever be over? I'm neither dead or alive. I am –

– undone. Ever repeating, ever present. For all eternity. Walking the streets of Cloisterham disguised among those who would search for me. They have no idea that I am –

– here. Under their feet. I never left. I never leave. I never stop. It never finishes. I am –

– here. Egypt. Far away and unaware. Blissful in my ignorance of what is happening back in –

– Cloisterham. In the water again. Lying in wait beneath the surface. I endure. Without end, without closure. I will not die. Not for long. I am –

– here. Above the water. Finding clues. Trying to stop it. Alive or dead. Dead or alive. Dead and alive. For ever and ever. I cannot live. I cannot die. I am –

– dead. In the dark. I am –

– alive. In the light. I am –

– …I am… –

– …I am.

Bibliography

Several of the original novels and articles were accessed either via the Bodleian Library's Special collections or directly from the Suzanet Research Library at the Charles Dickens Museum in London. In addition, several of the newspaper articles are preserved thanks to those early Dickensians who had the foresight to save and donate them to the Charles Dickens Museum – this includes B. W. Matz, Howard Duffield and Henry J. Glaisher. Where possible, page numbers have been provided for newspaper references, but in the case of those preserved as clippings this has not always been achievable. The original instalments of *Drood* as they first appeared can be found online in full at *The Drood Inquiry* (www.droodinquiry.com), while stories and articles from *All The Year Round* can be accessed freely at *Dickens Journals Online* (www.djo.org.uk).

Anon., 'Review of *The Mystery of Edwin Drood*', *The Athenaeum*, 2 April 1870, pp. 443-444

Anon., *The Times*, 2 April 1870, p. 4

Anon., 'The Magazines', *Illustrated London News,* 9 April 1870, p. 383

Anon., 'The Mystery of Rude Dedwin', *Judy*, 13 April 1870, p. 240

Anon., *Daily Telegraph*, 10 June 1870

Anon., *Pall Mall Gazette*, 10 June 1870

Anon., 'The Magazines', *Illustrated London News,* 11 June 1870, p. 618

Anon., *The Times,* 15 June 1870

Anon., 'The Late Charles Dickens', *The Period*, 25 June 1870, p. 84

Anon., 'The Magazines', *Illustrated London News,* 9 July 1870, p. 46

Anon., 'Edwin Drood', *Every Saturday: A Journal of Choice Reading*, 17 September 1870, p. 594

Anon., *The Saturday Review*, 1870, repr. in Collins, *Dickens: The Critical Heritage*, pp. 543-5

Anon., *Cornhill Magazine,* March 1884, pp. 308-317

Anon., 'The Very Latest: Descriptions of New Films that are ready for delivery to-day', *The Bioscope*, 11 February 1909, p. 13

Anon., 'The Mystery of Edwin Drood', *Supplement to the Bioscope*, 23 May 1912, p. xiv

Anon., 'The Trial of John Jasper for the Murder of Edwin Drood', *The Dickensian*, Vol 10, No. 1, January 1914, p. 10

Anon., 'Boom in Edwin Drood', *Daily Sketch*, 6 January 1914

Anon., 'A Literary Problem', *Midland Evening News,* 7 January 1914

Anon., 'John Jasper's Trial: Mystery of Edwin Drood Solved, "Manslaughter"', *Daily Star*, 8 January 1914

Anon., 'Mystery of Edwin Drood', *Dundee Advertiser*, 8 January 1914

Anon., 'Drood Mystery', *The Independent*, 9 January 1914

Anon., 'The Drood Verdict: How hard some people are to please; Mr Shaw's Comment', *Pall Mall Gazette*, 9 January 1914

Anon., 'Solving "Edwin Drood" Case', *The New York Dramatic Mirror,* 21 October 1914, p. 30

Anon., 'The Mystery of Edwin Drood', *The Bioscope*, 2 September 1915, p. 1009

Allen, Walter, *The English Novel: A Short Critical History* (London: Phoenix House, 1954)

Andrews, Malcolm, *Charles Dickens and His Performing Selves* (Oxford: OUP, 2007)

Aylmer, Felix, 'The Drood Case Re-opened', *The Dickensian*, Vol. 20, No. 4, October 1924, pp. 192-195

———, 'The Drood Case Re-opened. II. The Family Skeleton', *The Dickensian*, Vol. 21, No. 4, October 1925, pp. 205-209

———, *Dickens Incognito* (London: Rupert Hart-Davis, 1959)

———, *The Drood Case* (London: Rupert Hart-Davis, 1964

Bilham, D. W., 'Edwin Drood – to resolve a mystery?', *Dickensian*, Vol. 62, September 1966, pp. 181-183

BIBLIOGRAPHY

Blakeney, T. S., 'Problems of Edwin Drood', *Dickensian* Vol. 51, September 1955, pp. 182-185

Bleifuss, William W., 'A Re-examination of *Edwin Drood*', *Dickensian*, Vol. 50, June 1954, pp. 110-115

Boyd, Aubrey, 'A New Angle on the Drood Mystery', *Washington University Studies*, Vol. 9, Humanistic Studies, No. 1, 1922, pp. 35-85

Brend, Gavin, 'Response to "A Re-examination of *Edwin Drood*"', *The Dickensian*, Vol. 51, March 1955, pp. 87-88

———, '*Edwin Drood* and the Four Witnesses', *The Dickensian*, Vol. 52, Winter 1955, pp. 20-24

Bud, Rosa, *Edwin Drood Zombie*, www.fanfiction.net <https://www.fanfiction.net/s/7014786/1/Edwin-Drood-Zombie>, published 23 May 2011

Bulwer-Lytton, Edward, *A Strange* Story, *All The Year Round*, Vols. 5-6, Nos. 120-150, 10 August 1861–8 March 1862

Bulwer-Lytton, Robert 'The Disappearance of John Ackland', *All The Year Round*, Vol. 2 Nos. 42-46, 18 September-16 October 1869

Carter, Claire, 'A very modern ending for Dickens' final unfinished work as academics turn to crowd-sourcing to complete The Mystery of Edwin Drood': *Daily Mail* <http://www.dailymail.co.uk/news/article-2897308/A-modern-ending-Dickens-final-unfinished-work-academics-turn-crowd-sourcing-complete-Mystery-Edwin-Drood.html>, published online 5 January 2015

Chesterton, G. K., and F. G. Kitton, *Charles Dickens* (London: Hodder and Stoughton, 1903)

Chesterton, G. K., 'A Book of the Day. Mr Lang Detecting Again', *The Daily News*, 2 November 1905

———, *Charles Dickens* (London: Methuen, 1906)

Clark, William Archer, "Edwin Drood again" *Dickensian*, Vol. 33, Summer 1937, pp. 191-195

Collins, Philip, *Dickens and Crime*, 2nd Edn (London: Macmillan, 1965)

——— (ed.), *Charles Dickens: The Critical Heritage* (London: Routledge, 1971)

——— (ed.), Charles Dickens, *Sikes and Nancy and other public readings* (Oxford: OUP, 1983)

Collins, Wilkie, 'Wilkie Collins about Charles Dickens', *Pall Mall Gazette*, 20 January 1890, repr. Collins, *Dickens: The Critical Heritage*, pp. 587-8

Connor, Steven (ed), Charles Dickens, *The Mystery of Edwin Drood* (London: J. M. Dent, 1996)

Corfield, Wilmot, 'Edwin Drood', *Notes and Queries*, Vol. 7, 10 May 1913, pp. 362-3

Cox, Don Richard, *The Mystery of Edwin Drood: An Annotated Bibliography* (New York: AMS, 1998)

Dak, 'That Mystery', *The Dickensian*, Vol. 8, No. 12, December 1912, pp. 326-7

Daleski, H. M., *Dickens and the Art of Analogy* (London: Faber and Faber, 1970)

Dickens, Henry, Letter to G. F. Gadd, 2 February 1904

Dolby, George, *Charles Dickens as I knew Him,* 1885 (London: Everett & Co, 1912)

Donaghue, Denis, 'The English Dickens and *Dombey and Son*', in Ada Nisbet and Blake Nevius (eds.), *Dickens Centennial Essays* (Berkeley, Los Angeles, London: University of California Press, 1971), pp. 1-21

Dubberke, Ray, *Dickens, Drood and The Detectives* (New York: Vantage Press, 1992)

———, 'Edwin Drood by the Numbers', *The Dickensian*, Vol. 100, Summer 2004, pp. 132-137

Duffield, Howard, 'John Jasper – Strangler', *The Bookman*, February 1930, 581-55

F., H. H.,, 'Bazzard v. Helena Landless', *The Academy,* 9 September 1905, p. 934

Fildes, Luke, Letter to *The Times Literary Supplement*, 3 November 1905, p. 373

Foosemittee, *Drood*, www.fanfiction.net, < https://www.fanfiction.net/s/6856184/1/Drood>, published 30 March 2011

Ford, George H., *Dickens and His Readers: Aspects of Novel-Criticism since 1836* (1955) (New York: Norton, 1965)

Forster, John, *The Life of Charles Dickens: Volume Three* (London: Chapman and Hall, 1874)

Forsyte, Charles, *The Decoding of Edwin Drood: Fact-fict-ion solution to a classic problem* (London: Victor Gollancz Ltd, 1980)

Fruttero, Carlo, and Franco Lucentini, *The D Case,* trans. Gregory Dowling (San Diego, New York, London: Harcourt Brace, 1992)

Furneaux, Holly, *Queer Dickens: Erotics, Families, Masculinites* (Oxford: OUP, 2009)

Gadd, George, 'The History of a Mystery: A review of the solutions to Edwin Drood' *The Dickensian,* Vol. 1, September-December 1905

Gardiner, Gordon, *At the House of Dree* (Boston and New York: Houghton Mifflin, 1928)

Garfield, Leon, *The Mystery of Edwin Drood* by Charles Dickens, concluded by Leon Garfield (London: Andre Deutsch, 1980)

Gissing, George, *Charles Dickens: A Critical Study* (London: Gresham, 1902)

Guerrard, Albert, *The Triumph of the Novel: Dickens, Dostoevsky, Faulkner* (New York: OUP, 1976)

Hardy, Barbara, *Dickens: The Later Novels* (London: Longman, Green & Co, 1968)

Harris, Edwin, *John Jasper's Gatehouse* (Rochester: Mackays Ltd, 1932)

Hoel, Camilla Ulleland, *The Completion of* Edwin Drood*: Endings and Authority in Finished and Unfinished Narratives,* PhD Thesis submitted to The University of Edinburgh, 2012

Holmes, Rupert, *The Mystery of Edwin Drood Performance Script*, 1985
———, 'The History of the Mystery', www.rupertholmes.com, <http://www.rupertholmes.com/theatre/essdrood.html>, date accessed 10 June 2017

Hopsbaum, Philip, *A Reader's Guide to Charles Dickens* (London: Thames and Hudson, 1972)

Hughes, Gwyneth, 'Afterword', in Charles Dickens, *The Mystery of Edwin Drood* (London: BBC Books, 2012), pp. 275-9

Hurst, Greg, 'Readers to decide whodunit in Dickens "murder" mystery', *The Times*, 5 January 2015, p. 3

Hutton, Richard Holt, Review of 'The Mystery of Edwin Drood', *The Spectator*, 1 October 1870, repr. in Collins, *Dickens: The Critical Heritage*, pp. 547-550

James, Thomas Power, *The Mystery of Edwin Drood Complete* (Bratttleboro: T. P. James, 1874)

Johnson, Edgar, *Charles Dickens: His Tragedy and Triumph*, Two Volumes (London: Victor Gollancz, 1953)

Jolly, Emily, *An Experience*, *All The Year Round*, Vol. 2, Nos. 37 & 38, 14-21 August 1869

Joseph, Gerhard, 'Who Cares Who Killed Edwin Drood? Or, On the Whole, I'd Rather Be in Philadelphia', *Nineteenth-Century Literature*, Vol. 51, No. 2, September 1996, pp. 161-175

Kavanagh, Mary, *A New Solution of the Mystery of Edwin Drood* (London: John Long, 1919)

Kerr, Orpheus C., *The Cloven Foot, Being an Adaptation of the English Novel "The Mystery of Edwin Drood" by Charles Dickens to American Scenes, Characters, Customs and Nomenclature* (New York: Carleton, 1870)

Lang, Andrew, 'At the Sign of the Ship', *Longman's Magazine*, Vol. 46, September 1905, pp. 473-480

———, 'About Edwin Drood: A Dialogue', *The Cambridge Review*, No. 32, 2 March 1911, pp. 323-25

———, *The Puzzle of Dickens's Last Plot* (London: Chapman and Hall, 1905)

Leaver, H. R., *The Mystery of John Jasper* (Edmonton: Self-published, 1925)

Levett, J., Letter to B W Matz, 6 January 1914, held in the Charles Dickens Museum, London

Ley, J. W. T. (ed.), *The Trial of John Jasper*, (London: Chapman & Hall, 1914)

Lindsay, Jack, *Charles Dickens: A Biographical and Critical Study* (London: Andrew Dakers, 1950)

Longley, Katherine, *A Whispering Reed: Dickens's last novel, its making and purpose* (unpublished manuscript held in Senate House Library, MS1003/8/1)

Lonoff, Sue, 'Charles Dickens and Wilkie Collins', *Nineteenth-Century Fiction*, Vol. 35, No. 2, September 1980, pp. 150-170

Lord, Christopher, *The Edwin Drood Murders* (Portland: Harrison Thurman Books, 2013)

Love, Laurie, *Mr Jasper's Cadenza*, www.fanfiction.net <https://www.fanfiction.net/s/7743057/1/Mr-Jasper-s-Cadenza>, published 15 January-19 February 2012

Lucas, John, *The Melancholy Man: A Study of Dickens's Novels* (London: Methuen, 1970)

Madden, David, *The Mystery of Edwin Drood* (Milton Keynes: Unthank Books, 2011)

Makeham, John, Letter to *Daily News,* 17 June 1870

Matchett, Willoughby, and W. A. Fraser, Francis Studley, G. Forest, J. C. L. Clark, George F. Gadd, J. W. Wilson, 'Last Words on the Drood Mystery', *The Dickensian,* Vol. 4, No. 4, April 1908

Matz, B. W., Review of Walter's *Clues, The Dickensian*, Vol. 1, No. 7, July 1905, p. 184

———, 'Solving the "Mystery of Edwin Drood"', *The Dickensian*, Vol 1, No. 7, July 1905, pp. 184-185

———, 'The Mystery of Edwin Drood: A Bibliography', *The Dickensian*, Vol. 7, No. 5, May 1911, pp. 130-133

McKnight, Natalie, '"A little humouring of Pussy's points!"; or Sex – the *Real* Unsolved Mystery of *Edwin Drood*', *Dickens Quarterly*, Vol. 30, No. 1, March 2013, pp. 55-63

Miller, J. Hillis, *Charles Dickens: The World of his novels* (Cambridge, Massachusetts: Harvard University Press, 1965)

Mitchell, Charles, '*The Mystery of Edwin Drood*: The Interior and Exterior of Self'. *ELH*, Vol. 33, No. 2, June 1966, pp. 228-246

Monod, Sylvère, *Dickens the Novelist*, trans. Edward Wagenknecht (Norman, Oklahoma: University of Oklahoma Press, 1968)

Morford, Henry, *John Jasper's Secret, Being a Narrative of Certain Events Following and Explaining The Mystery of Edwin Drood* (London: Wyman and Sons, 1872)

Morgan, William de, Letter to B W Matz, 9 January 1914, held in the Charles Dickens Museum, London

Murfin, Ross, 'The Art of Representation: Collins' *The Moonstone* and Dickens' Example', *ELH*, Vol. 49, No. 3, Autumn 1982, pp. 653-672

Nayder, Lillian, *Unequal Partners: Charles Dickens, WIlkie Collins and Victorian Authorship* (Ithaca and London: Cornell University Press, 2010)

Nicoll, William Robertson, *The Problem of Edwin Drood: A Study in the Methods of Dickens*, 2nd Edn (London: Hodder and Stoughton, 1913)

O'Kane Mara, Miriam, 'Sucking the Empire Dry: Colonial Critique in *The Mystery of Edwin Drood*', *Dickens Studies Annual,* Vol. 32, 2002, pp. 233-246

Orwell, George, 'Charles Dickens', in *Inside the Whale and other essays* (London: Victor Gollancz, 1940), pp. 9-88

Paroissien, David (ed.), Charles Dickens, *The Mystery of Edwin Drood* (London: Penguin, 2002)

Partlow, Robert B. (ed.), *Dickens the Craftsman: Strategies of Presentation* (Carbondale and Edwardsville: Southern Illinois University Press, 1970)

Paulits, John, *The Mystery of Charles Dickens* (London: MX Publishing, 2012)

Pearl, Matthew *The Last Dickens* (London: Vintage, 2010)

Peruginni, Kate, *Pall Mall Magazine*, June 1906, reprinted in Nicol, *The Problem of 'Edwin Drood'*, pp. 28-43

Pope-Hennessy, Una, *Charles Dickens* (London: Chatto & Windus, 1945)

Praz, Mario, *The Hero in Eclipse in Victorian Fiction*, trans. Angus Davidson (Oxford: OUP, 1956)

Proctor, Richard, *Watched by the Dead: A loving study of Charles Dickens's half told tale* (London: W. H. Allen & Co., 1887)

———— (as Thomas Foster), 'Dickens's Story Left Half Told', *Knowledge*, Vol. 5, 27 June 1884, pp. 478-479

———— (as Thomas Foster), 'Dickens's Story Left Half Told. A Quasi-Scientific Inquiry into *The Mystery of Edwin Drood*', *Knowledge*, Vol. 6, 12 September 1884, pp. 209-10; 19 September 1884, pp. 235-6; 26 September 1884, pp. 257-8; 3 October 1884, pp. 276-7; 10 October 1884, pp. 297-8; 17 October 1884, pp. 313-4; 24 October 1884, pp. 340-2; 31 October 1884, pp. 356-8; 7 November 1884, pp. 386-7; 14 November 1884, pp. 400-01

Reece, Benny R., *The Mystery of Edwin Drood Solved* (New York: Vantage Press, 1989)

Reuter, Florizel Von, *In Search of Truth: Psychical Experiences of a Musician* (London: Simpkin Marshall Ltd and The Psychic Press, 1928)

Rose, Roman De La *Before the Shadow Falls*, www.fanfiction.net <https://www.fanfiction.net/s/8133983/1/Before-the-Shadow-Falls>, published 20 May 2012

————, *The Blossoming of the Bud*, www.fanfiction.net <https://www.fanfiction.net/s/7755271/1/The-Blossoming-of-the-Bud>, published 19 January – 11 March 2012

Rowland, Peter, *The Disappearance of Edwin Drood* (London: Constable, 1991)

S., R., letter to the editor, *Daily News*, 14 June 1870

Saunders, Montagu, *The Mystery in the Drood Family* (Cambridge: CUP, 1914)

Schiller, Laura, *Absolutely No Shame,* www.fanfiction.net <https://www.fanfiction.net/s/8796185/1/Absolutely-No-Shame>, published 15 December 2012

Sedgwick, Eve, 'Up the Postern Stair: *Edwin Drood* and the Homophobia of Empire', *Between Men: English Literature and Male Homosocial Desire* (New York: Columbia University Press, 1985), pp. 180-200

Seltzer, Beth, *Not Just the Facts: Victorian Detective Fiction's Critique of Information,* PhD Thesis submitted to Temple University, 2015

Sheldon, Georgie, *The Welfleet Mystery* (London: James Henderson and Sons, 1885)

Simcox, Edith (writing as H Lawreny), *The Academy*, 22 October 1870, repr. Collins, *Dickens: The Critical Heritage*, pp. 545-7

Simmons, Dan, *Drood* (London: Quercus, 2009)

Slater, Michael (ed.), *Dickens 1970* (London: Chapman and Hall, 1970)

————, *The Great Charles Dickens Scandal* (New Haven and London: Yale University Press, 2014)

Smith, Harry B., 'Sherlock Holmes Solves the Mystery of Edwin Drood', *Munsey's Magazine* Vol. 83, No. 3, December 1924, pp. 385-400

Squire, Lyn, *The Last Chapter* (Middletown, DE: NP, 2014)

Storey, Graham (ed.), *The Letters of Charles Dickens*, Volume Twelve 1868-1870 (Oxford: Clarendon Press, 2002)

Symons, Julian, *Charles Dickens* (London: Arthur Baker, 1951)

T., J., 'Boz', *The Englishwoman's Domestic Magazine*, 1 July 1870

Taylor, D. J., 'Who did it – and why?', *Guardian*, 21 March 2009

Thacker, John, *Antichrist in the Cathedral* (London: Vision Press, 1990)

Thurley, Geoffrey, *The Dickens Myth: Its Genesis and Structure* (London: Routledge & Kegan Paul, 1976)

Tomlin, E. W. F., 'Dickens's Reputation: a Reassessment', in E. W. F. Tomlin (ed.), *Charles Dickens 1812-1870: A Centennary Volume* (London: Weidenfeld and Nicolson, 1970), pp. 237-263

Vase, Gillian, *A Great Mystery Solved: A Sequel to The Mystery of Edwin Drood*, 3 Vols. (London: Remington and Co., 1878)

Walters, John Cuming, *Clues to Dickens's "Mystery of Edwin Drood"* (London: Chapman & Hall, 1905)

————, *The Complete Mystery of Edwin Drood: The history, continuation, and solution 1870-1912* (Boston: De Estes and Co, 1913)

Waugh, Arthur, *A Hundred Years of Publishing. Being a History of Chapman and Hall, Ltd* (London: Chapman and Hall, 1930)

Wilson, Angus, *The World of Charles Dicken* (London: Penguin, 1970)

Wilson, Edmund, 'Dickens: The Two Scrooges', *The Wound and the Bow: Seven Studies in Literature* (Cambridge: Riverside Press, 1941), pp. 1-104

Wing, George, '*Edwin Drood* and *Desperate Remedies*: Prototypes of Detective Fiction in 1870', *Studies in English Literature, 1500-1900*, Vol. 13, No. 4 (Autumn 1973), pp. 677-687

Yohalem, Jeffrey (head writer), 'Haunted House', *Assassin's Creed: Syndicate* (Ubisoft, 2015)

Notes

1. Malcolm Andrews, *Charles Dickens and His Performing Selves* (Oxford: OUP, 2007), p. 49.
2. Dickens talking to Charles Kent, cited in Philip Collins (ed.), Charles Dickens, *Sikes and Nancy and other public readings* (Oxford: OUP, 1983), p. 231.
3. Dickens cited in George Dolby, *Charles Dickens as I knew him,* 1885 (London: Everett & Co, 1912), pp. 448-449.
4. Dickens' contract with Chapman and Hall, reprinted in Arthur Waugh, *A Hundred Years of Publishing. Being a History of Chapman and Hall, Ltd* (London: Chapman and Hall, 1930), pp. 132-133.
5. Charles Dickens, Letter to John Forster, 6 August 1869, repr. in Graham Storey (ed.), *The Letters of Charles Dickens*, Volume Twelve 1868-1870 (Oxford: Clarendon Press, 2002).
6. Emily Jolly, *An Experience* (Part Two), *All The Year Round*, Vol. 2, No. 38, 21 August 1869, pp 280-288 (p. 281).
7. Robert Bulwer-Lytton, 'The Disappearance of John Ackland', *All The Year Round*, Vol. 2 Nos. 42-46, 18 September-16 October 1869.
8. Anon., *The Period*, 25 June 1870, p. 84.
9. J. T., 'Boz', *The Englishwoman's Domestic Magazine*, 1 July 1870.
10. Anon., *The Times,* 15 June 1870.
11. John Makeham. Letter to *Daily News,* 17 June 1870.
12. Anon,. 'What the Dickens next?', *John Bull,* 9 April 1870, p. 53.
13. Anon., 'The Magazines', *Illustrated London News,* 9 April 1870, p. 383.
14. Anon., *The Times,* 2 April 1870, p. 4.
15. ibid.
16. Anon., *The Athenaeum,* 2 April 1870, pp 443-444 (p. 443).
17. Anon., 'The Magazines', *Illustrated London News,* 9 April 1870, p. 383; *The Times,* 2 April 1870, p. 4.
18. Anon., 'The Magazines', *Illustrated London News,* 11 June 1870, p. 618.

19. R.S, letter to the editor, *Daily News*, 14 June 1870.
20. 'Edwin Drood', *Every Saturday: A Journal of Choice Reading*, 17 September 1870, p. 594.
21. 'The Magazines', *Illustrated London News,* 9 July 1870, p. 46.
22. *Pall Mall Gazette*, 10 June 1870.
23. *Daily Telegraph*, 10 June 1870.
24. Wilkie Collins, 'Wilkie Collins about Charles Dickens', *Pall Mall Gazette*, 20 January 1890, repr. Philip Collins (ed.), *Charles Dickens: The Critical Heritage* (London: Routledge, 1971), pp. 587-588 (p. 588).
25. 'Edwin Drood', *Every Saturday: A Journal of Choice Reading*, 17 September 1870, p. 594.
26. Richard Holt Hutton, Review of *'The Mystery of Edwin Drood',* The *Spectator,* 1 October 1870, repr. Collins, *Dickens: The Critical Heritage*, pp. 547-550 (p. 548).
27. Orpheus C. Kerr, *The Cloven Foot, Being an Adaptation of the English Novel "The Mystery of Edwin Drood" by Charles Dickens to American Scenes, Characters, Customs and Nomenclature* (New York: Carleton, 1870), pp. 14-15.
28. Kerr, p. 41.
29. 'The Mystery of Rude Dedwin', *Judy*, 13 April 1870, p. 240.
30. ibid.
31. ibid.
32. J. C. Walters, *The Complete Mystery of Edwin Drood: The history, continuation, and solution 1870-1912* (Boston: De Estes and Co, 1913), p. 213.
33. Kerr, 7.
34. Kerr, 7.
35. Kerr, 8.
36. Kerr, 9.
37. In 1905 George Gadd noted of the early completions that 'It may, or may not, be a tribute to our national modesty that none of these hasty attempts to assume the cloak of the Prophet is of British origin, but it is not the less certain that, for a number of years, America virtually held a monopoly in continuations of *Edwin Drood.*' George F. Gadd, 'The History of a Mystery: A review of the solutions to Edwin Drood', *The Dickensian,* Vol 1, No. 9 (September 1905), pp. 240-243 (p. 242).
38. Henry Morford, *John Jasper's Secret, Being a Narrative of Certain Events Following and Explaining The Mystery of Edwin Drood* (London: Wyman and Sons, 1872), p. 54.
39. Morford, pp. 63-4.

NOTES

40. Thomas Power James, *The Mystery of Edwin Drood Complete* (Bratttleboro: T. P. James, 1874), p. vii.

41. James, p. vii.

42. James, pp. viii-ix.

43. James, p. 488

44. James, p. ix.

45. James, p. x.

46. Aubrey Boyd, 'A New Angle on the Drood Mystery', *Washington University Studies*, Vol. 9, Humanistic Studies, No. 1, 1922, pp. 35-85 (p. 36).

47. John Forster, *The Life of Charles Dickens: Volume Three* (London: Chapman and Hall, 1874), pp. 425-6.

48. Gillian Vase, *A Great Mystery Solved: A Sequel to The Mystery of Edwin Drood*, 3 Vols. (London: Remington and Co., 1878), Vol. 1, preface.

49. Vase, Vol. 1, preface.

50. Vase, Vol. 1, preface.

51. Vase, Vol. 2, p. 292.

52. Vase, Vol. 2, pp. 294-5.

53. William Robertson Nicoll, *The Problem of Edwin Drood: A Study in the Methods of Dickens*, 2nd Edn (London: Hodder and Stoughton, 1913), p. xi.

54. Georgie Sheldon, *The Welfleet Mystery* (London: James Henderson and Sons, 1885), Preface.

55. Sheldon, p. 27.

56. Boyd, p. 36.

57. John Cuming Walters, *Clues to Dickens's "Mystery of Edwin Drood"* (London: Chapman & Hall, 1905), p. 21.

58. Thomas Foster, 'The Mystery of Edwin Drood', *Belgravia: A London Magazine,* Vol. XXXV, No. 140, June 1878 453-473 (p. 473).

59. Anon., *Cornhill Magazine,* March 1884, pp. 308-317 (p. 308).

60. Anon., *The Saturday Review*, 1870, repr. Collins, *Dickens: The Critical Heritage*, pp. 543-5 (p. 545); Edith Simcox (writing as H Lawreny), *The Academy*, 22 October 1870, repr. Collins, *Dickens: The Critical Heritage*, pp. 545-7 (p. 546).

61. First hit to Thomas Foster, 'Dickens's Story Left Half Told', *Knowledge*, 5, 27 June 1884, pp. 478-479. Response by H. E., 'Dickens's Story Left Half Told', *Knowledge*, 6, 25 July, 1884, p. 7. Prolonged response by Thomas Foster, 'Dickens's Story Left Half Told. A Quasi-Scientific Inquiry into *The Mystery of Edwin Drood*', *Knowledge*, Vol. 6, 12 September 1884, pp. 209-10; 19 September 1884, pp. 235-6; 26 September 1884,

pp. 257-8; 3 October 1884, pp. 276-7; 10 October 1884, pp. 297-8; 17 October 1884, pp. 313-4; 24 October 1884, pp. 340-2; 31 October 1884, pp. 356-8; 7 November 1884, pp. 386-7; 14 November 1884, pp. 400-01. Final (exhausted) response by H. E., 'Dickens's Story Left Half Told', *Knowledge*, 6, 28 November 1884, pp. 439-40.

62. Walters, *The Complete Mystery of Edwin Drood*, p. xxiv.

63. B. W. Matz, 'Solving the "Mystery of Edwin Drood", *The Dickensian*, Vol 1, No. 7, July 1905, pp. 184-185 (p. 184); Montagu Sanders, *The Mystery in the Drood Family* (Cambridge: CUP, 1914), p. vii.

64. Richard Proctor, *Watched by the Dead: A loving study of Charles Dickens's half told tale* (London: W. H. Allen & Co., 1887), pp.136-7.

65. Proctor, p. iv.

66. Walters, *Clues,* p. 29.

67. Walters, *Clues,* p. 72.

68. Walters, *Clues,* p.113.

69. Walters, *Clues,* Foreword.

70. B.W. Matz, Review of Walter's *Clues, The Dickensian*, Vol. 1, No. 7, July 1905, p. 184.

71. Andrew Lang, *The Puzzle of Dickens's Last Plot* (London: Chapman and Hall, 1905).

72. H. H. F., 'Bazzard v. Helena Landless', *The Academy,* 9 September 1905, p. 934.

73. G. K. Chesterton, 'A Book of the Day. Mr Lang Detecting Again', *The Daily News*, 2 November 1905.

74. Andrew Lang, 'At the Sign of the Ship', *Longman's Magazine*, Vol. 46, September 1905, pp. 473-480; 'About Edwin Drood: A Dialogue', *The Cambridge Review*, No. 32, 2 March 1911, pp. 323-25.

75. M. R. James, 'The Edwin Drood Syndicate', *The Cambridge Review,* 27, (30 November 1905), pp. 123-5; (7 December 1905), pp. 142-44 (p. 144).

76. Lang, 'At the Sign of the Ship', p. 474; p. 478.

77. Don Richard Cox's annotated bibliography of *The Mystery of Edwin Drood* notes seventeen separate instances in which Holmes and *Drood* crossed paths. See Don Richard Cox, *The Mystery of Edwin Drood: An Annotated Bibliography* (New York: AMS, 1998), p. 651.

78. G. K. Chesterton and F. G. Kitton, *Charles Dickens* (London: Hodder and Stoughton, 1903), p. 3.

79. E. W. F. Tomlin, 'Dickens's Reputation: a Reassessment', in E. W. F. Tomlin (ed.), *Charles Dickens 1812-1870: A Centenary Volume* (London: Weidenfeld and Nicolson, 1970), pp. 237-263 (p. 259).

80. G. K. Chesterton, *Charles Dickens* (London: Methuen, 1906), p. 238.

81. Chesterton, *Charles Dickens*, p. 239.

82. George Gissing, *Charles Dickens: A Critical Study* (London: Gresham, 1902), p. 68.
83. Gissing, pp. 68-9.
84. Gadd, 'The History of a Mystery'.
85. Walters, *Clues,* pp.15-16.
86. Luke Fildes, Letter to *The Times Literary Supplement*, 3 November 1905, p. 373.
87. Fildes.
88. Kate Peruginni, *Pall Mall Magazine*, June 1906, reprinted in W Robertson Nicol, *The Problem of 'Edwin Drood': A Study in the Methods of Dickens* (London, New York, Toronto: Hodder and Stoughton, 1912), pp. 28-43 (p. 34).
89. Henry Dickens, Letter to G. F. Gadd, 2 February 1904.
90. Dak, 'That Mystery', *The Dickensian*, Vol. 8, No. 12, December 1912, pp.326-7.
91. The same issue in which Dak's poem appears also tells us that Augustus Ovey gave a lecture on 5 November 1912 at Clifford's inn, 'Round about Rochester with Charles Dickens, his homes, his haunts, his characters', in which '*Pickwick, Great Expectations,* and *Edwin Drood*, of course, afforded most of the material upon which the Lecture and selection of pictures was based.' Anon., 'The Dickens Fellowship: London' *The Dickensian*, Vol. 8, No. 12, December 1912, p. 332.
92. B. W. Matz, 'The Mystery of Edwin Drood: A Bibliography', *The Dickensian*, Vol. 7, No. 5, May 1911, pp. 130-133.
93. Walters, *The Complete Mystery of Edwin Drood*, p. 213.
94. Walters, *The Complete Mystery of Edwin Drood*, p. 213.
95. Wilmot Corfield, 'Edwin Drood', *Notes and Queries*, Vol. 7, 10 May 1913, pp. 362-3.
96. Anon., 'The Very Latest: Descriptions of New Films that are ready for delivery to-day', *The Bioscope*, 11 February 1909, p. 13.
97. Anon., 'The Mystery of Edwin Drood', *Supplement to the Bioscope*, 23 May 1912, p. xiv.
98. ibid., p. xiv.
99. Anon., 'Solving "Edwin Drood" Case', *The New York Dramatic Mirror,* 21 October 1914, p. 30.
100. ibid., p. 30.
101. Anon., 'The Mystery of Edwin Drood', *The Bioscope*, 2 September 1915, p. 1009.
102. ibid., p. 1009.
103. ibid. p. 1009.
104. Anon., 'Solving "Edwin Drood" Case', *The New York Dramatic Mirror,* 21 October 1914, p. 30.

105. Anon., 'The Mystery of Edwin Drood', *The Bioscope*, 2 September 1915, p. 1009.

106. Anon., 'Boom in Edwin Drood', *Daily Sketch*, 6 January 1914.

107. Anon., 'The Trial of John Jasper for the Murder of Edwin Drood', *The Dickensian*, Vol 10, No. 1, January 1914, p. 10.

108. 'Who Murdered Edwin Drood?' Uncredited press clipping from 1914, preserved in the Charles Dickens Museum, London.

109. George Bernard Shaw, letter to B. W. Matz, 28 November 1913.

110. 'A Literary Problem', *Midland Evening News,* 7 January 1914.

111. J. Levett, letter to B. W. Matz, 6 January 1914.

112. Anon., 'Mystery of Edwin Drood', *Dundee Advertiser*, 8 January 1914.

113. Anon., 'John Jasper's Trial: Mystery of Edwin Drood Solved, "Manslaughter"', *Daily Star*, 8 January 1914.

114. William de Morgan, Letter to B. W. Matz, 9 January 1914.

115. J. W. T. Ley (ed.), *The Trial of John Jasper*, (London: Chapman & Hall, 1914), p. 79.

116. 'The Drood Verdict: How hard some people are to please; Mr Shaw's Comment', *Pall Mall Gazette*, 9 January 1914

117. ibid.

118. ibid.

119. Anon., 'Drood Mystery', *The Independent*, 9 January 1914.

120. Further trials have been held in Philadelphia, 29 April 1914; Toronto, 10 March 1921; Montreal, 28th April 1931.

121. Mary Kavanagh, *A New Solution of the Mystery of Edwin Drood* (London: John Long, 1919), p. 7.

122. Kavanagh, p. 7.

123. Kavanagh, pp. 11-12.

124. Kavanagh, p. 28.

125. Kavanagh, p. 31.

126. Kavanagh, pp. 31-2.

127. Kavanagh, p. 7.

128. Saunders, *The Mystery in the Drood Family*, p. 159.

129. Boyd, 49.

130. Boyd, 83-84.

131. Boyd, 37.

132. Boyd, 35, fn.

133. Felix Aylmer, 'The Drood Case Re-opened', *The Dickensian* Vol. 20, No. 4, October 1924, pp. 192-195 (p. 192).

134. Aylmer, 'The Drood Case Re-opened', p. 192; Felix Aylmer, 'The Drood Case Re-opened. II. The Family Skeleton', *The Dickensian*, Vol. 21, No. 4, October 1925, pp. 205-209 (p. 207).

135. Katherine Kelly "John Jasper" *Dickensian* Vol. 19, No. 1, January 1923, pp. 34-36 (p. 36).

136. Katherine Kelly, Response to 'The Drood case Re-opened': *The Dickensian,* Vol. 21, No. 1, January 1925, pp. 20-21 (p. 20).

137. Kelly, Response to 'The Drood case Re-opened', p. 21.

138. Harry B. Smith, 'Sherlock Holmes Solves the Mystery of Edwin Drood', *Munsey's Magazine* Vol. 83, No. 3, December 1924, pp. 385-400 (p. 385).

139. Arthur Conan Doyle, cited in Florizel Von Reuter, *In Search of Truth: Psychical Experiences of a Musician* (London: Simpkin Marshall Ltd and The Psychic Press, 1928), p. 315.

140. H. R. Leaver, *The Mystery of John Jasper* (Edmonton: Self-published, 1925), p.5.

141. Leaver, p. 5.

142. Leaver, p. 13.

143. Leaver, p. 59.

144. Boyd, 71.

145. Una Pope-Hennessy, *Charles Dickens* (London: Chatto & Windus, 1945), p. 478

146. Mario Praz, *The Hero in Eclipse in Victorian Fiction*, trans. Angus Davidson (Oxford: OUP, 1956), p. 139.

147. Lillian Nayder, *Unequal Partners: Charles Dickens, WIlkie Collins and Victorian Authorship* (Ithaca and London: Cornell University Press, 2010), p. 184.

148. Howard Duffield, 'John Jasper – Strangler', *The Bookman*, February 1930, 581-55 (p. 588).

149. Edward Bulwer-Lytton, *A Strange* Story, originally published in 31 parts in *All The Year Round,* Vols. 5-6, Nos. 120-150, 10 August 1861–8 March 1862 (part 16, Vol. 6, No. 23, November 1861, Ch. 31, p. 199).

150. Cox, p. viii.

151. Gordon Gardiner, *At the House of Dree* (Boston and New York: Houghton Mifflin, 1928), p. 124. Marginalia by Howard Duffield from his personal copy held at the Charles Dickens Museum, London.

152. Edwin Harris, *John Jasper's Gatehouse* (Rochester, Mackays Ltd,1932).

153. Willoughby Matchett, W. A. Fraser, Francis Studley, G. Forest, J. C. L. Clark, George F. Gadd, J. W. Wilson, 'Last Words on the Drood Mystery', *The Dickensian,* Vol. 4, No. 4, April 1908, pp. 98-104; William Archer Clark "Edwin Drood again" *Dickensian*, Vol. 33, Summer 1937, pp. 191-195.

154. Boyd, 36-7.

155. George H. Ford, *Dickens and His Readers: Aspects of Novel-Criticism since 1836* (1955) (New York: Norton, 1965), p. 175.

156. Ford, p. 175.

157. See Michael Slater, *The Great Dickens Scandal* (New Haven and London: Yale, 2012) for further details on how the reports gathered in number at this time.

158. Ford, p. 167.

159. Philip Collins, *Dickens and Crime*, 2nd Edn (London: Macmillan, 1965), p. 310.

160. Denis Donaghue, 'The English Dickens and *Dombey and Son*', in Ada Nisbet and Blake Nevius (eds.), *Dickens Centennial Essays* (Berkeley, Los Angeles, London: University of California Press, 1971), pp. 1-21 (p. 1).

161. Edmund Wilson, 'Dickens: The Two Scrooges', *The Wound and the Bow: Seven Studies in Literature* (Cambridge: Riverside Press, 1941), pp. 1-104, p. 1.

162. Wilson, p. 2.

163. Wilson, p. 2.

164. Wilson, p. 2; p. 85.

165. Wilson, p. 93.

166. Wilson, p. 85.

167. Wilson, p. 84.

168. Wilson, p. 101.

169. Wilson, p. 102.

170. Wilson, p. 103.

171. Wilson, p. 99.

172. Wilson, p. 1.

173. Forster, p. 425.

174. Wilson, p. 64.

175. Wilson, p. 95.

176. Wilson, p. 64.

177. Wilson, p. 102.

178. Ford, p. 167.

179. Wilson, p. 100.

180. Jack Lindsay, *Charles Dickens: A Biographical and Critical Study* (London: Andrew Dakers, 1950) p. 5; Julian Symons, *Charles Dickens* (London: Arthur Baker, 1951) p. 81.

181. Lindsay, p. 397; Symons, p. 82.

182. Edgar Johnson, *Charles Dickens: His Tragedy and Triumph*, Two Volumes (London: Victor Gollancz, 1953), Vol. II, p. 1140.

183. Johnson, Vol. II, p. 1140.

184. Ford, p. 175

185. Richard M. Baker, *The Drood Murder Case: Five Studies in Dickenvs's Edwin Drood* (Berkeley and Los Angeles: University of California Press, 1951).

NOTES

186. Richard M. Baker, 'What Might Have Been: A Study for Droodians. Part One.' *Nineteenth Century Fiction*, Vol. 4, No. 4, March 1950, pp. 275-297 (p. 278).

187. William W. Bleifuss, 'A Re-examination of *Edwin Drood*', *Dickensian*, Vol. 50, June 1954, p. 110.

188. Bleifuss, p. 110.

189. Bleifus, p. 114.

190. Bleifus, p. 177.

191. Bleifus, p. 27.

192. T. S. Blakeney, 'Problems of Edwin Drood', *Dickensian,* Vol. 51, September 1955, pp. 182-185 (p. 182).

193. Blakeney, p. 184.

194. Gavin Brend, 'Response to "A Re-examination of *Edwin Drood*"', *The Dickensian*, Vol. 51, March 1955, pp. 87-88, p. 87.

195. Brend, 'Response to "A Re-examination of *Edwin Drood*"', p. 88.

196. Blakeney p. 183; Brend, 'Response to "A Re-examination of *Edwin Drood*"', p. 88.

197. Gavin Brend, '*Edwin Drood* and the Four Witnesses', *The Dickensian*, Vol. 52, Winter 1955, 20-24.

198. Brend, '*Edwin Drood* and the Four Witnesses', p. 24.

199. Brend, '*Edwin Drood* and the Four Witnesses', p. 24.

200. Brend, '*Edwin Drood* and the Four Witnesses', p. 23.

201. Brend, '*Edwin Drood* and the Four Witnesses', p. 21.

202. Brend, '*Edwin Drood* and the Four Witnesses', p. 22.

203. Brend, '*Edwin Drood* and the Four Witnesses', p. 20.

204. Brend, '*Edwin Drood* and the Four Witnesses', p. 21.

205. John Keir Cross, 'Was this the end of Edwin Drood?', *TV Times* Vol. 20, No. 256, 23 September 1960, pp. 6-7 (p. 7).

206. Cross, p. 7.

207. Cross, p. 7.

208. Anon., 'The Mystery of Edwin Drood', *TV Times* Vol. 20, No. 256, 23 September 1960, p. 32.

209. Donald Sinden, cited in John K. Newnham, 'A "Wolf" in Uncle's Clothing', *TV Times* Vol. 20, No. 256, 23 September 1960, pp. 6-7 (p. 6).

210. Newnham, p. 6.

211. Anon., 'The Mystery of Edwin Drood', *TV Times*, Vol. 21, No. 262, 4 November 1960, p. 32.

212. ibid.

213. Anon., 'The Mystery of Edwin Drood', *TV Times*, Vol. 21, No. 263, 11 November 1960, p. 32.

214. Ngaio Marsh, interviewed by David Griffiths, 'New Twist to the Edwin Drood Tale', *TV Times,* Vol. 21, No. 261, 28 October 1960, pp. 10-11 (p. 11).
215. Marsh in Griffiths, p. 11.
216. Marsh in Griffiths, p. 11
217. Griffiths, p. 10; Cross, p. 7.
218. Collins, *Dickens and Crime*, p. 284.
219. Collins, *Dickens and Crime*, p. 291.
220. Collins, *Dickens and Crime*, p. 301.
221. Collins, *Dickens and Crime*, p. 290.
222. Collins, *Dickens and Crime*, p. 313.
223. Collins, *Dickens and Crime*, p. 308.
224. Collins, *Dickens and Crime*, p. 308.
225. Collins, *Dickens and Crime*, p. 309.
226. Collins, *Dickens and Crime*, p. 310.
227. Collins, *Dickens and Crime*, p. 309.
228. Collins, *Dickens and Crime*, p. 319.
229. Philip Collins, Foreword, John Thacker, *Antichrist in the Cathedral* (London: Vision Press, 1990), pp. 7-9 (p. 8).
230. Felix Aylmer, *Dickens Incognito* (London: Rupert Hart-Davis, 1959).
231. Slater, *The Great Charles Dickens Scandal*, p. 135.
232. Felix Aylmer, *The Drood Case,* (London: Rupert-Hart-Davis, 1964, p. 1.
233. Aylmer, *The Drood Case*, p. 1.
234. Aylmer, *The Drood Case*, p. 2.
235. Aylmer, *The Drood Case*, p. 14.
236. Aylmer, *The Drood Case*, pp. 29-30.
237. Aylmer, *The Drood Case*, p. 169.
238. Aylmer, *The Drood Case*, p. 3.
239. Aylmer, *The Drood Case*, p. 38.
240. Aylmer, *The Drood Case*, p. 30.
241. Philip Hopsbaum, *A Reader's Guide to Charles Dickens* (London: Thames and Hudson, 1972), p. 280.
242. George Orwell, 'Charles Dickens', in *Inside the Whale and other essays* (London: Victor Gollancz, 1940), pp. 9-88 (p. 73).
243. Walter Allen, *The English Novel: A Short Critical History* (London: Phoenix House, 1954), p. 152.
244. D. W. Bilham, 'Edwin Drood – to resolve a mystery?', *Dickensian*, Vol. 62, September 1966, pp. 181-183 (p. 183).
245. Charles Mitchell, '*The Mystery of Edwin Drood*: The Interior and Exterior of Self'. *ELH*, Vol. 33, No. 2, June 1966, 228-246.

246. J. Hillis Miller, *Charles Dickens: The World of his novels* (Cambridge, Massachusetts: Harvard University Press, 1965), p. 321.

247. Barbara Hardy, *Dickens: The Later Novels* (London: Longman, Green & Co, 1968), p. 37.

248. See Tomlin, *Charles Dickens 1812-1870*; Nisbet and Nevius, *Dickens Centennial Essays*; Robert B. Partlow (ed.), *Dickens the Craftsman: Strategies of Presentation* (Carbondale and Edwardsville: Southern Illinois University Press, 1970); and Michael Slater (ed.), *Dickens 1970* (London: Chapman and Hall, 1970). Each of these collections, wide-ranging as they are in their topics, contain only a handful of references to *Drood*.

249. John Lucas, *The Melancholy Man: A Study of Dickens's Novels* (London: Methuen, 1970), p. 317.

250. Angus Wilson, *The World of Charles Dickens*, (London: Penguin, 1970), p. 291.

251. H. M. Daleski, *Dickens and the Art of Analogy* (London: Faber and Faber, 1970), p. 336.

252. Geoffrey Thurley, *The Dickens Myth: Its Genesis and Structure* (London: Routledge & Kegan Paul, 1976), p. 329.

253. Thurley, p. 350.

254. Thurley, p. 350.

255. George Wing, 'Edwin Drood and Desperate Remedies: Prototypes of Detective Fiction in 1870', *Studies in English Literature, 1500-1900*, Vol. 13, No. 4, Autumn 1973, pp. 677-687 (p. 686).

256. Pope-Hennessy, p. 477.

257. Ford, p. 122

258. Sue Lonoff, 'Charles Dickens and Wilkie Collins', *Nineteenth-Century Fiction*, Vol. 35, No. 2, September 1980, pp. 150-170 (p. 161).

259. Ross Murfin, 'The Art of Representation: Collins' *The Moonstone* and Dickens' Example', *ELH*, Vol. 49, No. 3, Autumn 1982, pp. 653-672 (671).

260. Albert Guerrard, *The Triumph of the Novel: Dickens, Dostoevsky, Faulkner* (New York: OUP, 1976), p. 3.

261. Charles Forsyte, *The Decoding of Edwin Drood: Fact-fict-ion solution to a classic problem* (London: Victor Gollancz Ltd, 1980), p. 30.

262. Edward Blishen, Introduction, *The Mystery of Edwin Drood* by Charles Dickens, concluded by Leon Garfield (London: Andre Deutsch, 1980), p. ix.

263. Blishen, in Garfield, p. ix.

264. Forsyte, p. 26.

265. Forsyte, p. 26.

266. Forster, Vol. III, pp. 425-6.
267. Blishen, in Garfield, p. xv.
268. Forsyte, p. 104.
269. Forsyte, p. 209.
270. Garfield, p. 316.
271. Forsyte, p. 106.
272. Blishen, in Garfield, p. xiii.
273. Garfield, front inlay.
274. Katharine Longley, *A Whispering Reed: Dickens's last novel, its making and purpose* (unpublished manuscript held in Senate House Library, MS1003/8/1), pp. 154-155.
275. Roy Roussel, 'The Completed Story in *The Mystery of Edwin Drood*', *Criticism*, Vol. 20, Fall 1978, pp. 383-402 (p. 383).
276. Roussel, p. 384.
277. Eve Sedgwick, 'Up the Postern Stair: *Edwin Drood* and the Homophobia of Empire', *Between Men: English Literature and Male Homosocial Desire* (New York: Columbia University Press, 1985), pp. 180-200.
278. Sedgwick, p. 199.
279. Thacker, p. 12.
280. Marilyn Thomas, '*Edwin Drood*: A Bone Yard Awaiting Resurrection', *Dickens Quarterly*, Vol 2, No. 1, March 1985, pp. 12-18 (p. 18).
281. Thacker, p. 149.
282. Thacker, p. 150.
283. Miriam O'Kane Mara, 'Sucking the Empire Dry: Colonial Critique in *The Mystery of Edwin Drood*', *Dickens Studies Annual,* Vol. 32, 2002, pp. 233-246 (p. 244).
284. Rupert Holmes, 'The History of the Mystery', www.rupertholmes.com, <http://www.rupertholmes.com/theatre/essdrood.html>, date accessed 10 June 2017.
285. Holmes, 'The History of the Mystery'.
286. Rupert Holmes, *The Mystery of Edwin Drood Performance Script,* Appendix 11, p. 71.
287. Holmes, *The Mystery of Edwin Drood Performance Script*, Act 2, Scene 5, p. 22.
288. Holmes, *The Mystery of Edwin Drood Performance Script*, Act 1, Scene 3, p. 23.
289. Holmes, *The Mystery of Edwin Drood Performance Script*, Act 1, Scene 4, p. 27.
290. Holmes, *The Mystery of Edwin Drood Performance Script*, Appendix 15, p. 75.
291. Holmes, in conversation with the author, 6 June 2017.

292. Holmes, *The Mystery of Edwin Drood Performance Script,* Appendix 15, p. 75.

293. Benny R. Reece, *The Mystery of Edwin Drood Solved* (New York: Vantage Press, 1989), Back Inlay.

294. Reece, p. 3.

295. Reece, p. 3.

296. Reece, pp. 3-4.

297. Reece, p. 5.

298. Reece, p. 51.

299. Reece, p. 6.

300. Peter Rowland, *The Disappearance of Edwin Drood* (London: Constable, 1991), p. 175.

301. Ray Dubberke, *Dickens, Drood and The Detectives* (New York: Vantage Press, 1992), p. 134.

302. Carlo Fruttero and Franco Lucentini, *The D Case,* trans. Gregory Dowling (San Diego, New York, London: Harcourt Brace, 1992), p. 7.

303. Fruttero and Lucentini, p. 23.

304. Fruttero and Lucentini, p. 318.

305. Fruttero and Lucentini, p. 445.

306. Timothy Forder (dir.), *The Mystery of Edwin Drood*, First Standard Media, 1993.

307. Gerhard Joseph, 'Who Cares Who Killed Edwin Drood? Or, On the Whole, I'd Rather Be in Philadelphia', *Nineteenth-Century Literature*, Vol. 51, No. 2, September 1996, pp. 161-175 (p. 170).

308. Steven Connor (ed.), Charles Dickens, *The Mystery of Edwin Drood* (London: J. M. Dent, 1996), p. 286.

309. David Paroissien (ed.), Charles Dickens, *The Mystery of Edwin Drood* (London: Penguin, 2002), p. xxxiii.

310. Connor, p. xxxv.

311. Cox, pp. ix-x.

312. Ray Dubberke, 'Edwin Drood by the Numbers', *The Dickensian*, Vol. 100, Summer 2004, pp. 132-137.

313. Dubberke, 'Edwin Drood by the Numbers', p. 134.

314. Mark Gattis, 'The Unquiet Dead', *Dr Who,* Season 1, Episode 2 (2005).

315. Lyn Squire, *The Last Chapter* (Middletown, DE: NP, 2014), p. 43.

316. Jed Rubenfeld, cited in Matthew Pearl, *The Last Dickens* (London: Vintage, 2010), back cover.

317. D. J. Taylor, 'Who did it – and why?', *Guardian*, 21 March 2009.

318. Christopher Lord, *The Edwin Drood Murders* (Portland: Harrison Thurman Books, 2013).

319. David Madden, *The Mystery of Edwin Drood* (Milton Keynes: Unthank Books, 2011), p. xiv.

320. Gwyneth Hughes in discussion with David Madden and the author, *The Mystery of Edwin Drood: Solutions and Resolutions*, Conference held by University of Buckingham at Senate House, London, September 2014.

321. Gwyneth Hughes, 'Afterword', in Charles Dickens, *The Mystery of Edwin Drood* (London: BBC Books, 2012), pp. 275-9 (p. 279).

322. Hughes, 'Afterword', p. 279.

323. Holly Furneaux, *Queer Dickens: Erotics, Families, Masculinites* (Oxford: OUP, 2009), p. 170.

324. Furneaux, p. 167.

325. Furneaux, p. 127.

326. Furneaux, p. 166.

327. Nayder, p. 198.

328. Nayder, p. 183.

329. Nayder, p. 187.

330. Camilla Ulleland Hoel, *The Completion of* Edwin Drood*: Endings and Authority in Finished and Unfinished Narratives,* PhD Thesis submitted to The University of Edinburgh, 2012, p. 110

331. Hoel, p. 185.

332. Beth Seltzer, *Not Just the Facts: Victorian Detective Fiction's Critique of Information,* PhD Thesis submitted to Temple University, 2015, p. 166.

333. Seltzer, p. 163.

334. Seltzer, p. 173.

335. Connor, p. 306.

336. www.droodiana.ru

337. www.droodinquiry.com

338. https://cloisterhamtales.wordpress.com

339. Greg Hurst, 'Readers to decide whodunit in Dickens "murder" mystery', *The Times*, 5 January 2015, p. 3.

340. Anonymous comment on Claire Carter, 'A very modern ending for Dickens' final unfinished work as academics turn to crowd-sourcing to complete The Mystery of Edwin Drood': *Daily Mail* <http://www.dailymail.co.uk/news/article-2897308/A-modern-ending-Dickens-final-unfinished-work-academics-turn-crowd-sourcing-complete-Mystery-Edwin-Drood.html>, published online 5 January 2015.

341. Peter the Painter, comment on Carter.

342. Henry Noel, comment on Carter.

343. Colonel Steve Zodiac, comment on Carter.

344. Earwig-O, comment on Carter.

345. Catdog71, comment on Carter.

346. Jeffrey Yohalem (head writer), 'Haunted House', *Assassin's Creed: Syndicate* (Ubisoft, 2015).

347. Yohalem.

348. Rosa Bud, *Edwin Drood Zombie,* www.fanfiction.net < https://www.fanfiction.net/s/7014786/1/Edwin-Drood-Zombie>, published 23 May 2011.

349. Foosemittee, *Drood*, www.fanfiction.net, <https://www.fanfiction.net/s/6856184/1/Drood>, published 30 March 2011.

350. Roman De La Rose, *Before the Shadow Falls*, www.fanfiction.net, <https://www.fanfiction.net/s/8133983/1/Before-the-Shadow-Falls>, published 20 May 2012; Laura Schiller, *Absolutely No Shame,* www.fanfiction.net, < https://www.fanfiction.net/s/8796185/1/Absolutely-No-Shame>, published 15 December 2012.

351. Roman De La Rose, The Blossoming of the Bud, www.fanficton.net, <https://www.fanfiction.net/s/7755271/6/The-Blossoming-of-the-Bud>, published 11 March 2012, Chapter Six.

352. Laurie Love, *Mr Jasper's Cadenza*, www.fanfiction.net, < https://www.fanfiction.net/s/7743057/1/Mr-Jasper-s-Cadenza>, published 15 January-19 February 2012, Chapter Two, Author's note.

353. Love, Chapter One, Author's note.

354. Love, Chapter Two.

355. Natalie McKnight, '"A little humouring of Pussy's points!"; or Sex – the *Real* Unsolved Mystery of *Edwin Drood*', *Dickens Quarterly*, Vol. 30, No. 1, March 2013, pp. 55-63 (p. 58).

356. Sylvère Monod, *Dickens the Novelist*, trans. Edward Wagenknecht (Norman, Oklahoma: University of Oklahoma Press, 1968), p. 499.

357. Hopsbaum, pp. 279-281

358. Olivia Griffiths, email to the author, 2 June 2015.

Index

INDEX

Dickens, Charles
  Bicentenary 2012, 139-40
  Death 1870, xvi, 1-11, 19, 93, 151, 163-4
  Death (centenary of) 1970, 42, 81, 108
  Style (and emulation of) 15-16, 22-23, 114-5
Dickens, Charles (Jnr), 10, 18, 19, 24-5, 92, 99
Dickens, Henry, 47, 80
Dickens, Kate *see* Perugini, Kate
Dickens Fellowship, 35, 42-3, 54-57, 59, 70, 102
Dickensian, The, 35, 42-44, 47-9, 55, 64-5, 67, 73, 91, 101, 107, 130, 134, 135, 146, 147
Dickson-Carr, John, 95-7
Digital Humanities *see* Online responses
Dombey and Son, xviii
Dostoevsky, Fyodor, xvii, 85-6, 88-9, 99, 107, 109-10, 112-3, 132
Downs, Sarah Elizabeth *see* Sheldon, Georgie
Doyle, Arthur Conan, 40, 66, 90, 91, 128
  see also Sherlock Holmes
Dr Who, 135
Drood Inquiry, The, 148-52, 168
Dubberke, Ray, 129, 131, 134-5
Duffield, Howard, 68-71, 75, 83-4, 98, 103, 105, 112, 120, 129, 134, 148

Eroticism, 142-3, 155-7

Fanfiction, x, 153-7
Fildes, Luke, 10, 19, 46, 47, 92-3, 99, 148
Film *see* Screen Adaptations

Ford, George, 74-5, 80, 87, 110
Forder, Timothy, 131-2
Forster, John, xvii, 10-11, 23-4, 28, 34, 37-8, 45-7, 58, 59, 62, 72, 83-4, 86, 89-90, 92-4, 97, 99, 105, 107-9, 111-2, 115-6, 119, 121-2, 123, 131, 136, 138, 139, 140-1, 142, 149, 158, 164, 169
Forsyte, Charles, 111-5, 128, 131, 140, 141
Foster, Thomas *see* Proctor, Richard
Fruterro, Carlo and Lucentini, Franco
  The D Case (*La Verita sul caso D*), 73, 129-131, 136, 141-2, 146-7, 157-8
Furneaux, Holly, 142-3

Gadd, George, 47, 49
Gads Hill, 3
Garfield, Leon, 111-5, 131, 140, 141
Gilbert, Arthur, 51
Gissing, George, 43, 82-3, 144
Great Expectations, 37, 65, 94

Hard Times, 106
Hardy, Barbara, 108
Hardy, Thomas, 109
Harris, Edwin
  John Jasper's Gatehouse, 71-2
Hoel, Camilla Ulleland, 145-6, 168
Holmes, Rupert, 122-6, 129, 131, 141-2, 146, 157-8
Homosocial, 119-121, 124-5, 142-3
Hughes, Gwyneth, 140-2, 144-5, 154, 156, 158

Internet *see* Online responses
Irreverent, The, xiv, 122-158, 162, 167-70

199